VOLUME 524

NOVEMBER 1992

THE ANNALS

of The American Academy *of* Political
and Social Science

RICHARD D. LAMBERT, *Editor*
ALAN W. HESTON, *Associate Editor*

POLITICAL ISLAM

Special Editors of this Volume

CHARLES E. BUTTERWORTH

University of Maryland
College Park

I. WILLIAM ZARTMAN

School of Advanced International Studies
Johns Hopkins University
Washington, D.C.

⑤ SAGE PUBLICATIONS *NEWBURY PARK   LONDON   NEW DELHI*

Editorial Office: 3937 Chestnut Street, Philadelphia, PA 19104.

For information about membership* (individuals only) and subscriptions (institutions), address:

SAGE PUBLICATIONS, INC.
2455 Teller Road
Newbury Park, CA 91320

From India and South Asia, write to:	From the UK, Europe, the Middle East and Africa, write to:
SAGE PUBLICATIONS INDIA Pvt. Ltd.	SAGE PUBLICATIONS LTD
P.O. Box 4215	6 Bonhill Street
New Delhi 110 048	London EC2A 4PU
INDIA	UNITED KINGDOM

SAGE Production Staff: LINDA GRAY, LIANN LECH, and JANELLE LeMASTER

*Please note that members of The Academy receive THE ANNALS with their membership.

Library of Congress Catalog Card Number 91-67480
International Standard Serial Number ISSN 0002-7162
International Standard Book Number ISBN 0-8039-4687-2 (Vol. 524, 1992 paper)
International Standard Book Number ISBN 0-8039-4686-4 (Vol. 524, 1992 cloth)
Manufactured in the United States of America. First printing, November 1992.

The articles appearing in THE ANNALS are indexed in *Book Review Index, Public Affairs Information Service Bulletin, Social Sciences Index, Current Contents, General Periodicals Index, Academic Index, Pro-Views,* and *Combined Retrospective Index Sets.* They are also abstracted and indexed in *ABC Pol Sci, Historical Abstracts, Human Resources Abstracts, Social Sciences Citation Index, United States Political Science Documents, Social Work Research & Abstracts, Sage Urban Studies Abstracts, International Political Science Abstracts, America: History and Life, Sociological Abstracts, Managing Abstracts, Social Planning/Policy & Development Abstracts, Automatic Subject Citation Alert, Book Review Digest, Work Related Abstracts, Periodica Islamica,* and/or *Family Resources Database,* and are available on microfilm from University Microfilms, Ann Arbor, Michigan.

Information about membership rates, institutional subscriptions, and back issue prices may be found on the facing page.

Advertising. Current rates and specifications may be obtained by writing to THE ANNALS Advertising and Promotion Manager at the Newbury Park office (address above).

Claims. Claims for undelivered copies must be made no later than three months following month of publication. The publisher will supply missing copies when losses have been sustained in transit and when the reserve stock will permit.

Change of Address. Six weeks' advance notice must be given when notifying of change of address to ensure proper identification. Please specify name of journal. Send address changes to: THE ANNALS, c/o Sage Publications, Inc., 2455 Teller Road, Newbury Park, CA 91320.

The American Academy of Political and Social Science

3937 Chestnut Street   Philadelphia, Pennsylvania 19104

Origin and Purpose. The Academy was organized December 14, 1889, to promote the progress of political and social science, especially through publications and meetings. The Academy does not take sides in controverted questions, but seeks to gather and present reliable information to assist the public in forming an intelligent and accurate judgment.

Meetings. The Academy occasionally holds a meeting in the spring extending over two days.

Publications. THE ANNALS is the bimonthly publication of The Academy. Each issue contains articles on some prominent social or political problem, written at the invitation of the editors. Also, monographs are published from time to time, numbers of which are distributed to pertinent professional organizations. These volumes constitute important reference works on the topics with which they deal, and they are extensively cited by authorities throughout the United States and abroad. The papers presented at the meetings of The Academy are included in THE ANNALS.

Membership. Each member of The Academy receives THE ANNALS and may attend the meetings of The Academy. Membership is open only to individuals. Annual dues: $42.00 for the regular paperbound edition (clothbound, $60.00). California residents must add 7.25% sales tax on all orders ($45.05 paperbound; $64.35 clothbound). Add $9.00 per year for membership outside the U.S.A. Members may also purchase single issues of THE ANNALS for $13.00 each (clothbound, $18.00). California residents: $13.94 paperbound, $19.31 clothbound. Add $1.50 for shipping and handling on all prepaid orders.

Subscriptions. THE ANNALS (ISSN 0002-7162) is published six times annually—in January, March, May, July, September, and November. Institutions may subscribe to THE ANNALS at the annual rate: $132.00 (clothbound, $156.00). California institutions: $141.57 paperbound, $167.31 clothbound. Add $9.00 per year for subscriptions outside the U.S.A. Institutional rates for single issues: $24.00 each (clothbound, $29.00). California institutions: $25.74 paperbound, $31.10 clothbound.

Second class postage paid at Thousand Oaks, California, and additional offices.

Single issues of THE ANNALS may be obtained by individuals who are not members of The Academy for $17.00 each (clothbound, $26.00). California residents: $18.23 paperbound, $27.89 clothbound. Add $1.50 for shipping and handling on all prepaid orders. Single issues of THE ANNALS have proven to be excellent supplementary texts for classroom use. Direct inquiries regarding adoptions to THE ANNALS c/o Sage Publications (address below).

All correspondence concerning membership in The Academy, dues renewals, inquiries about membership status, and/or purchase of single issues of THE ANNALS should be sent to THE ANNALS c/o Sage Publications, Inc., 2455 Teller Road, Newbury Park, CA 91320. Telephone: (805) 499-0721; FAX/Order line: (805) 499-0871. *Please note that orders under $30 must be prepaid.* Sage affiliates in London and India will assist institutional subscribers abroad with regard to orders, claims, and inquiries for both subscriptions and single issues.

Printed on recycled, acid-free paper

THE ANNALS

of The American Academy *of* Political
and Social Science

RICHARD D. LAMBERT, *Editor*
ALAN W. HESTON, *Associate Editor*

--------- FORTHCOMING ---------

WHITE-COLLAR CRIME
Special Editors: Gilbert Geis and Paul Jesilow
Volume 525   January 1993

FREE TRADE IN THE WESTERN HEMISPHERE
Special Editor: Sidney Weintraub
Volume 526   March 1993

RELIGION IN THE NINETIES
Special Editor: Wade Clark Roof
Volume 527   May 1993

See page 3 for information on Academy membership and
purchase of single volumes of **The Annals.**

CONTENTS

PREFACE .... *Charles E. Butterworth and I. William Zartman*   8

THE GOLDEN AGE:
THE POLITICAL CONCEPTS OF ISLAM ....*Ira M. Lapidus*   13

POLITICAL ISLAM: THE ORIGINS ....*Charles E. Butterworth*   26

POPULAR ISLAM ....*Patrick D. Gaffney*   38

MILITANT ISLAM AND THE
POLITICS OF REDEMPTION ....*Mary-Jane Deeb*   52

CONSERVATIVE AND
TRADITIONAL BROTHERHOODS ....*John Obert Voll*   66

STATE ISLAM AND COMMUNAL PLURALITY ....*Nazih N. Ayubi*   79

THE CLERGY'S CONCEPTS OF
RULE IN EGYPT AND IRAN ....*Shahrough Akhavi*   92

MONARCHS, MULLAS, AND MARSHALS:
ISLAMIC REGIMES?..........................*Ibrahim A. Karawan*   103

ISLAMICIST UTOPIA AND DEMOCRACY ....*Lahouari Addi*   120

ISLAM IN THE STATES OF THE FORMER USSR ....*Vitaly Naumkin*   131

AN AFRICAN CASE STUDY OF
POLITICAL ISLAM: NIGERIA ....*John Hunwick*   143

POLITICAL ISLAM IN ASIA: A CASE STUDY ....*Alain-Gérard Marsot*   156

MAGHREBI IMMIGRATION TO EUROPE:
DOUBLE INSERTION OR DOUBLE EXCLUSION? ....*Rémy Leveau*   170

DEMOCRACY AND ISLAM:
THE CULTURAL DIALECTIC ....*I. William Zartman*   181

BOOK DEPARTMENT   192

INDEX   231

BOOK DEPARTMENT CONTENTS

INTERNATIONAL RELATIONS AND POLITICS

OBERDORFER, DON. *The Turn: From the Cold War to a New Era:*
The United States and the Soviet Union, 1983-1990;
FEINBERG, RICHARD F. et al. *From Confrontation to Cooperation:*
U.S. and Soviet Aid to Developing Countries. Donald M. Snow 192

TRACHTENBERG, MARC. *History and Strategy.* David L. Schalk 193

AFRICA, ASIA, AND LATIN AMERICA

FORESTA, RONALD A. *Amazon Conservation in the Age of*
Development: The Limits of Providence. Ronald M. Schneider 194

HAERI, SHAHLA. *Law of Desire: Temporary*
Marriage in Shi'a Islam. William O. Beeman 195

HOURANI, ALBERT. *A History of the Arab Peoples.* Don Peretz 197

HUNTER, F. ROBERT. *The Palestinian Uprising:*
A War by Other Means. Charles S. Kamen 198

KOHLI, ATUL. *Democracy and Discontent:*
India's Growing Crisis of Governability. Craig Baxter 198

NESTER, WILLIAM R. *The Foundation of Japanese Power:*
Continuities, Changes, Challenges. Charlotte G. O'Kelly 199

TAPPER, NANCY. *Bartered Brides: Politics, Gender and*
Marriage in an Afghan Tribal Society. Benedicte Grima 200

VAILLANT, JANET G. *Black, French, and African:*
A Life of Leopold Sedar Senghor. Dickson A. Mungazi 201

EUROPE

CHRISTIAN, DAVID. *Living Water: Vodka and Russian*
Society on the Eve of Emancipation. Dan Usher 203

EDWARDS, JOHN CARVER. *Berlin Calling: American*
Broadcasters in Service to the Third Reich. Daniel J. Leab 205

GILLINGHAM, JOHN. *Coal, Steel and the Rebirth of Europe,*
1945-1955: The Germans and French from Ruhr Conflict
to Economic Community. Karl H. Cerny 206

KENNETT, LEE. *The First Air War: 1914-1918.* George H. Quester 207

MERRIMAN, JOHN M. *The Margins of City Life: Explorations*
on the French Urban Frontier, 1815-1851. Paul M. Hohenberg 207

UNITED STATES

BELLAH, ROBERT N., RICHARD MADSEN, WILLIAM M. SULLIVAN,
ANN SWIDLER, and STEVEN TIPTON. *The Good Society.* Fred Rotondaro 209

CARSON, MINA. *Settlement Folk: Social Thought and*
the American Settlement Movement, 1885-1930. Richard H. Collin 209

CORNELIUS, JANET DUITSMAN. *When I Can Read My Title Clear:*
Literacy, Slavery, and Religion in the Antebellum South. Kenneth W. Goings   210

HAYWOOD, ROBERT C. *Victorian West:*
Class and Culture in Kansas Cattle Towns;
WILLIAMS, MARILYN THORNTON. *Washing "The Great Unwashed":*
Public Baths in Urban America,1840-1920. Olive Checkland   211

SCHUMAKER, PAUL. *Critical Pluralism, Democratic*
Performance, and Community Power. Robert E. Calvert   212

WHITE, SHANE. *Somewhat More Independent: The End of*
Slavery in New York City, 1770-1810. John A. Hardin   214

SOCIOLOGY

ANDERSON, ELIJAH. *Streetwise: Race, Class, and*
Change in an Urban Community. Reynolds Farley   215

GOODWIN, MARJORIE HARNESS. *He—Said—She—Said:*
Talk as Social Organization among Black Children. Loren Schweninger   217

JENCKS, CHRISTOPHER and PAUL PETERSON, eds.
The Urban Underclass. A. Reza Vahabzadeh   218

KADISH, MORTIMER R. *Toward an Ethic of*
Higher Education. Daniel G. Solorzano   218

PESHKIN, ALAN. *The Color of Strangers, the Color of Friends:*
The Play of Ethnicity in School and Community. Daniel Mitchell   219

SNOW, CATHERINE E., WENDY S. BARNES, JEAN CHANDLER,
IRENE F. GOODMAN, and LOWRY HEMPHILL. *Unfulfilled Expectations:*
Home and School Influences on Literacy. Valerie E. Lee   220

TYACK, DAVID and ELISABETH HANSOT. *Learning Together:*
A History of Coeducation in American Public Schools. Joe W. Trotter   222

ECONOMICS

BURTON, LLOYD. *American Indian Water Rights and*
the Limits of Law. David Lewis Feldman   223

SLOANE, ARTHUR A. *Hoffa.* Ronald L. Filippelli   224

PREFACE

Political Islam has been seen by some as the successor to the Communist threat, a creeping mobilization that confronts the "Great Satan" of Western civilization and modernization. To others, it is nothing to worry about— merely an inherent aspect of religious practice wherever there are Muslims. This study aims to steer a careful path between these two inadequate perceptions.

Islam is, indeed, a religious belief that covers all aspects of life and denies the validity of any philosophical separation between "church" and state. "*Islam din wa dawla*" ("Islam is religion and state") is a basic precept subscribed to by all Muslims as part of their faith. But the fact that this identity contains two distinct elements in its predicate indicates that those elements are actually separate, and the ultimate relation between the two can take many variations. Otherwise, there would be no concern at the present time —as opposed to other periods in history—over the political forms of Islam.

On the other hand, some of the ways in which political Islam manifests itself at the end of the twentieth century are specifically anti-Western, consciously revolutionary, avowedly antisecularist and antimodernist, even intentionally violent. Probably the biggest contradiction within this extreme form of political Islam is the fact that it consists not of a single movement but of a plethora of groups and liaisons divided above all by national origins. Within different countries, even the most extreme forms differ widely; moreover, when particular groups have been totally successful in seizing power, none of the governments they have formed resembles any other. Indeed, like any religious movement, the desire to foster unity and orthodoxy proves to be the greatest guarantee of division and heterodoxy.

Somewhere in the broad terrain between the normal and the extreme form of religion and politics in Islam lies the reality of the phenomenon under investigation. Its manifestations are varied and contradictory, and no single expression can be taken as evidence of the nature of the whole. There are peaceful Islamic intellectual circles and violent terrorist groups, political parties that have won and lost by pursuing the democratic process and those dedicated to eradicating the democratic regime by which they seek to come to power. Similarly, there are interpreters and adherents who profess to live by the unchanged Word of the seventh century, just as there are those who seek new meanings appropriate to the twentieth. The articles presented in this volume bring that diversity to light; they identify the nuances within its stark threat and the myriad details of its current practices.

None of the articles focuses on the everyday beliefs of the millions of Muslims around the world as these relate to their personal perception of themselves and of God. There is no reason to do so, for their God is universally

8

recognized to be the same as the God of Jews and Christians, and it is acknowledged that human understanding of this God derives initially from the same scriptural sources while going beyond them to provide a newer and somewhat different revelation. Though these commonalities and differences of belief are not addressed here, they should be kept in mind. After all, they form the basis for the political manifestation of the religion that is the subject of investigation.

At the outset, some definitional distinctions appear warranted. The term "fundamentalism" is avoided in the following articles primarily because it is objected to by the subjects of study themselves as a Christian—and therefore inappropriate—term. There might be some value to using it, nonetheless, since a single term would underline the fact that literal application of past scripture to current daily life is an element present in many religions—an element present in various strengths at various times and thus not just a variation applied to Islam. On the other hand, a specific term highlights the specific features of this particular tendency, and so the term "Islamicist" is used to refer to those who strive to bring politics into line with Islamic precepts. "Islamic," by contrast, is used to refer to religious and specifically Quranic prescriptions, and "Muslim" is used to refer merely to the general practice of the religion without any particular implication of either politics or piety.

The articles forming this study are about political Islam, the religiously based efforts of some Muslims to relate to state power. In bringing out the specific nature of the common subject, our coauthors define and analyze political Islam in several different ways. Thus the following 14 articles fall into six general groupings: political Islam viewed across time, nonofficial manifestations of political Islam, official attitudes to and ways of dealing with political Islam, political Islam empowered, accounts of political Islam apart from the Middle East, and the interplay between culture and politics with respect to political Islam.

Differently stated, the study attempts to offer a survey of Islamic attitudes and practices at the hand of the state both in instances where governments have become Islamic and those where they seek to control the expression of Islamicist tendencies. It also looks at Islamic organizations that govern their own affairs as fraternities and independent societies outside of direct state control or opposition. In addition, it examines oppositional forms of political Islam, either as the low-culture form of religion opposed to the official or high-culture version, or as parties and movements designed to seize power by various means in order to create an Islamic political order. Moreover, focusing on the way Islamic regimes interact with Islamic groups seeking to have a greater say in rule or with non-Islamic groups calling for greater recognition, the study examines the state and the larger community both in general and in particular. Finally, it considers what is theoretically involved in calling for greater attention to empowering Islam.

POLITICAL ISLAM ACROSS TIME

In the article that opens this study, Ira M. Lapidus looks at Middle Eastern states over time. Though he notes how influential Islam was in the premodern era, Lapidus argues that it has little national sway today. Tracing the development of two Islamic paradigms for rule, he urges that most states in the Middle East have now opted for a political life in which Islam is relegated to private practice and thus deprived of influence over official political life.

Charles E. Butterworth agrees with the way Lapidus views the influence of Islam on Middle Eastern politics in the premodern era, but he then seeks to discover what those calling for a greater Islamic role in politics today have in mind. Arguing that there is nothing new about such a demand, Butterworth sketches a general history of political discourse within the Islamic tradition to buttress his point and proposes a novel way for proponents of liberal democracy to reassess their criticism of unabashedly Islamic regimes.

NONOFFICIAL MANIFESTATIONS
OF POLITICAL ISLAM

Taking issue with recent journalistic attempts to capture popular Islam, Patrick D. Gaffney proposes that we begin by looking at the way Islam has evolved through history. His analysis leads him to distinguish between official and popular Islam and thus to emphasize the way the populace has had recourse to Sufism, rather than activism, over the ages. He concludes by noting that popular Islam now seems to point in two directions. First, it serves as the basis for a comprehensive teaching advanced by those who would challenge the present status quo; second, it continues to capture the lived experiences of the masses of Muslims, that is, the populace.

Militant Islamic movements in Algeria, Tunisia, Libya, the Occupied Territories, and Lebanon are the focus of Mary-Jane Deeb's article. She begins by noting five broad conditions that seem to be common to all of these movements, then turns to a detailed consideration of how each has emerged. In the course of her presentation, she notes the concepts and causes embraced by each and strives to discern how these also link the different movements.

Casting an eye on the way Sufi brotherhoods have functioned in West Africa, North Africa, Russia, the Sudan, and Egypt in the last century as well as in this one, John Obert Voll shows how they have preserved Islamic piety and how they represent popular expressions of Islam. Like Patrick Gaffney, Voll sees the Sufi brotherhoods as offering significant solace to the populace at times when Islam was out of favor by providing a sense of continuity. In his article, Voll explains the origins and functions of several brotherhoods, then details the way some have come to play a role in the growing move toward the Islamization of society and politics.

OFFICIAL ATTITUDES TO POLITICAL ISLAM

Nazih N. Ayubi paints a broad picture of Islam empowered. Looking at the role of the *'ulama'* in a number of different regimes that proclaim themselves Islamic, he first sketches the major differences between Sunnite and Shiite regimes, then turns to a consideration of the way non-Muslim minorities are treated in all Islamic states. To make his argument more persuasive, Ayubi turns from time to time to recent history and even looks back to medieval jurisprudence. A salient feature of his article is his intelligent use of recent analyses from the pens of scholars living in the Arab Middle East and writing in Arabic.

In contrast, Shahrough Akhavi looks at two particular cases of how proponents of Islam discern its relationship to political power. In Egypt, about ten years ago, the leader of al-Azhar issued a formal religious reply to a pamphlet written by the revolutionary leader implicated in Sadat's assassination. Noting how the religious leader sought in this instance to defend secular rule, urging that in Egypt it was perfectly compatible with the aspirations of Muslims, Akhavi contrasts that writing with Khomeini's powerful *Islamic Government*, the treatise meant to justify the Islamic regime that he intended as the proper Islamic replacement for the rule of the Shah.

POLITICAL ISLAM EMPOWERED

Ibrahim A. Karawan denies the existence of a monolithic model of Islamic government or governance. Insisting that it makes more analytic sense to speak of a diversity of Islamic regimes, he shows that the Islamic regimes of Saudi Arabia, Iran, the Sudan, and Pakistan evince three different types of regime: a conservative dynastic regime, a populist authoritarian regime, and a military authoritarian regime. Karawan is, nonetheless, equally intent upon noting that all three share in using religious symbolism to gain legitimacy.

Identifying himself as "neither a Western politician nor an Algerian army officer" but as a somewhat theoretical academic, Lahouari Addi considers what changes must take place in contemporary Islamic societies for an Islamicist polity to be formed. His reflections center on the missed opportunity of the Islamic Salvation Front in Algeria, on what might have been and at what price. In the process, he notes the tensions between the conditions for democracy based on political parties and a regime—calling itself popular or not—based on the conviction that it rules in accordance with divine will.

POLITICAL ISLAM OUTSIDE THE MIDDLE EAST

Four articles are devoted to instances of political Islam in countries outside of the Middle East. Vitaly Naumkin discusses the way Islam managed to survive in Central Asia and other parts of the former USSR under the Communist regime and pays special attention to the role of the local *'ulama'*. Though not well educated in Islamic doctrine, they succeeded in carrying on a tradition that has now come into its own. Indeed, under the right conditions, Naumkin thinks we could well see Islamicists coming to power in Kazakhstan, Tadzhikistan, and Uzbekistan.

The focus of John Hunwick's article is Nigeria. He discusses the relationship of Islam to politics within that nation since it became independent in 1960. Religion first appeared on the political scene in 1977 when proposals to create a federal *shari'a* court unleashed protest from Christian members of the Constituent Assembly on the draft constitution. Since then, Muslims and Christians have become increasingly polarized, and Hunwick predicts that Nigeria will continue to be plagued by religious violence.

Alain-Gérard Marsot's article focuses on the role of Islam in the politics of Asia. He notes first that the majority of Muslims live in Asia, not the Middle East. For him, Islamic resurgence is a response to the global issue of modernization and development. Recounting the history of the spread of Islam to Asia, Marsot discusses the events that first encouraged conversion to Islam, namely, the spread of Islam, European colonialism, and population patterns.

Rémy Leveau addresses the issue of immigration from North Africa to Europe and the problems created as a new culture seeks to take root in an older, established one. Islamic identity remains powerful within the Maghrebian community in Europe, and this sometimes creates tensions between those who demand cultural and religious recognition and the state, which—due to historical precedents such as the Iranian revolution—fears political Islam. Leveau concludes by suggesting that a European communitywide immigration policy should be established, in part to filter and slow immigration from the South and in part to end the discrimination against Muslims currently practiced in Europe.

THE CULTURE AND POLITICS OF POLITICAL ISLAM

I.William Zartman's concluding article addresses the issue of the confrontation between political Islam and Western democracy. He traces the modern resurgence of political Islam to problems facing states that have adopted Western, secular, and materialistic polities. Insisting that there is no inherent incompatibility between Islam and democracy since Islam does not prescribe how rulers should be chosen but only that they should be pious, he concedes that some currents of political Islam nonetheless monopolize the national religion and allow only those subscribing to what they deem the true path a place in power.

CHARLES E. BUTTERWORTH

I. WILLIAM ZARTMAN

ANNALS, *AAPSS*, 524, November 1992

The Golden Age:
The Political Concepts of Islam

By IRA M. LAPIDUS

ABSTRACT: The present role of Islam in Middle Eastern politics is not a continuation but a reconstruction of the historical paradigms. In the premodern era, there were two Islamic paradigms. One was of an integral state and society unified under the political and moral leadership of a charismatic religious teacher; the other, of a society divided between state and religious institutions and differentiated political and religious elites, the latter being the custodians of the true Islam. The second tradition made room for purely secular monarchical concepts and a secular political culture. In the modern era, the historical Islamic paradigms have little influence on state formation. Even the avowedly Islamic states do not really hark back to the past but represent, for the most part, contemporary national states appealing to a new concept of national-state Islam.

Ira M. Lapidus is professor of history and chairman of the Center for Middle Eastern Studies at the University of California at Berkeley. Author of Muslim Cities in the Later Middle Ages; A History of Islamic Societies *and other works, he is a past president of the Middle East Studies Association of North America and has been a fellow of the National Endowment for the Humanities, the Center for Advanced Study in the Behavioral Sciences, and other institutions.*

THE Islamic revival is once again of urgent importance. Now, in the midst of a worldwide Muslim struggle over the role that Islam should play in contemporary societies, we are faced with compelling questions: How much does this revival reflect the desire to return to a golden age of the Muslim past? How much is it a contemporary phenomenon? Indeed, what is the Islamic and, in particular, the Middle Eastern political heritage, and what is its impact in the present?

THE FIRST GOLDEN AGE

The Middle Eastern Islamic heritage provides not one but two basic constellations of historical society, two golden ages, two paradigms, each of which has generated its own characteristic repertoire of political institutions and political theory. The first is the society integrated in all dimensions, political, social, and moral, under the aegis of Islam. The prototype is the unification of Arabia under the leadership of the Prophet Muhammad in the seventh century. The Prophet brought together the Meccans who left their home to join his community, the Medinans who accepted Islam, individual Arabians who emigrated to Medina, fractions of clans, converts made among the aristocratic families of Mecca, and various tribes in western Arabia; he unified a disparate and fragmented population into a single community. The Prophet functioned, on the one hand, as an economic and political leader and, on the other, as an exemplar of individual righteousness and morality. In this community, no distinction was made between religion and religious authority and the state and secular authority.[1]

The concept of an undifferentiated political religious community was carried over from the Prophet to the early caliphs. The Rashidun, who ruled from 632 to 660, did not inherit the Prophet's capacity to receive revelation, but their authority to implement and execute revealed law was considered as great as his authority to pronounce it.[2] Most Muslims, though for different reasons, believe that the first civil war (656-60), brought this authority to an end and that ever after the office of the caliphate was corrupted. The Shiites believe that it fell into the hands of inappropriate successors, for only Ali and the family of Ali could rightfully be caliphs; the Sunnites accept the actual historical succession but believe that later rulers were secular, self-serving kings—neither true caliphs nor true representatives of the community bequeathed by the Prophet.

Nonetheless, this image of the Prophetic community has inspired ever-renewed movements to restore the wholeness of the *umma* (community of Muslims). Shiites and Kharijites have struggled to restore the leadership of the rightful Imam. Repeatedly, Sunnite reformers have risen up to overthrow corrupt governments and set up a state committed to an Islamic morality. Sufi heroes have at-

1. W. Montgomery Watt, *Muhammad at Mecca* (New York: Oxford University Press, 1953); *Muhammad at Medina* (New York: Oxford University Press, 1955).

2. Patricia Crone and Martin Hinds, *God's Caliph* (New York: Cambridge University Press, 1986).

tempted to establish their authority, acting self-consciously in imitation of the Prophet. These reformers, like the Prophet himself, commonly found their supporters in tribal or other factionalized societies. Like the Prophet, they attempted to integrate individuals, families, clans, lineages, and clientele groups into a unified body. Such movements include, in North Africa, the Fatimids, the Almoravids, the Almohads, and the Sa'di and Alawite dynasties in Morocco; the Safavid dynasty in Iran; and, throughout the Muslim world, Berber Zawaya lineages, Evliadi among Turkomans, and Sufi-led movements such as the Sanusiyya. All of these movements exemplify the impulse to re-create, under religious leadership, the ideal community exemplified in the first golden age of Islam.[3] Nowadays, neo-Islamic movements, still inspired by the same underlying concept, take up the old ideal. Now this ideal, however, is supported not by tribal and rural communities but by the urban petite bourgeoisie, petty traders, craftspeople, *bazaaris*, and mobile and sometimes déraciné students.

THE SECOND GOLDEN AGE

The second historical paradigm is the imperial Islamic society, built not on Arabian or tribal templates but on the differentiated structures of previ-

3. On revivalist movements, see Ira M. Lapidus, *A History of Islamic Societies* (New York: Cambridge University Press, 1988), pp. 257-59, 563-68; John Voll, *Islam: Continuity and Change in the Modern World* (Boulder, CO: Westview Press, 1982); Fazlur Rahman, *Islam* (Chicago: University of Chicago Press, 1979), pp. 193-224.

ous Middle Eastern societies. By the advent of Islam, Middle Eastern societies had already been organized into differentiated tribal, state, and church institutions. After the Arab conquests, the early caliphate underwent a similar differentiation. Tribal armies were displaced by newly recruited client forces who were expected to be more dependent upon, loyal to, and obedient to their rulers; and tribal chiefs were replaced by administrative cadres drawn from the conquered populations. At the same time, the caliphate was transformed from the charismatic succession to the religious authority of the Prophet into an imperial institution and a regime governed not by religious norms but by the laws of political survival. As the caliphate took on an increasingly secularized political identity, the religious heritage of the Prophet came to be embodied in his companions and their disciples and successors, scholars, and holy men. Eventually, the caliphs retained only a nominal role as the official representatives of Islam and the official fount of state and religious authority, while the Muslim populace came to be organized into schools of law, theological sects, Shiite communities, Sufi lineages, and brotherhoods representing the legacy of the Prophet.

Such religious groups were commonly independent of state regimes. Most withdrew from participation in government and were concerned with community solidarity, worship, education, law, personal morality, and the upholding of the symbols of Islam. While religious scholars maintained their aspiration for an ideal society in which state and community were integrated as in the time of the Prophet, they were not actually committed to bringing it about in practice. In return for state support, they commonly legitimized reigning governments and taught acceptance and submission to the common people.

By the eleventh century, Middle Eastern states and religious communities were highly differentiated. States were officially committed to the defense and patronage of Muslim worship, education, law, and *jihad*, but they were not inherently Islamic institutions. It was widely recognized that these states operated on the basis of non-Islamic legitimation. Conquering regimes, be they Arab or Turkish, looked back to tribal ancestry as the basis of dynastic legitimacy. By the cultivation of local languages, poetic traditions, architectural motifs, musical themes, and cultic practices, Middle Eastern states asserted independence from Islam and identified themselves as cosmopolitan, imperial, and patrimonial regimes legitimated by non-Muslim civilization.[4]

Thus, despite the common statement that Islam is a total way of life defining political as well as social and family matters, most Muslim societies did not conform to this ideal. They were in fact built around separate institutions of state and religion.

The separation of state and religion yields a second image of the golden age of Islam. This image is embedded in the Ottoman empire; it

is an image of a world-conquering empire, establishing the dominion of Islam over all peoples and fulfilling the Islamic "providence" or "manifest destiny" to rule the world. This was a golden era of security, preeminence, and world domination. This was a golden age also because the Ottoman empire upheld the true practice of Islam. It was the protector and patron, indeed the organizer and master, of the scholars and holy men who managed Muslim education, Muslim legal and judicial affairs, and Muslim worship.[5]

The practical tradition of separation of state and religion also generated a sociopolitical theory. Muslim political theorists, such as al-Baqillani, al-Mawardi, and Ibn Taimiyya, devised a theory of the caliphate that symbolized the ideal existence of the unified *umma*, while at the same time allowing for historical actualities. The conclusion of their theorizing was that the state was not a direct expression of Islam but a secular institution whose duty it was to uphold Islam. The community of scholars and holy men were the ones who truly carried on the legacy of the Prophet.[6]

---

4. Lapidus, *History of Islamic Societies*, pp. 137-80; A.K.S. Lambton, *Theory and Practice in Medieval Persian Government* (London: Variorum Reprints, 1980); H. Busse, *Chalif und grosskönig, die Buyiden im Iraq* (Beirut: Franz Steiner Verlag, 1969).

5. On the Ottoman empire, see Halil Inalcik, *The Ottoman Empire: The Classical Age, 1300-1600* (London: Weidenfeld & Nicolson, 1973); H.A.R. Gibb and Harold Bowen, *Islamic Society and the West* (New York: Oxford University Press, 1954, 1957).

6. Yusuf Ibish, *The Political Doctrine of al-Baqillani* (Beirut: American University Press, 1966); al-Mawardi, *Les Statuts gouvernementaux*, trans. E. Fagnan (Algiers: Adolph Jourdan, 1915); Ibn Taymiya, *Ibn Taymiya on Public and Private Law in Islam* (Beirut: Khayats, 1968); Henri Laoust, *Essai sur les doctrines sociales et politiques de Taki-d-Din Ahmad b. Tamiya* (Cairo: L'Institut française d'archéologie orientale, 1939).

In this tradition, the realm of Islamic authenticity lies within the soul of the individual and in the relations of individuals to each other within small communities. This is the Islam that sees holiness and religion as incompatible with state power. Politics are expected to be violent and corrupt. The control of the state is justified only by conquest; obedience is legitimated by the need to submit, to minimize further warfare, and to prevent anarchy in society, but the state cannot embody a religious ideal. This renunciation of political utopianism may help explain some cases of acquiescence to patrimonial regimes and the relative weakness of democratic or other secular utopian movements in the present-day Middle East.

THE NON-ISLAMIC POLITICAL HERITAGE

This second paradigm allows for a differentiated nonreligious concept of political authority. Alongside the Islamic concept of the caliph as the upholder of Islam, there is a concept of political rationality inherently valid in its own terms as a source of political behavior. This level of political thinking is expressed in the Persian political heritage in which the ruler is the shadow of God on earth and bears a divine authority independent of religion. He both upholds order and serves as a moral example to his subjects. Rulership and statehood, in a sense, serve a religious purpose apart from Islam and apart from the spokesmen of the religious establishment.[7]

7. On Persian political theory, see E.I.J. Rosenthal, *Political Thought in Medieval Is-*

Furthermore, behind the formal and literary concepts of the state and the ruler, there were also working assumptions, axioms, and premises about the nature and organization of political power that did not reach the level of formal theory but are nonetheless crucial to understanding Middle Eastern politics. One is that state power is not an expression of the total society but rather the prerogative of certain individuals or groups. Control of the state belonged to certain families, tribes, dynasties, or military castes. Not only did some groups rule over others, but elites and subjects were of a totally different standing. Government was the prerogative of the one and not of the other. In Middle Eastern societies, there was a caste-like bifurcation between the military elite and the subject population.[8]

A further assumption of Middle East political systems was that, within the ruling elite and between the ruling elite and the various segments of the subject population, the exercise of political power was organized through networks of clients and retainers. These networks were bound together by subjective obligations, such as the oath of allegiance or gratitude, rather than by legal or

lam (New York: Cambridge University Press, 1958); al-Jahiz, *Le livre de la couronne,* trans. Charles Pellat (Paris: Société d'édition "Les belles lettres," 1954); Nizam al-Mulk, *The Book of Government or Rules for Kings,* trans. H. Darke, 2d ed. (London: Routledge & Kegan Paul, 1960); Kai Ka'us b. Iskandar, *A Mirror for Princes: The Qabus Nama,* trans. Reuben Levy (New York: E. P. Dutton, 1951).

8. On the rulers and the ruled, see Gibb and Bowen, *Islamic Society and the West,* passim.

other formal, institutional, or hierarchical considerations.[9]

Between rulers and subjects, political power was brokered by intermediary notables. For example, in the Mamluk empire of Egypt and Syria, state-appointed governors cultivated local notables, appointed them to offices, contributed to their religious and charitable causes, and organized public works in return for cooperation in maintaining public order and facilitating taxation. The governors similarly cultivated ties with youth gangs, fraternities, and the populace of town quarters.[10] In Middle Eastern societies with a strong tribal component, Sufis played the intermediary role. Muslim holy men—sometimes charismatic teachers, sometimes the custodians of local shrines, sometimes the members of holy lineages, sometimes affiliated with brotherhoods—facilitated the selection of tribal chiefs, mediated disputes, organized long-distance trade, and otherwise helped in the administration of rural populations.[11]

9. For example, see Roy Mottahedeh, *Loyalty and Leadership in an Early Islamic Society* (Princeton, NJ: Princeton University Press, 1980).
10. Ira M. Lapidus, *Muslim Cities in the Later Middle Ages*, 2d ed. (New York: Cambridge University Press, 1984).
11. On the social and political functions of Sufism, see Lapidus, *History of Islamic Societies*, pp. 168-72, 254-57, 261-64. For further examples, see V. N. Basilov, "Honour Groups in Traditional Turkmenian Society," in *Islam in Tribal Societies: From the Atlas to the Indus*, ed. A. A. Ahmed and D. M. Hart (London: Routledge & Kegan Paul, 1984), pp. 220-43; Julia Clancy-Smith, "Saints, Mahdis and Arms: Religion and Resistance in Nineteenth-Century North Africa," in *Islam, Politics, and Social Movements*, ed. Edmund Burke and Ira M. Lapidus (Berkeley: University of California

Thus we have not one but two paradigms, two concepts of the Muslim golden age. One looks to a unified state and society under the leadership of the caliph, whose authority extends to all realms of personal and public concern. This is the integralist conception of Islam. The second, in both its classic and Ottoman versions, tacitly recognizes the institutional division between the structures of state and religion. In this paradigm, Muslims look to the religious sphere for personal and communal fulfillment, to Islam as a personal and social ethos and not a concept or institution of the political regime. Finally, the differentiation of state and religion allows for an imperial and secular notion of the state and for the incorporation of Middle Eastern but not Islamic institutions and concepts into the theory, legitimation, and operation of political regimes.

ISLAM IN THE MODERN ERA

The modern era has brought a radical transformation of political and social institutions and inevitably of the ideas that shape, accompany, and reflect these institutions. There is a renewed struggle over the role that Islam should play in the constitution of contemporary Muslim societies. The role of the historical culture is being reconstructed by political struggle. There are two main arenas for the contestation over Islamic and traditional political values: the domain of the state, its definition, legit-

Press, 1988), pp. 60-80; Charles C. Stewart with E. K. Stewart, *Islam and Social Order in Mauritania* (New York: Oxford University Press, 1973).

imation, and institutional organization; and the domain of the civil or nonstate society.

THE ISLAMIC STATES

In the domain of the state, the avowedly Islamic states are a conspicuous minority. Only Saudi Arabia, Morocco, Iran, and Pakistan today profess to be legitimated or regulated by Islamic norms. The contemporary Islamic states, however, do not simply return to either of the two traditional paradigms. Absent from contemporary political rhetoric is any appeal to the concept of the caliphate.

Saudi Arabia and Morocco are in many ways closest to the traditional image of Islamic states and Muslim rulers. This is due to the continuity of premodern regimes. The Saudi state was founded in the eighteenth century by the alliance of a religious reformer, deliberately copying the precedents of the Prophet, and a tribal chieftain, using allegiance to the principles of reformed Islam, as the basis of an integrated state. The Saudi state continues to use Islam as the basis of its legitimacy, reinforced by the seizure of Mecca and Medina in 1926, by control and patronage of the pilgrimage, and by the sponsorship of international Islamic educational, missionary, and political activities. Combining religious teaching with the formation of a polity transcending tribal groups, the Saudi state seems to repeat the early Islamic experience, but the community of the Prophet was based upon his sole leadership, while the Saudi

state is based on a separation of authority and an alliance between religious and secular chieftains. While the Saudi rulers have tried to take on the religious aura of imams, there remains a lingering division between political authority vested in the state and religious authority vested in the 'ulama'—the descendants of ibn 'Abd al-Wahhab.[12]

The Moroccan regime is also based on the Islamic identity of the monarch, who is considered a caliph, an executor and defender of Islam, a personal descendant of the Prophet, a bearer of Sufi virtues, a charismatic holy man, and a dispenser of baraka, of God's blessing in the world. He is the high priest of the great Moroccan Islamic festivals such as the birthday of the Prophet and the celebration at the end of Ramadan. Like the Saudi regime, the Moroccan government is one of the few Middle Eastern or Islamic states to have survived the colonial era and the transition to the national state. It survives because the French helped preserve the monarchy as a vehicle of colonial control, while the sultans managed to maintain themselves as the personification of Moroccan national identity. While the sultan continues to bear the Islamic marks of legitimacy, his political power is actually based on

12. R. Bailey Winder, *Saudi Arabia in the 19th Century* (New York: Octagon Books, 1965); J. S. Habib, *Ibn Sa'ud's Warriors of Islam: The Ikhwan of Najd and Their Role in the Creation of the Sa'udi Kingdom* (Leiden: E. J. Brill, 1978); William Ochsenwald, "Saudi Arabia and the Islamic Revival," *International Journal of Middle East Studies*, 13:271-86 (1981).

the administrative strength of a modern territorial national state.[13]

Similarly, Islamic Iran is not built on a return to past models but rather on a radically new concept of the Islamic state. The Islamic Republic of Iran is based on a modern type of national state, constructed between 1925 and 1979, on the same organizational bases and secular concepts as Turkey. It differs in that it was the one Middle Eastern country in which the religious elites remained a powerful social and political force, antagonistic to the state elites; laid claim to direct political authority; and were able to mobilize mass support to overthrow the state. The Iranian Islamic republic, much as it is Islamic in identity, remains a national state in terms of its institutional bureaucratic structure and the kinds of economic and political policies it pursues.[14]

So Pakistan, despite its nominal Islamic affiliation, is also a modern national state. It originates in an Islam that has been defined in nationalist political terms but excludes the personal and moral dimensions of Muslim religiosity. The leaders of the movement to establish an independent Pakistan were entirely secularized in their education and life-styles and had no commitment to Islam in the traditional personal or local communal sense. Their rhetoric was Muslim in form, but the content was wholly nationalistic.

A nationalist concept of Pakistan expressed in religious and Muslim rather than in secular terms was necessary for various reasons. First, religiously based nationalism was the only rhetorical solution to the political dilemma of the Muslim elites of the Indian subcontinent. They used Islam to differentiate themselves from the Hindu Indian nationalist movement and to carve out a domain in which Muslim military and bureaucratic chieftains and Muslim merchant leaders would have a territory of their own and a more favorable opportunity to maintain their position in the postcolonial era. Second, Islam was essential to unify a population divided by tribal, ethnic, linguistic, caste, and local differences.[15]

13. Abdullah Laroui, *Les origines sociales et culturelles du nationalism marocain, 1830-1912* (Paris: F. Maspero, 1977); J. P. Halstead, *Rebirth of a Nation: The Origins and Rise of Moroccan Nationalism, 1912-1944* (Cambridge, MA: Harvard University Press, 1967).

14. Nikki R. Keddie, *Roots of Revolution: An Interpretive History of Modern Iran* (New Haven, CT: Yale University Press, 1981); H. Algar, *Religion and State in Iran, 1785-1906: The Role of the Ulama in the Qajar Period* (Berkeley: University of California Press, 1972);

idem, "The Oppositional Role of the Ulama in Twentieth-Century Iran," in *Scholars, Saints and Sufis*, ed. Nikki R. Keddie (Berkeley: University of California Press, 1972), pp. 231-55; S. Akhavi, *Religion and Politics in Contemporary Iran: Clergy-State Relations in the Pahlavi Period* (Albany: State University of New York Press, 1980); Said A. Arjomand, "Shi'ite Islam and the Revolution in Iran," *Government and Opposition*, 16:293-316 (1981); idem, "Traditionalism in Twentieth-Century Iran," in *From Nationalism to Revolutionary Islam*, ed. Said A. Arjomand (New York: Macmillan in association with St. Anthony's College, Oxford, 1984), pp. 195-232; idem, *The Turban for the Crown* (New York: Oxford University Press, 1988).

15. Leonard Binder, *Religion and Politics in Pakistan* (Berkeley: University of California Press, 1961); R. S. Wheeler, *The Politics of Pakistan* (Ithaca, NY: Cornell University Press, 1970).

THE SECULAR
NATIONAL STATES

Apart from these cases of Islam refashioned, it is striking how little influence the historical Islamic traditions have had on modern state formation. The Islamic heritage is no longer invoked, is largely ignored, and is sometimes expressly repudiated. In the great waves of state building that followed World War I and World War II, old empires were liquidated and replaced by new national states built around secular cultural identities. In Turkey, Tunisia, Egypt, Syria, Iraq, and Jordan, Islam was disestablished. It is no longer the officially supported religion of the state. Though these states sometimes give special consideration to Muslim symbols and Muslim practices, Islam no longer legitimates the state and no longer defines its moral and social vision. All of these states abolished the *millet* system and set up secular educational and judicial systems, which actually compete with the primary functions of Islam. Muslim religious life, in general, became separated from state institutions and flourishes as a differentiated element of the "civil society."[16]

The Turkish state was the most radical example of modern secularization. The republic of Ataturk was founded on nationalist and republican principles and undertook a veritable cultural revolution to liquidate

the attachment of the Turkish people to their Islamic past. It included changing the script in which Turkish was written so as to make the Ottoman language inaccessible. Muslim religious organizations were disestablished; formal instruction of Islam was abolished; changes in style of dress were mandated; and a new legal code replaced the *shari'a*. Perhaps the most important change was the increased scope given for the participation of women in public life. All of these transformations, including the idea of constitutional government, the standards of technical, social, and political modernity, and the concept of the total mobilization of society to reach its economic and political goals, were of European inspiration.[17]

Furthermore, these states strive for secular national identities. The nationalist concept did not rise spontaneously from the people or the historical culture but came into being as the preferred doctrine of opposition intelligentsia in the late nineteenth and early twentieth centuries. The primary reason for the adoption of nationalism was that Middle Eastern intelligentsias wanted to reject the political dominance of an older generation of Ottoman or Qajar imperial rulers and the moral dominance of Islam. Furthermore, nationalism served to articulate domestic opposition to European colonial rule precisely because Europeans accepted it as the basis of political society. Thus

16. Lapidus, *History of Islamic Societies*, pp. 571-717; idem, "Islam and Modernity," in *Patterns of Modernity*, ed. S. N. Eisenstadt (London: Frances Pinter, 1989), pp. 89-115; Michael S. Hudson, *Arab Politics: The Search for Legitimacy* (New Haven, CT: Yale University Press, 1977).

17. R. D. Robinson, *The First Turkish Republic* (Cambridge, MA: Harvard University Press, 1965); Lord Kinross, *Ataturk: The Rebirth of a Nation* (London: William Morrow, 1964).

nationalism conveniently expressed the opposition of a new elite both to the older imperial and religious elites of their own societies and to their colonial rulers.

Nationalism also had another, symbolic importance. For cosmopolitan, mobile, educated persons who had been taken out of the matrix of small, family-centered communities and launched into the world of cities, international contacts, foreign languages, and global political concerns, the concept of a national state became a homeland of the mind. For people who no longer belonged to the older order, and for whom the colonial political societies could offer only positions of subordination to a foreign elite, nationalism defined a new identity.

With the formation of modern states and the coming of independence, nationalism was diffused from the elites to the masses. For these masses, now subject to new state regimes bent on the social and economic transformation of their societies, nationalism would again serve as a concept replacing loyalties to more parochial family, village, and religious associations.[18]

18. On Turkish nationalism, see D. Kushner, *The Rise of Turkish Nationalism 1876-1908* (London: Frank Cass, 1977); Ziya Gökalp, *Turkish Nationalism and Western Civilization* (New York: Columbia University Press, 1959). On Arab nationalism, see Albert Hourani, *Arabic Thought in the Liberal Age* (New York: Cambridge University Press, 1983); Sylvia Haim, ed., *Arab Nationalism: An Anthology* (Berkeley: University of California Press, 1976); Zeine N. Zeine, *The Emergence of Arab Nationalism* (Delmar, NY: Caravan Books, 1973); C. E. Dawn, *From Ottomanism to Arabism: Essays on the Origins of Arab Nationalism* (Urbana: Illinois University Press, 1973);

For the masses, nationalism takes elements of the traditional culture borrowed from linguistic, ethnic, tribal, and religious identities and fuses them into a new concept of political identity. We find fused into Arab nationalism the Arabic language and its literary achievements, the saga of the Arab conquests and the early Arab empires, tribal and family ties that are still traced back to pre-Islamic Arabia, and, of course, the Arab identification with Islam.

Still, nationalism is not an age-old concept but a modern synthesis of elements of cultural traditions that previously did not belong together. In the Middle Eastern past, national, ethnic, or linguistic identities had never been important bases for political solidarity. Before the modern era, Middle Eastern peoples defined political loyalty in terms of family, lineage, or tribal ties, in terms of clientele obligations, in terms of religious affiliation, and in terms of service to the state. While Middle Eastern cultures recognized that there were important linguistic and ethnic differences between populations, these differences were never the basis of political action.

ISLAMIC ORIENTATIONS
IN MODERN SOCIETIES

Still, in the contempory situation there is a subtle, if negative, role for

Philip S. Khoury, *Urban Notables and Arab Nationalism: The Politics of Damascus, 1860-1920* (New York: Cambridge University Press, 1983); William Cleveland, *The Making of an Arab Nationalist: Ottomanism and Arabism in the Life and Thought of Sati' al-Husri* (Princeton, NJ: Princeton University Press, 1971).

Islam and for the historical political culture in shaping the general orientations, attitudes, dispositions, and practices of Middle Eastern states. The historical orientations within Islamic culture may affect the role of modern states in economic development. For example, an important strand in the Islamic tradition may contribute indirectly to the limited commitment of many contemporary Middle Eastern regimes to economic development. Both rulers and subjects often expect the state to be concerned with the maintenance of power and the exploitation of their populations, but not necessarily with economic development as the primary goal. These expectations may also reflect the traditional attitude of Muslim societies that high status is gained from education, piety, or power, to which money may contribute but is not the defining component. As opposed to European cultures, where the accumulation of wealth was the central value and was validated by high status for successful merchants and entrepreneurs, in Middle Eastern societies maintenance of power and religious piety seem to have been the dominant values.

Furthermore, modern states can be seen as an expression of the historical separation of state and Islam. This separation allows the state to be a purely political and power-based entity. Stripped of its Islamic functions, the modern state no longer has a transcending importance as the locus of ultimate values and is no longer expected to fulfill the ultimate religious yearnings of its subjects and citizens. All hope of salvation has been concentrated in the nonstate realm, in the religiocivil community, and in personal piety. This leads again, in practice, to an acceptance of the state as necessary for political power, military security, and public order, but it removes the expectation that the state itself can be a source of worldly justice and dignity. Utopian expectations that the state can embody genuine secular democratic, socialist, or egalitarian ideals are also subverted.

In these circumstances, not the Islamic but the "unspoken premises" of the Middle Eastern cultural tradition come to the fore. Many Middle Eastern states are authoritarian, military, and patrimonial regimes run by means of clienteles. For example, many features of the Turkish republic and the Ataturk program may be derived from the patrimonial premises of the Ottoman empire. In present-day Syria and Iraq, one may see a similar assumption of state power by small cliques operating through clienteles, and the continuation of the traditional expectation that the state is the prerogative of segmented elites.

Many factors help perpetuate the grip of patrimonial premises upon modern statecraft. Not only past cultural orientations but also the continuation into the modern era of small and insecure bourgeoisies, weak landowning classes, and tribal and factional divisions within society all combine to perpetuate institutional features and cultural assumptions that derive from the unspoken Middle Eastern political tradition.

ISLAM AND IDENTITY

While Islam has a limited role in the construction of contemporary national states, it has a pervasive importance in the constitution of civil society, society outside the state, and, therefore, a profound potential for the reconstruction of modern states in Islamic or neo-Islamic terms. Despite the success of secular national states, Middle Eastern identities have never been fully secularized. Rather Islam has been parochialized in national terms. Today nationalism is the single most important bearer of Islam. For example, the concept of Turkish national identity includes kinship to the Turks of Inner Asia, the Hittite ancestry of Turkish peoples in Anatolia, a history of the dominance of Turkish-speaking military elites, and also the historical allegiance of Turkish peoples to Islam. Latent Islamic identifications are the ultimate basis of Turkish national identity. In Turkey, Greeks, Armenians, and Jews, though Turkish speaking, have not been accepted as part of the nation. What makes Turks Turks, in the minds of many, is Islam, just as what makes Arabs Arabs for many Arabs is being Muslim. Much of the emotional power of nationalism in the Middle East is derived from the capacity of Islam to signify social solidarity and channel the force of Muslim faith into national commitments.[19]

In some cases Islam enters into the formation of national identity in a more direct way. Since the nineteenth century, throughout North Africa, Islamic reformism has been particularly important in overcoming parochial, localistic identifications and creating a broader sense of identity among the populations of Tunisia, Algeria, and Morocco. The reform movements created a new universal standard of religious values and religious practices; they stressed the importance of education, literate knowledge, and responsible commitment to Islamic social goals. These sentiments helped create a sense of commonality and political solidarity and became the basis of national identifications throughout North Africa.[20]

Islam continues to define national identities precisely because it remains the basis of local community life and personal religious belief. There are strong trends in all Middle Eastern countries toward new types of Islamic communal activities. Ethnic associations, religious congregations, welfare associations, charities, discussion groups, educational organizations, women's groups, economic cooperatives, and paramilitary training organizations have become more common.[21]

19. See note 18. See also James Piscatori, *Islam in a World of Nation-States* (New York: Cambridge University Press, 1986).

20. On Islam and nationalism in North Africa, see Ali Merad, *Le reformisme musulman en Algerie de 1923 à 1940* (Paris: Mouton, 1967); P. Shinar, "The Historical Approach of the Reformist 'Ulama' in the Contemporary Maghrib," *Asian and African Studies* (Jerusalem), 7:181-210 (1971); Abdullah Laroui, *Les origines du nationalisme marocain*; J. P. Halstead, *Rebirth of a Nation*; E. E. Evans-Pritchard, *The Sanusi of Cyrenaica* (New York: Oxford University Press, 1949).

21. See Morroe Berger, *Islam in Egypt Today* (New York: Cambridge University Press, 1970); Gilles Kepel, *Muslim Extremism in Egypt* (Berkeley: University of California Press, 1985).

Furthermore, even where Islamic movements are not strongly organized, Islam remains important as a personal or private religion. While it no longer regulates the public world, it continues to be vital to people's ethical and psychological needs. In highly secularized Middle Eastern societies, Islam becomes more and more a quest for meaning without being linked to political purposes. In these milieus, a new kind of Islamic community emerges, one that is based on personal piety rather than on commitment to political institutions, and an Islam of private belief and private social identity that is dissociated from the communal political matrix in which such identity was once embedded.[22]

This reconstruction of Islam has important implications for political and social behavior. First, Islam, especially in its reformist and revivalist versions, is the basis for a more fully self-disciplined and self-directed autonomous personality. The neo-Islamic movements seem to cultivate in their members a sense of social responsibility, moral dynamism, and an active engagement in the affairs of the society with a view to Islamizing contemporary Muslim populations. They provide through religious identity a sense of dignity, self-esteem, and self-discipline. This focusing of individual loyalties upon religious values is a critical factor in mobilizing people for moral, social, and political action.

Finally, and perhaps most important, Islam is the basis of political opposition movements. These movements appeal precisely to the excluded elements in the formation of modern political states, to the petite bourgeoisie or *bazaaris*, and sometimes to workers, students, and rural migrants to cities; they have a new urban class base in contrast to the historically rural character of reformist movements. They try to define the principles of a new Muslim morality by going back to the Quran and the *sunna*, but their idea is not to create a prescriptive program of detailed rules for behavior but to find general values to allow people living in new social conditions to reorganize their daily lives. These movements also attempt to meet the need for social solidarity in disorganized populations. They build up extensive networks of cells or chapters and mosques, schools, clinics, clubs, cooperative workshops, and industries. Ultimately, they aspire to the creation of an Islamic state.

Yet the goals of many of these movements are not, strictly speaking, political. The movements are not committed to particular institutions or to political principles such as democracy and equality. They are concerned rather with individual morality and ethical behavior, and to them the state is simply the force that encourages or requires the people to adhere to Islamic norms. The true domain of Islam is still the righteous small community and the ethical individual.

22. For postmodern Islam, see Lapidus, *History of Islamic Societies*, pp. 551-70, 879-917.

ANNALS, *AAPSS*, 524, November 1992

Political Islam:
The Origins

By CHARLES E. BUTTERWORTH

ABSTRACT: Seeking to understand why Islamicists prize the non-democratic and even nonliberal political rule to be found in revelation-based politics, the article first considers the older Arabic and Islamic analysis of political regimes and their goals. Then it investigates why, in a more recent past, thoughtful thinkers within that same cultural milieu called for independence while endorsing non-democratic and nonliberal regimes. Finally, it suggests why thinkers today continue to do the same. The goal is not to apologize for Islamicist doctrines in the present or in the recent or distant past but to point to the problems with current Western analyses and critiques of political Islam.

Professor of government and politics at the University of Maryland, College Park, Charles E. Butterworth specializes in medieval Islamic political philosophy. His publications include critical editions of most of the Middle Commentaries written by Averroes on Aristotle's logic; translations of books and treatises by Averroes, Alfarabi, and Alrazi, as well as Maimonides; and studies of different aspects of the political teaching of these and other thinkers in the ancient, medieval, and modern traditions of philosophy.

BEFORE rushing to castigate as benighted, backward, and hopelessly illiberal those Middle Eastern peoples who long to govern themselves by religious laws and thus to ensure a higher level of communal moral decency, we modern Westerners would do well to pause and reflect momentarily on our own cultural origins. Though now almost universally rejected in the West as a valid description of the proper attitude toward government and its functionaries, the following admonition once held great sway among faithful Christians:

Let every soul be subject to the governing authorities. For there is no authority except from God, and those that exist have been instituted by God. Therefore the one resisting authority goes against what God has appointed, and resisters will incur judgment.[1]

Nor is it all that different from the injunction laid upon pious Muslims:

Oh, you who believe, obey God and obey the Apostle and those charged with authority among you. If you disagree among yourselves about anything, refer it to God and the Apostle.[2]

Not until sometime after Marsilius of Padua (c. 1275-1342) were Paul's strictures forsaken and the famous advice offered by Jesus about distinguishing between the things belonging to Caesar and those belonging to God raised to the elevated rank it occupies today.[3] Though of a piece with the prophet Samuel's dire predictions about the harsh demands a king would make upon his subjects,[4] Jesus' suggestion is not consonant with the larger Old Testament teaching about the need for the faithful to let themselves be guided in all matters by God. Nonetheless, by the late fourteenth or fifteenth century, we Westerners began to turn away from the notion that political authority is divinely inspired. Whatever the reasons for that change—deeper understanding of the base demands of politics on rulers, however honorable their intentions; conviction that political and temporal concerns differ

---

1. See Rom. 13:1-2; here and in what follows, the translation is my correction of the Revised Standard Version. The next two verses (13:3-4) explain why Paul insists so adamantly on obedience to authority: "For rulers are not a terror to good conduct, but to bad. Would you have no fear of the one who is in authority? Then do what is good, and you will receive his approval. For he is God's servant for your good. But if you do wrong, be fearful, for he does not bear the sword in vain; he is the servant of God to execute His wrath on the wrongdoer." The rest of the exhortation (13:5-7) is also worth considering.

2. See Quran 4:59; the translation is my own.

3. See Matt. 22:15-22: "Then the Pharisees went and took counsel how to entangle him in his talk. And they sent their disciples to him, along with the Herodians, saying, 'Teacher, we know that you are true, teach the way of God truthfully, and concern yourself about no one; for you do not regard the rank of men. Tell us, then, what do you think: Is it lawful to pay taxes to Caesar, or not?' But Jesus, aware of their malice, said, 'Why do you test me, you hypocrites? Show me the money for the tax.' And they brought him a dinar. And Jesus said to them, 'Whose likeness and inscription is this?' They said, 'Caesar's.' Then he said to them, 'Render, then, Caesar's things to Caesar and the things that are God's to God.' When they heard it, they were astonished; and they went away and left him." Note especially verse 21, that is, the next to the last sentence. See also Matt. 17:24-27 and compare with Mark 12:13-17, esp. 17, and Luke 20:19-26, esp. 25. Again, the translation is my correction of the Revised Standard Version.

4. See 1 Sam. 8:10-21, 1-9.

radically from spiritual and moral ones; doubt about the existence of a divine or natural order—it finds a clear and all too familiar expression in the middle of the eighteenth century with Rousseau's famous, albeit completely unsubstantiated, assertion that "man is born free."[5]

It is the major sentiment standing behind our repugnance for political regimes that take their bearing from revelation, that is, for regimes that are or would be self-consciously Islamicist. Convinced that natural human freedom—and the equality that necessarily accompanies it—must be respected and preserved by a political regime if it is to be deemed legitimate, we condemn those regimes that aim at instilling moral virtues and sacrificing human liberty for a higher goal.[6] Although particular actions—for example, Ayatollah Khomeini's sentence of death against Salman Rushdie—or promises of actions to be taken—such as the Algerian Islamic Salvation Front's declaration that once in power it would put an end to the very democratic systems that allowed it to come to power—reveal all too clearly the lack of patience that Islamicist regimes have for the freedoms and procedures we Westerners hold to be essential hallmarks of good government, it is also utterly manifest that, precisely because those hallmarks are merely procedural, they are not the only guarantors of good government.

For this reason, it is appropriate to inquire why others prize the nondemocratic and even nonliberal political rule that is to be found in revelation-based politics. To this end, I propose first to consider the older Arabic and Islamic analyses of political regimes and their goals. Then I will explain why, in a more recent past, thoughtful thinkers within that same cultural milieu called for independence while endorsing nondemocratic and nonliberal regimes. Finally, I will suggest why thinkers today continue to do the same. There is no intent here to apologize for Islamicist doctrines in the present or in the recent or distant past, for such apologetics would serve no purpose. If anything, my approach merely points to the failure in current Western analysis of political Islam to pay sufficient attention to the rhetorical transformations that arguments for something like an Islamic regime have undergone in the course of history as the character of the audience addressed has changed over time and as the goal pursued by the various speakers has been altered.

5. See Jean-Jacques Rousseau, *Social Contract*, bk. 1, chap. 1. The complete phrase reads: "Man is born free, and everywhere he is in chains" (my translation). *Social Contract* was published in 1762.

6. See, for example, Leonard Binder, *Islamic Liberalism: A Critique of Development Ideologies* (Chicago: University of Chicago Press, 1988), pp. 1-4; also Francis Fukuyama, *The End of History and the Last Man* (New York: Free Press, 1992), passim.

THE DISTANT PAST

There is little need to insist that Islam offers as much practical as it does spiritual guidance to the faithful. Whether we look back to the community founded by the Prophet Muhammad while he was in Medina (622-30) or to the way it was continued during the two years after he returned to Mecca, whether we think about the tradition of the four rightly guided caliphs (632-61)—the first successors to Muhammad—or about the caliphs who guided the Umayyad (661-750), Abbasid (750-1258), and Spanish Umayyad (756-1031) empires, or whether we consider the princes and commanders who ruled the Arab and Berber dynasties in Spain and North Africa (1031-1492) and the sultans who ruled the Ottoman empire (1453-1918), we see political rule linked with religion. From the very opening of the Quran and the plea that the Lord of the universe show the faithful the straight path to the assurance that He has made of Muslims "a balanced nation that [they] may be witnesses to people" and on to the promise that He will bring victory to those who enter His religion, the close link between Islam and power is evident.[7]

During the Golden Age of Islam, referred to in this *Annals* issue in the article by Ira Lapidus, numerous thinkers argued that Islam should be joined to politics. Nominally, of course, it was joined. The rulers were supposed to represent a continuation of the Prophet Muhammad's rule; they were his successors and, as such, something like the vicegerents of God. Yet, as Lapidus notes, there was a great gap between intention and achievement, between what was supposed to be and what actually was. Jurists, theologians, and philosophers sought in their writings as well as in their deeds to resolve this discrepancy. They addressed them-

7. See Quran 1:2-4, 5; 2:143; 110:1-2; the translation is mine.

selves to a small, but learned, audience, namely, to individuals schooled in the sciences of Islam (the sayings and deeds of the Prophet, jurisprudence, and theology), in grammar as well as in poetry and literature, and in philosophical writings.

The jurists and theologians strove to make revealed doctrine more apparent. With a jurist like al-Mawardi (c. 985-1058), this resulted in explanations of the qualities needed for a person to become a caliph, the ways matters of state could be administered without infringing on revealed laws, or the conditions that must be met for military incursions to be in accordance with Quranic strictures. Neither al-Mawardi nor any of his fellow jurists raised the larger questions of whether it was appropriate to change political rule itself or how a wise ruler might expand the liberty of his subjects. In the writings of a sometime theologian like al-Ghazali (1058-1111), we find a defense of doctrines of the faith and attacks upon groups and individuals whose thinking appeared to threaten the well-being of the community. Even in his efforts to quicken religious faith, the emphasis is on particular issues— above all, on morals—rather than on how a ruler intent upon following in the path of the Prophet might best fashion his regime. Furthermore, in speaking about moral improvement, al-Ghazali dwells on personal endeavor; he pays no attention to how laws or institutions might shape moral conduct.

For reflections on the goals of political life and how a regime might be structured to achieve them, we must turn to the philosophers. Our best guides in such matters are Alfarabi (870-950), Avicenna (980-1037), and Averroes (1126-98), not least because they dare to look back beyond the advent of Islam to the wisdom of Greece in order to suggest what can make political life best. In looking back, however, they never forget the importance of revelation and its influence on politics.

Alfarabi draws attention to this new phenomenon in his *Enumeration of the Sciences* by setting forth two accounts of political science. Both presuppose the validity of the traditional separation between the practical and the theoretical sciences, but neither is adequate for the radically new situation created by the appearance of revealed religion. The first account puts forth a political science that is simply practical.[8] It begins abruptly, not be defining political science and its general scope or what it consists of, but by stating what political science investigates, namely, the distinctively human things: voluntary actions and ways of life. The investigation looks back to what leads to these actions and ways of life

as well as forward to why the actions are performed.

The first political science thus provides a general overview of individual and civic human morality without ever leaving the immediate domain in which humans find themselves. At no point does it look beyond human beings and human things. This first political science also shows why political association is beneficial. In addition, it sets forth the general guidelines that thoughtful individuals can use to judge between different regimes.

The second account of political science goes beyond the practical limits of the first without presenting a fully theoretical political science. Indeed, even though this political science is said to include the "theoretical and practical sciences," such exclusive attention is paid to what it has to say about actions that nothing is said about how it handles opinions, especially the theoretical opinions set forth in religion.[9] Alfarabi designates it at first as political philosophy, explaining that it is limited to investigating general rules and to giving general descriptions or patterns for determining the voluntary actions and ways of life it investigates. This second political science starts, then, from where the first political science left off; it presupposes the investigations already undertaken by the first political science and moves from them to the formulation of general rules and patterns.

From this sketch it should be manifest that neither the first nor the second account of political science in

8. See 'Uthman Amin, ed., *Ihsa' al-'Ulum li-al-Farabi* (Cairo: Dar al-Fikr al-'Arabi, 1949). Fauzi Najjar has translated the work into English; see *Enumeration of the Sciences* in *Medieval Political Philosophy: A Sourcebook*, ed. Ralph Lerner and Muhsin Mahdi (New York: Free Press of Glencoe, 1963), pp. 22-30. The following interpretation develops a suggestion made by Muhsin Mahdi in "Science, Philosophy, and Religion in Alfarabi's *Enumeration of the Sciences*," in *The Cultural Context of Medieval Learning*, ed. J. E. Murdoch and E. D. Sylla (Dordrecht: B. Reidel, 1975), pp. 113-47, esp. pp. 144-45. The first account of political science occurs in *Enumeration of the Sciences*, 102:4-104:15.

9. The second account is set forth in *Enumeration of the Sciences*, 104:16-107:4.

the *Enumeration of the Sciences* can lead to the kind of rulership or to the royal craft needed for the new phenomenon of revealed religion. Nor can either speak about the opinions or actions that the jurisprudence and theology of revealed religion address. Such a rulership or royal craft can come only from a political science that would both combine theoretical and practical sciences along with prudence and show how they are to be ordered in the soul of the ruler. This kind of political science would be more theoretical than the one first set forth in the *Enumeration of the Sciences* and go beyond the understanding of the sciences presupposed in the second one, an understanding that is based on what has preceded in the *Enumeration of the Sciences*.[10] In his other writings—most notably in his *Book of Religion*, but also in the *Political Regime*, the *Aphorisms of the Statesmen*, and the *Principles of the Opinions of the Inhabitants of the Virtuous City*—Alfarabi develops this broader political science. It speaks of religious beliefs as opinions and of acts of worship as actions and notes that both are prescribed by a supreme ruler or prophet for a community.

Opening with a discussion of religion centered in political community, then moving to political science, the *Book of Religion*[11] presents Alfarabi's

restructuring of political science. As in the *Enumeration of the Sciences*, two accounts are provided, but here they are preceded by an account of virtuous religion. It begins with a description of a supreme ruler whose goals are similar to those of the Prophet and an analysis of his prescriptions. The reasons for everything done by this supreme ruler are traced back to philosophy so incessantly that religion appears to depend on philosophy, theoretical as well as practical. Similarly, the art of jurisprudence, presented as providing for what the supreme ruler did not accomplish before his death, is portrayed as both dependent on practical philosophy and a part of political science.[12] Obliged to say something about practical philosophy, Alfarabi complies by again offering two accounts of political science. The deficiencies of the first resemble those that came to light in the *Enumeration of the Sciences*, but the second account provides what is needed by presenting a political science that can offer a comprehensive view of the universe and indicate what kind of practical acumen permits the one who possesses this understanding, either the supreme ruler or a successor endowed with all of his qualities, to rule wisely. Able to explain the various ranks of all the beings, it also stresses the importance of religion for uniting the citizens and for helping them attain the virtues that prolong decent political life.[13]

This view of the harmony between good government and the activity of the Prophet finds similar expression

10. See Mahdi, "Science, Philosophy, and Religion," p. 137.

11. See Alfarabi, *Kitab al-Millah wa Nusus Ukhra*, ed. Muhsin Mahdi (Beirut: Dar al-Mashriq, 1968). An English translation of this work by Charles E. Butterworth is in the new edition of *Medieval Political Philosophy: A Sourcebook*, ed. Ralph Lerner and Muhsin Mahdi (New York: Free Press of Glencoe, forthcoming).

12. See *Book of Religion*, paras. 5, 10.

13. See ibid., paras. 15-27, esp. para. 27 end.

in Avicenna's most extensive discussion of politics, that set forth at the very end of the *Metaphysics* in his *Shifa*.[14] It differs from any of the accounts to be found in Alfarabi because Avicenna is silent on the different sorts of virtuous and vicious regimes, rulerships, and civic communities. He says nothing about what distinguishes them or how to bring them about. He is equally silent about what would cause each one to cease to exist and how each one might be transformed into one opposed to it. Political science for Avicenna, at least insofar as it is presented here, centers around an explanation of the political characteristics of prophecy and divine law.

Nonetheless, the attention he gives those two subjects leads him to raise questions fundamental to politics: the nature of law, the purpose of political community, the need for sound moral life among the citizens, the importance of providing for divorce as well as for marriage, the conditions for just war, the considerations that lie behind penal laws, and the goal of human life. Avicenna's description of the way the political community arises and the provisions made for it by a ruler as wise as a prophet shows why traditional Islamic political rule is praiseworthy and alludes to what is wrong with regimes that prize freedom, the pursuit of wealth, or conquest rather than adherence to moral virtue. To underline his purpose, Avicenna constantly refers to the ruler who sets down the laws he praises here as one who gives "traditional law" (calling this lawgiver a *sannin* and his law *sunna*) or as one who gives "divine law" (calling this lawgiver a *shari'* and his law *shari'a*).

For reasons too involved to discuss here, Averroes perceives his task differently from either of his two predecessors. Seeing the pursuit of philosophy threatened in his day and saddened by the bickering between the proponents of different religious factions or sects, he attempts to show why philosophical investigation was warranted by the divine law. In the most famous of his works, *The Decisive Treatise*, he likens the lawgiver to a physician: just as the latter strives to preserve the health or cure sicknesses of the body, so does the former for the soul.[15] The lawgiver, like the physician, knows what preserves health and prevents sickness. He understands what good health is and how it can be achieved as well as how to preserve it. Because those whom he seeks to heal do not understand these things, he speaks to them in language they can understand. He no more enters into the details or the premises of his actions than the physician does of his. To gain the people's acceptance of his prescriptions, he uses whatever kind of speech the people can most readily understand— again, as does the physician.

14. See Avicenna, *Kitab al-Shifa, al-Ilahiyyat*, ed. G. Anawati and S. Zayid (Cairo: al-Hai'a al-'Amma li-Shu'un al-Matabi' al-Amiriyya, 1960). The discussion of politics occurs in bk. 10, chaps. 1-5.

15. See Averroes, *Kitab Fasl al-Maqal*, ed. George F. Hourani (Leiden: E. J. Brill, 1959). An English translation by Hourani is to be found in *Medieval Political Philosophy* (1963), pp. 163-86. For what follows, see the translation by Charles E. Butterworth forthcoming in the new edition of *Medieval Political Philosophy*, paras. 53-56.

The problem, notes Averroes, is that many jurists and theologians do not understand that the lawgiver or prophet spoke indirectly and thus try to explain things to the people that only confuse them. By this analogy, Averroes shows why one cannot interpret all the words of the Prophet literally and points to the need for those so qualified to investigate the health and sickness of the soul as well as the ways to preserve or attain the one and avoid or repel the other. To do so is to understand the Prophet's goal with respect to the people for whom he legislated, for the Prophet's prescriptions are his laws, and they presuppose political community. Like Alfarabi and Avicenna before him, then, Averroes seeks to preserve philosophical inquiry because it provides the understanding and explanation of what is sound about that legislation.

None of these philosophers explicitly rails against the rulers of the day, although Averroes does suggest on occasion that things are not as good as they might be in "these cities in this time of ours."[16] Their goal is not to urge radical change or to cajole actual rulers to act better by offering advice about how to rule, but to show what goals are to be pursued by a good ruler and what conduces to the achievement of those goals. For them, the purpose of living together in community is to acquire the human excellences impossible to at-

16. This occurs above all in his *Commentary on Plato's "Republic"*; see Charles E. Butterworth, *Philosophy, Ethics, and Virtuous Rule: A Study of Averroes' Commentary on Plato's "Republic"* (Cairo: American University in Cairo Press, 1986), pp. 12-13, 87-88.

tain in solitary existence, and they investigate how the prescriptions of the Prophet as well as the practices traditionally derived from them lead to these excellences. Because the goal of association is excellence, intellectual as well as moral, rule by one who has such excellence is preferable. Though it is admittedly difficult to find rulers so qualified, rule by such a one remains the standard. Similarly, the pursuit of excellence—not the pursuit of freedom, wealth, or conquest—remains the standard. The philosophers of the Arabic or Islamic distant past stand out as guides to that goal, guides ever cognizant of its arduous demands and abundant riches. Moreover, acutely aware of the intellectual and moral differences between individuals and the groups they constitute, these philosophers see no reason to expect much from popular government.

THE RECENT PAST

Apart from Ibn Khaldun and perhaps Mulla Sadra, political reflection in the Arabic or Islamic tradition languished during the next six and a half centuries. Philosophical speculation was focused on metaphysical questions and issues of personal morality. When it did turn to politics, it usually took the form of particular advice to rulers and was directed to questions that would help them preserve their own reign. Only with the advent of Jamal al-Din al-Afghani (1837-97) does it return to the larger questions raised by Alfarabi, Avicenna, and Averroes.

Al-Afghani is troubled by the weakness that characterizes the Islamic world in his day. Dominated by Western imperialist powers, even in their own lands, Arab and Muslim rulers seem to have lost all memory of the grandeur and greatness that were once theirs and to have no idea of how they might regain their former rank. His challenge to thoughtful Muslims, first formulated in lectures to university audiences and then distributed in occasional articles read by an educated few, won him the sympathy of Muhammad 'Abduh (1849-1905). These two eventually joined forces to launch—from Paris, because no Arab or Muslim country would tolerate al-Afghani's presence —a short-lived journal known as *al-'Urwa al-wuthqa* (The most solid link). In it, they argue vigorously for independence from foreign domination but see no reason to replace monarchic rule with popular government. It is their conviction that the Arab and Muslim populaces are not yet sufficiently disciplined to govern themselves well and thus still need the tutelage of a ruler who will train them in the skills needed for self-government.[17] Their total silence elsewhere in their writings about the possibility of future self-rule need not be taken as evidence that the promise here is no more than a diplomatic ploy to preserve the goodwill of otherwise sympathetic Westerners. Indeed, al-Afghani's generous concession to Ernest Renan that philosophy and religion must always be in conflict also strengthens the case for

postponing democracy, for he makes it clear that Middle Eastern peoples will not soon be ready to forsake religious guidance.[18]

The same theme is developed more extensively by 'Abduh. In fact, he bases his own political teaching on an attempt to explain the reasonableness of letting political life be guided by Islamic precepts. His famous *Risalat al-tawhid* (Treatise on unity) presents a coherent exposition of how Islam helps human beings to live together in society so that they may eventually attain the happiness intended for them by the Creator. 'Abduh focuses on the assistance that God offers mankind by sending prophets who show us how to get along in political community. By drawing our attention to something higher than self-preservation or immediate gain, they teach us how to work together without harming one another or causing evil. In learning to honor such a higher Being, we are prompted to love one another as fellow creatures of that Being, to control our desires, redirect our passions, and regulate our actions. Almost like another Alfarabi, 'Abduh explains what prompts the opinions the prophets ask us to believe and the actions they urge us to perform.

Whereas al-Afghani addresses his explanations to anyone who will listen, even to the supremely confident readers of the *Journal des débats*, his primary audience is those learned Near and Middle Easterners, Mus-

17. See "Madi al-umma wa hadiruha wa 'ilaj 'ilaliha" [The nation's past, its present, and the treating of its ills], in *al-'Urwa al-wuthqa* (Cairo: Dar al-'Arabi, 1957), pp. 13-21; al-Afghani, "al-Hukuma al-istibdadiyya" [Despotic government], *Misr*, 2/33 (1879).

18. See Ernest Renan, "L'Islamisme et la science," *Journal des débats*, 30 Mar. 1883; Jamal al-Din al-Afghani, "Réponse à M. Renan," ibid., 18 May 1883; Ernest Renan's own reply to al-Afghani in ibid., 19 May 1883.

lim or Christian, who suffer the degradation of imperialist rule. Even so, his references are primarily Muslim, and the past age of glory he recalls is distinctly one of Muslim hegemony. That tendency is taken further by 'Abduh, with his emphasis on the soundness of living according to Islamic precepts; but the audience is still a learned one. With Hasan al-Banna (1906-49), as with Abu al-A'la al-Mawdudi (1903-80) before him, the audience and the teaching change radically. Both speak to the masses, al-Mawdudi in order to defend Islam and to show how easily it can be applied to all problems of daily life, al-Banna in order to reform Muslims and to awaken them to what they can be as self-reliant and fully conscious followers of their faith. The change in audience and in goal are reflected in the quality of the arguments both offer, namely, ones far more rhetorical and hortatory than analytical or measured.

Each sees a need for founding an Islamic political regime. Al-Mawdudi considers it the only rule under which Muslims can live freely and fully as Muslims and thus deems it essential that the Quranic provisions for personal and communal virtue be implemented. For al-Banna, it makes no sense to deny Muslims the right to national liberation natural to all peoples; moreover, only a Muslim regime can fight against the atheism, pursuit of pleasure, self-centeredness, and relentless profit seeking that he believes will destroy all of Western society. In addition, each is responsible for the formation of groups that seek to carry out the teachings of the founder. Yet whereas the Islamic

groups patterned on al-Mawdudi's teaching arose almost accidentally, Hasan al-Banna founded the Muslim Brotherhood from the very beginning in order to spread his call to other Muslims more readily and more efficiently.

THE ISSUE BEFORE US

The spokesmen for Islamic government who succeed al-Mawdudi and al-Banna share with them the desire to speak to a larger audience and the willingness to make popular arguments. But instead of railing against non-Muslim and Western colonial or imperialist powers, these spokesmen denounce the Muslim rulers who came to power after Near and Middle Easterners were moved to act on the teachings of al-Afghani, 'Abduh, al-Mawdudi, and al-Banna. Whereas al-Mawdudi and al-Banna simply ignore the philosophical teachings of the distant tradition on which al-Afghani and 'Abduh are only too happy to rely for guidance as well as for evidence of a rich cultural past, new spokesmen such as Sayyid Qutb (1906-66) and Ruhollah Khomeini (1900-89) dismiss the older philosophers as having been too influenced by a foreign tradition to be of any assistance in an authentic Muslim undertaking. Though they thereby demonstrate that they have learned nothing from Averroes' *Decisive Treatise* and its famous rebuke of al-Ghazali for this same error, they are not in the least concerned. Their goals are to defend Islam against the aspersions cast upon it by Westerners who have failed to understand its merits, to bring about a thorough

moral change in Muslims themselves, and to achieve truly Islamic
self-rule rather than an imitation of
socialism, as in the Egypt of Nasser
combated by Qutb, or an unbridled
capitalist consumerism, as in the
Iran of the Shah as portrayed by
Khomeini.

Now others too numerous to name
follow the lead of Qutb and
Khomeini. Shahrough Akhavi discusses Egypt's 'Abd al-Salam Faraj in
his contribution to this volume, and
Mary-Jane Deeb speaks of Tunisia's
Rached Ghannouchi, Lebanon's Muhammad Hussain Fadhlallah, and
Ahmad Yassin, the founder of Hamas
in the Occupied Territories. Even
were we to add the names of Egypt's
Shaykh Kishk and Mustafa Mah-
moud, the list would still not be exhausted. All those now calling for Islamic politics share the desire to replace errant rulers who have failed to
enforce or to abide by the teachings
of Islamic divine law, the shari'a, as
well as to improve the material and
spiritual well-being of fellow Muslims through encouraging their
closer adherence to Islamic precepts.
But despite opportunities for practical reflection afforded by current instances of Islamic rule in nations as
diverse as Pakistan, Saudi Arabia,
and Iran, these spokesmen have yet
to set forth clear ideas about how
Islamic government should function.
Their rhetoric, addressed now more
than ever to the unlearned masses of
citizens, speaks only of what might
be and ignores the practical, procedural issues of how these goals are to
be reached without harming citizens
along the way. It also ignores the
major question of how to provide for

prudent decisions once the goal of Islamic government has been reached.
To some extent, the failure to address
such issues is also a result of overriding concern with reaching the goals.

Yet, properly understood, it is
against precisely this tendency to ignore procedural safeguards that
Western criticism of political Islam is
addressed. There are other objections, of course. We in the West are
more concerned with safeguarding
freedom than with providing for citizen virtue. That is partly due to a
prevailing confusion about what
ought to be called virtue, one that has
its roots in the thinkers to whom we
turn for guidance about classical liberalism. Though they teach us that
the greatest goods are life, liberty,
and the pursuit of either property or
happiness, they have little to say
about the pursuit of virtue. Similarly,
the high regard in which we hold life
and freedom leads us to look dimly on
coercive inducements to virtuous
conduct—especially when those inducements threaten life or limb.

To the latter kind of procedural
objections, proponents of Islamic government have a ready answer: the
penalties are meant to serve as vivid
signs that there are boundaries or
limits that human conduct should
not transgress, and before the divine
law that calls for such penalties is
instituted, Muslims subject to them
must undergo a thorough moral reform. For such thinkers—and those
in this path are only too happy to cite
the teaching of Hasan al-Banna with
approval—the basic preliminary to
an official return to Islamic law must
be a thorough moral reform of the
citizenry carried out at all levels of

society. But the Western criticism is not merely procedural, at least not in this sense. It goes deeper, for it raises the very question of whether moral improvement is the proper concern of government or not. Until at least the days of Muhammad 'Abduh, the philosophical foundations for considering moral improvement a proper concern of government were clear; since then, the cogent philosophical defense tends to have been rejected, but the theological one goes back to basically the same principles.

When all of these objections have been met, there is still another reason behind the Western criticism of political Islam. Whatever Western attitudes are today about imperialism and colonialism, it is clear that the West still considers itself as deserving to set the tempo for the rest of the world to follow. Patent as this is in the title and basic premise of Fukuyama's best-seller or in Binder's acknowledged presupposition that the whole world—and especially the Islamic part of it—must become politically liberal, it also prevails in the analyses of those who seek to explain what is truly fearful about calls for political Islam. Shireen T. Hunter insists, for example, that we should not consider these calls or the movements they engender as aberrations "in the social, economic, and political development of the Muslim world" that will soon pass away but should rather be alarmed about "the fundamentalists' animosity toward the great-power domination of the present international order."[19] To this there are only two replies. One calls for greater tolerance with respect to the basic presuppositions of those who look to religion for guidance and thus serves as an especially appealing rejoinder to the proponents of liberalism.[20] The other, set forth here, points to the goals sought by those in favor of Islamicism and argues for their validity both because they are part of a higher understanding of politics that we Westerners once embraced and because the political liberalism we now follow has not shown them to be without benefit but merely difficult to achieve.

19. See Shireen T. Hunter, "Islamic Fundamentalism: What It Really Is and Why It Frightens the West," *SAIS Review*, 6:189-91, 199-200 (1986). See also R. Hrair Dekmejian, "Anatomy of Islamic Revival: Legitimacy Crisis, Ethnic Conflict, and the Search for Islamic Alternatives," *Middle East Journal*, 34:1-3 (1980); Lucien S. Vandenbroucke, "Why Allah's Zealots? A Study of the Causes of Islamic Fundamentalism in Egypt and Saudi Arabia," *Middle East Review*, 16:32, 38 (1983); Raymond A. Hinnebusch, Jr., *Egyptian Politics under Sadat: The Post-Populist Development of an Authoritarian-Modernizing State* (Cambridge: Cambridge University Press, 1985), pp. 199-200; Hassan Bakr A. Hassan, "Islamic Revivalism and Its Impact on the Middle East and the Superpowers," in *Culture and International Relations*, ed. Jongsuk Chay (New York: Praeger, 1990), pp. 207-8.

20. See Mona Abul-Fadl, *Islam and the Middle East: The Aesthetics of a Political Inquiry* (Herndon: International Institute of Islamic Thought, 1990), pp. 38-39 and passim. In this light, Rousseau's single negative dogma needed in civil religion is instructive; see *Social Contract*, bk. 4, chap. 8, last three paras.

ANNALS, *AAPSS*, 524, November 1992

Popular Islam

By PATRICK D. GAFFNEY

ABSTRACT: The current wave of religiously motivated protest movements throughout the Islamic world has frequently been associated with popular Islam. This concept of a popular, as opposed to an official, practice has deep roots, however, extending back to the formative period of the Muslim tradition. Classically, the emergence of a clerical elite defined in terms of their functions in the fields of law, education, and administration as well as religion coincided with the rise of a parallel folk piety inspired by Sufism which adapted Islam to local circumstances. The sweeping changes of the last two centuries have undermined many of the old religious institutions belonging to both these spheres. But the overall structures of social relations have largely remained within the context of the nation-state. With few and short-lived exceptions, rural peasants and urban masses who continue to regard Islam as the primary basis for their identity have not responded positively to the summons of the current revival. On the other hand, Islamicists, despite divisions among themselves, have established their importance. Popular Islam persists therefore as a vital concept pointing in two directions.

Patrick D. Gaffney is currently an associate professor in the Department of Anthropology and a faculty fellow at the Kroc Institute for International Peace Studies at the University of Notre Dame. He has conducted extensive field research, especially in Egypt. His publications include articles on the ethnography of Islamic preaching, the history of religious bureaucracies, the function of mosques, social movements, popular culture, and human rights.

THE term "popular Islam" suggests a variety of meanings across different fields of discourse. Most generally, it occurs as a term of contrast. It describes one set of phenomena presumably associated with the populace or the masses over against another set joined to the elite. On another level, however, as a unit of analysis, popular Islam also serves as a symbolic index for the assertion of authority. It is evoked with respect to such contested areas as orthodoxy, authenticity, legitimacy, social justice, modernity, alignment, popularity, and accountability.

With respect to the sociopolitical aspects of religion, the term appears with both of these connotations. In most classical contexts, referring to beliefs and practices as popular usually denotes complexes held to be aberrant, such as the veneration of saints; the use of amulets, charms, and oracles; or the often spectacular performances of certain Sufi brotherhoods. This conservative approach typically dismisses these activities as products of ignorance or superstition. The late shaykh of al-Azhar, Dr. Abd al-Halim Mahmud, for instance, held popular Islam to be a sort of oxymoron. It consisted simply of abuses, which he disparaged as "the religion of the streets," which needed reform.

For those who study religion from an anthropologically informed perspective, the term is essentially neutral, conveying empirical facts. In general, "popular Islam" alludes to the derivative and synthetic patterns of the little tradition characteristic of communities on the periphery rather than at the center of a putative Islamic civilization. The category includes those forms of Islamic expression typical of the commoners in urban neighborhoods, villages, or tribal settings. Presumably it reflects the adaptations of localized social structures and indigenous cultural values to the so-called great tradition of the literate, urban upper class, which supposedly embodies the normative standard.

Increasingly, however, the term "popular Islam" has prompted considerable debate over its definition and its usefulness. Nevertheless, most scholars continue to agree on the importance of distinguishing between what Abdul Hamid el-Zein has called different "Islams" even while controversy persists over terminology, methods, and interpretation.[1]

More recently, popular Islam has arisen as a concept of major significance in discussions of the ideological, social, political, and economic tensions that currently challenge many regimes and to some extent the entire international order of the contemporary Middle East. Here, in addition to serving as a term of description and analysis with sometimes contradictory applications, popular Islam is frequently connected with various militant groups that manifest this link in all manner of names, titles, and slogans. Explicit evocations of a "popular" base by Arabic designa-

1. Abdul Hamid el-Zein, "Beyond Ideology and Theology: The Search for the Anthropology of Islam," in *Annual Review of Anthropology*, ed. Bernard J. Siegel (Palo Alto, CA: Annual Reviews, 1977), pp. 227-54; J.D.Y. Peel and C. C. Steward, eds., *"Popular Islam" South of the Sahara* (Manchester: Manchester University Press, 1985); Jacques Waardenburg, "Official and Popular Religion in Islam," *Social Compass*, 25(3-4):315-41 (1978).

tions such as "popular front" (*jabha sha'biyya*) or, in Persian, of the "masses" (*tudeh*) are usually avoided since they are tainted as Marxist vocabulary. But Islamicist groups often project an equivalent image of populism by resort to other phrases.

For instance, names may connote the broadest possible appeal regardless of a group's limited scope or the exclusive nature of its actual membership. Illustrations include Hizballah, or Party of God, a militant nucleus of marginalized Lebanese Shiites; Jama'at al-Muslimin, or Society of Muslims, a tiny clandestine band once operating in Upper Egypt; and Ittijah al-Islami, or Islamic Trend, a Tunisian protest movement made up largely of students, young intellectuals, and middle-class businessmen. Thus popular Islam has come to be variously identified with the perceived properties of everything signaled by Islamic fundamentalism.

Unfortunately, this largely journalistic or propagandistic use of popular Islam has severely reduced the concept's richness and its protean implications on several scores. First, it has led to an overall shrinking of focus. As a result, use of the term frequently encourages mistaken impressions of uniformity, continuity, or even inevitability with regard to events billed as Islamic in quite different settings. Sometimes wildly distorted misunderstandings of both historical forces and sociological scale follow. The naive anticipation, widely echoed a decade ago, of a Middle Eastern domino effect, with the Islamic Republic in Iran as the ready paradigm advancing ineluctably upon other lands, exemplified this myopia.

Second, the conflation of popular Islam with a quite small number of actual revolutionary elements tends to freeze the elusive and dynamic aspects represented by the concept. It flattens into one dimension the many facets of consciousness and the diverse avenues for mobilization relevant to the long-established contrast between popular and official Islam. Furthermore, it overlooks the fluid character of the relationships that define this pairing not as static entities but as formal institutions and informal frameworks that may change places over time, that may depend upon and reinforce each other, or that may fuse and eventually reappear only to divide again along new lines.

Finally, to confine a discussion of popular Islam to "sacred rage" (*ghadba li-allah*) risks both confusion and diversion. It invites the drawing of false conclusions based on errors of the sort that Georg Simmel warned against as the misplacing of the "teleological accent." To single out a few banner incidents chosen on the basis of the size of the headlines they generate often feeds an impression that politicized Islam is the reason behind the general instability throughout the region, whereas, in fact, this perception mistakes effect for cause.

ISLAM AS POPULAR
AND OFFICIAL

The relation of Islamic militancy to the uncertain status quo is indirect. While dissident activism expressed in religious terms does pose an acknowledged security dilemma, this movement is far more the result than the origin of these troubles. Islamic resurgence represents a reaction to a tangled history of regional domestic interaction that has left the peoples of the Middle East generally feeling fragmented, violated, frustrated, and demoralized. The causes of these problems are revealed not in the tactics of any particular confrontation, but in the contradictions between ideals and expectations, on the one hand, and present life circumstances, on the other.

Because Islam by definition encompasses both the mundane and the spiritual, it is not surprising that it should play a central and public role among Muslims. What is remarkable is the changing character of the Islam that asserts these moral and political prerogatives. Clearly, the right to represent Islam and to speak authoritatively in its name is now contested by differing parties. Some view the outcome of this struggle in uncompromising and absolutist terms, including, not infrequently, the sounding of millennial evocations naming the Madhi or, for Shiites, the Imam.

But the language of Islam is also deeply embedded in the fabric of both official functions and everyday activity. Virtually all Muslim nations prescribe Islam as the state religion, and they directly subsidize mosques together with their clergy, as well as religious schools, publications, and special festivals. Thus to presuppose that popular Islam as a concept always belongs on one side or the other of a given crisis situation, whether it be the government—as in Iran, the Sudan, Libya, and Saudi Arabia—or the opposition—as in Algeria, Tunisia, Egypt, and Syria—is to deprive

the term at the outset of a great deal of its potential value.

To recover the usefulness of the contrast between these two levels, one high and the other low, requires therefore a pulling back from the contemporary barricades and the stridency of rhetorical battlegrounds. Assuming this more detached perspective, the background of this conventional dualism can be traced in two directions.

First, in doctrinal terms, the revealed texts themselves specify a division within the *umma*, that is, the idealized community, on the basis of piety. In the Quran (49:14-17), for instance, an explicit distinction is made between "Muslims" (*muslimun*) and "believers" (*mu'minun*). The former epithet refers to those who have technically converted by proclaiming their submission to God and his Prophet but who are lax in the performance of faith's duties. The latter term denotes those who have dedicated themselves wholly in obedience to carrying out the will of the creator. Believers are declared morally superior to mere Muslims. Interestingly, in its original context this dichotomy also includes a social marker, for these verses are addressed in reproach specifically to bedouins.

Second, this dualism asserts itself historically. Comparable divisions arose after the death of the Prophet that specify social gradations based on the closeness of followers to the Messenger of God when he lived. The measure for such status was understood to entail one's biography and behavior as modeled on the Prophet's words and deeds. But piety was also implicit in one's knowledge of those remembered precedents that came to be known as traditions (*hadith*). As the Islamic imperium rapidly expanded, bringing with it the complexities of governing an extensive polyglot realm, the rivalries of tensions within that first generation of Muslims that had been redirected outward began to resurface within the community. Civil war erupted, shattering the pristine unity of the *umma*.

After defeating the legitimists who had supported Ali, the fourth and last of the Rightly Guided Caliphs, the triumphant Umayyads established a dynasty in Damascus based as much on tribal loyalties as on religion. Only after this rupture did a self-conscious corpus of Islamic norms begin to emerge, replacing the earlier "silent" living practice. Remarking on this development, Fazlur Rahman points to it as the pivotal moment in Islamic history, when "the Sunna was being explicitly formulated not only in respect to its content but also in the concept of the Sunna itself."[2] Simultaneously and by consequence, the opposing concept of innovation, or *bid'a*, was also gaining definite doctrinal and jural status.

The codification of the *sunna*, which together with the Quran constitutes the two sources of the *shari'a*, or "Islamic law," occurred over the next three centuries. Accompanying this process was the forging of the great legal and theological sciences specific to Islam. A distinct social class of scholars trained in these disciplines also began to establish itself. Increasingly, its members assumed important functions throughout urban Islamic society, especially in the fields of law, education, and administration, in addition to religion. By the eleventh century, a vast system with the *madrasa*, or "school," as its core institution had evolved into the formation of the *'ulama'*, or "scholars," as a corporate status group comparable to the clergy of medieval Europe. This learned elite constituted the origin of what has since become known as establishment or official Islam.

LEGALISTIC AND MYSTICAL AUTHORITY

Theories of political order formulated in the classical era tend to portray the *'ulama'* as responsible for assuring that no ruler acts in a way that prevents the application of the *shari'a*. As the guardians, arbiters, and teachers of the law, they embodied the aspiration for a just and virtuous community even while caliphs from roughly the tenth century onward saw their authority steadily usurped by successions of military chiefs and provincial autocrats. Thus, as the Abbasid empire waned and finally collapsed, these religio-juridical specialists continued to represent the source of Islamic legitimacy for any power elite. This role had several public ritual elements. As preachers, they regularly confirmed a ruler's authority by pronouncing his name in an obligatory blessing at the Friday sermon. Likewise, by custom, they ratified the loyalty of the people upon the inauguration of new ruler through an oath known as the *bai'a*.

2. Fazlur Rahman, *Islam* (Garden City, NY: Doubleday, 1968), p. 60.

During this same period, while these men of the pen flourished, separate yet parallel developments were occurring among the rural and lower classes. For the Muslim masses, the legalistic refinements of the 'ulama' grew increasingly remote and irrelevant to their needs. Coinciding with the rise of sophisticated Islamic jurisprudence and speculative theology, a second trend had taken root that concentrated directly on the spiritual and mystical dimensions of Islam. Thus, throughout the same long summer and autumn of the Abbasid golden age, an extensive Sufi tradition was also being elaborated.

Marked by its own distinctive beliefs, institutions, and forms of organization, often fusing with other lines of solidarity such as kin groups, village and neighborhood bonds, or guild membership, this Sufi ethos came to permeate the entire fabric of popular life. Open to inspiration from Jewish, Christian, Gnostic, Hindu, and animist sources, while always borrowing freely from the learning of 'ulama' who were themselves frequently drawn by the charisma and lore of the salahun, or "holy men," Sufism produced a satisfying vision of divine-human relations. In fact, in many settings, its teachings and ritual practices all but engulfed the legalistic form of religion. It was primarily through Sufism and not the shari'a that Islam spread gradually across central Asia, into the subcontinent, to Indonesia, and across sub-Saharan Africa.

Moreover, Sufism, in addition to its abundant esoteric and introspective features, produced its own coherent, if sometimes implicit, theories on the use and abuse of power. One such subterranean doctrine asserts that the world is governed by unseen holy men whose authority derives from their proximity to the Prophet, his family, and his friends. Those who succeed in winning and maintaining the favor of these saints find that their patron not only guides and protects them but bestows blessings that may include miracles.[3]

Concomitant with these notions is the belief that certain rulers are placed in power and then sustained through similar mystical patronage. Amounting to a claim of divine right, this conviction is central among Shiites for whom the "hidden Imam" acts as a determinant political idea. But it also plays a formidable role, notably during crises situations, in the popular appeal of King Hassan of Morocco, for example, or King Hussein of Jordan, both of whom cite pedigrees as descendants of the Prophet.[4]

Finally, this bifurcation is widely reflected in Islam's great philosophical heritage. Alfarabi, Avicenna, Averroes, and others who built upon the ethics and politics of Greeks typically characterize the "city" as divided into two distinct orders, "the elect few and the common masses" (al-khassa wa al-'amma). Likewise, the seminal thesis of Ibn Khaldun

3. Edward B. Reeves, *The Hidden Government: Ritualism, Clientism, and Legitimation in Northern Egypt* (Salt Lake City: University of Utah Press, 1990); Clifford Geertz, *Islam Observed: Religious Development in Morocco and Indonesia* (Chicago: University of Chicago Press, 1968).

4. Dale F. Eickelman, "Religion in Polity and Society," in *The Political Economy of Morroco*, ed. I. William Zartman (New York: Praeger, 1987), pp. 84-97.

rests on the dyadic interaction of two populations, that of the desert and that of the city, which undergo cyclic transformations through the changing structures of their solidarity.[5]

ISLAM AS A POLITICAL IDEOLOGY

The dramatic spread of the Ottoman empire out of Anatolia starting in the early sixteenth century only exacerbated Islam's dichotomous character. The two-tiered quality of its society was formalized in the evolution of sultanism, which drew clear boundaries between an elite stratum consisting of the court, with its appended military and its civilian administration, over against a popular stratum made up of the administered. These stark divisions were reinforced by numerous markings. Historians of Turkish literature point, for instance, to the gap that separated palace culture, which was "esoteric both in language and subject matter . . . comprehensible to but a selected few . . . unconcerned with the happenings of day to day life," from a "folk" culture in local vernaculars.[6]

Law was likewise partitioned. The shari'a or its functional derivative, which was understood popularly as Islam, served as the moral foundation for ordinary community relationships while a second system of qanun laws emanated from the Sul-

tan, the great lawgiver. An economic border also split the society in that Ottoman officials did not pay taxes, whereas, with few exceptions, all others did. Ottoman clergy were also bifurcated. However, as the empire declined in the face of external pressures from European imperialism and internal ethnic and regional assertiveness, their status, especially at the upper tier of the societal gulf, began to erode markedly.

Even while the clergy's traditional role as intermediaries between the elite and the masses persisted, the 'ulama' as a learned class were steadily losing their rapport with the wider populace. Their place as advocates for justice on the part of the community was being taken over by others whose authority rested not on their academic competence but on their spiritual leadership within the realm of the popular brotherhoods.

The sweeping transformations that brought an uneasy end to Ottoman hegemony in the nineteenth and twentieth centuries also had a profound impact on the social contours of religion. Most decisive was the mass appeal of nationalism, which was variously grafted onto Islam during the colonial period. A host of initiatives urged reforms in order to revive the umma and to check the overwhelming advance of Western influence and exploitation seen as undermining the integrity of traditionally Muslim lands. This surge of nationalist enthusiasm began with secular elites, such as the Young Turks, who sought to strengthen and modernize their own societies through education, industry, political change, and social progress modeled

5. E.I.J. Rosenthal, Political Thought in Medieval Islam (New York: Cambridge University Press, 1962).

6. Walter Andrews, Poetry's Voice, Society's Song (Seattle: University of Washington Press, 1985), p. 16, cited in Serif Mardin, "The Just and the Unjust," Daedalus, 120(3):118 (1991).

along Western lines. But the rhetoric of the spokesmen for this new future was thoroughly steeped in such Islamic ideals as liberty, justice, unity, honor, responsibility, order, and *maslaha* or "public welfare."[7]

This translation of aspirations, rooted in the idiom of religion made into a political ideology articulated by an emerging indigenous elite, prompted fundamental changes in many spheres including the diminution of many attitudes and practices that were long synonymous with popular Islam. The meteoric decline of the influence of Sufi organizations that coincided with the ascent of the nationalist agenda has been seen by many as a process of virtually direct conversion. Marshall Hodgson has remarked, for instance, that the "toning down of all of the more emotional, and much of the more collective side of religion [meant that] as emotions were withdrawn from cult, they were invested in politics."[8]

POPULAR ISLAM
AND NATIONALISM

In many cases this redirecting of fervor from the spiritual to earthly rituals spurred armed conflicts. Rebellions

7. Serif Mardin, *The Genesis of Young Ottoman Thought: A Study in the Modernization of Turkish Political Ideas* (Princeton, NJ: Princeton University Press, 1962); J. M. Ahmad, *The Intellectual Origins of Egyptian Nationalism* (New York: Oxford University Press, 1960); Tamara Sonn, *Between Qur'an and Crown: The Challenge of Political Legitimacy in the Arab World* (Boulder, CO: Westview Press, 1990).

8. Marshall G. S. Hodgson, *The Venture of Islam: The Gunpowder Empires and Modern Times* (Chicago: University of Chicago Press, 1974), 3:285.

and liberation struggles have brought *jihad* and the modern iconography of revolution (*thawra*) together in the forging of "popular" regimes in the Middle East. At times, allegedly grass-roots religious movements attained power—such as was claimed in Pakistan, Saudi Arabia, Libya, and lately Iran—so that a "purified" or "reformed" religious practice is, at least initially, formally installed.

But this purported reshaping of popular Islam into a lasting political system has inevitably failed. The realities of inequality, underdevelopment, ethnic and sectarian division, lack of opportunity, unemployment, poverty, factionalism, corruption, censorship, autocratic rule, and disregard for human rights have arisen out of the crucible of postcolonial Third World experience to dash the original exalted hopes at least for the many have-nots. Just as nationalism has brought about independence, as well as the political fragmentation of the Islamic world, so, too, colonial rule and its successor, the world market system, have brought some tokens of modernity along with a degrading economic dependency and moral vulnerability.

These complex processes also dealt catastrophic blows to the traditionally sanctioned structures that had bridged the gap between popular and official Islam. As the monopolies held by the religious establishment over such fields as education, welfare services, and the courts ended, and as they lost control of their once considerable resources, derived from mortmain trusts known as *waqf*, their political relevance dimmed as well. With nationalism supplanting religion as the focus for loyalty, the perennial distinction between popular and official Islam seemed to slip from view. First, collective energy was fixed on the expulsion of foreign masters whose illegitimacy was most fully demonstrated in their exclusion from the *umma*, now constituted as the burgeoning nation. Then later, in the 1950s and 1960s, the immediacies of economic and social development combined with regional hostilities, particularly broad support for the struggle of the Palestinians, caused the older divisions to pass into the background.

Of course, a variety of specifically Islamic reform efforts accompanied this crystallizing of political nationalism, exhibiting two general tendencies. One of these, later dubbed Islamic modernism, envisaged the prevailing European ideas of progress, liberty, justice, equality, and scientific education as entirely compatible with Islam and it sought to transplant them onto Muslim soil. Its founding visionary, Shaykh Rifa'a al-Tahtawi (1801-73), is credited with having masterfully invested the banal term for "birthplace" (*watan*) with a new meaning as the equivalent to the French "*patrie.*" In his influential writings, he incorporated all the ardor, pride, and loyalty of European patriotism in Islam, coining the axiom which has since become proverbial: "Love of country is a branch of the faith."

The second was a conservative countermove intent upon resisting the perceived alien and hostile values imported from the West. Wahhabism, in its many variants, represents this effort, which had perhaps its most

forceful leader in Hasan al-Banna, who started the Society of the Muslim Brothers. He called upon Muslims to throw off the debilitating encrustations that had sullied their communal life and resulted in defeat and degradation. They were to draw inspiration directly from the purity of early Islam, establishing an "Islamic nation" (*watan Islami*) through the comprehensive application of the *shari'a.* By doing so, he insisted, Muslims would regain the strength and prosperity of that blessed original era when the community was united and Islam reigned triumphant.

Neither Islamic modernism nor its traditionalist counterpart, which came to be known broadly as Islamic fundamentalism, were ever really mass movements. Both, however, strongly influenced public opinion, especially among the educated youth and *evolués* who had earlier embraced the cause of nationalism but continued to ask questions about its ultimate direction. Both also contributed to the general restlessness that mounted through the middle of this century as the anticipated benefits of national independence in both moral and material terms were constantly postponed. Through newspapers, books, and pamphlets, but most cogently through the spread of a distinctly modern form of association, the *jama'iyya*, or "voluntary benevolent society," the tenets of a loosely conceived Islamic alternative were advanced. These practical and highly flexible associations served as a channel for local religiously motivated initiatives to establish schools, clubs, cooperatives, welfare services, and, most notably, mosques.

It has been the rapidly accelerating increase in the number of mosques sponsored by these associations that has lately charged with extraordinary significance a double classification system that had been evolving quietly throughout this century. In brief, while details vary from country to country, a general distinction has emerged that defines mosques as either belonging to the government (*masjid hukumi*) or as independent or, as it is often translated, somewhat misleadingly, "private" (*masjid ahli*).

In theory, this distinction points to the agency that subsidizes and therefore administers the mosque. But practically, the difference for Muslims in recent decades has revolved more around the two types of preachers involved. In the first case, it is a religious functionary, trained in an official institute and then appointed and supervised by the state. Those who preach in independent mosques, by contrast, are chosen by a given mosque's patron, which in the case of a *jama'iyya*, is its congregation. Thus mosques of this second type have often provided platforms for dissent in the absence of other public vehicles for effective protest.

But it gravely oversimplifies matters to say that this distinction between mosques reproduces the contrast of official and popular Islam. For, in fact, many prominent Islamicist spokesmen hold pulpits in government mosques, where they preach sermons brimming with half-submerged cues conveying unmistakable sympathy for increasing Islamization. Most are moderates, but not all, including the renowned Shaykh Abd al-Hamid Kishk of Cairo. Although long banned from his country's broadcast media and frequently restrained in other ways, including occasional arrest, not only does this pyrotechnic orator, known for his barbed and defiant indictments of officials, continue to preach regularly before crowds of thousands at a government mosque, but his sermons on bootlegged cassette recordings enjoy a colossal circulation from Marrakech to Muscat.[9]

ISLAMIC STATES AND MUSLIM CITIZENS

Seen in retrospect, the Six Day War of 1967 was the cataclysm that toppled the collective confidence in the golden promises of nationalism throughout the Islamic world. In confronting the humiliation, the deprivation, and the utter perplexity that followed what seemed an incomprehensible military defeat, an incisive moral verdict was discerned. In the 1970s, the Islamicist agenda began to find a newly receptive public especially among that same educated class that had imbibed the imported tonics of liberating socialism or liberal capitalism, only to find them toxic.[10] Many were inclined to return to religious imperatives and they re-

---

9. Gilles Kepel, *Muslim Extremism in Egypt: The Prophet and Pharaoh* (Berkeley: University of California Press, 1985), pp. 172-90; Johannes J. G. Jansen, *The Neglected Duty: The Creed of Sadat's Assassins and Islamic Resurgence in the Middle East* (New York: Macmillan, 1986), pp. 121-50.

10. Jalal Al-i Ahmad, *Occidentosis: A Plague from the West* (Berkeley, CA: Mizan Press, 1984).

sponded favorably to the refurbished slogan of the Muslim Brothers, "Islam is the solution."

Numerous regimes sought to co-opt this groundswell while some leaders attempted to harness it for short-term political motives. Sadat was one of the latter as he encouraged Islamicist consolidation and activism in the early 1970s as a foil to the strong Arab socialist cadres on campuses, within the party, and in professional syndicates. But by the late 1970s, in Egypt and elsewhere, after Islamicist forces had far exceeded their limited usefulness to those in power, it had become extremely difficult to contain the mounting enthusiasm. This trend has since continued, although not by the repetition of Iran's unique experience.

Thus Saad Eddin Ibrahim, reviewing trends in the 1980s, has concluded that "religious popularism is proving to be the functional equivalent of Nasser's national socialism."[11] But the mobilization this experienced observer here calls "popularism" must not be confounded with popular Islam in the broadest sense. For to do so would be to ignore vital differences in the historical context of these two movements and to presuppose a "privileging of ideology" at the expense of attention to social dynamics that supply the concept of popular Islam with its greatest advantages.[12]

Clearly, those currently claiming to speak for Islam in political contests regard themselves as representatives of the moral authority rooted in a united community of believers. The state, presumably, is their adversary. But this perception of a solid bloc of Islamicists in conflict with a fixed opponent, the government, can be quite misleading. For one thing, such a static view renders bizarre or literally incoherent a sequence of headlines such as "Algeria Chooses Islam"[13] when noting election returns, only to be followed shortly thereafter with "Algeria Sends Muslims a Message"[14] when reporting that the Islamic Salvation Front had been suppressed. Here, references to the rulers, the nation, the religion, and some of its adherents collide in a free-for-all of semantic slippage.

In fact, not only does the Islamicist movement remained divided along the familiar lines of traditionalism and modernism already noted, but many positions have grown more radical. Islamic fundamentalists have been increasingly influenced by theorists such as Abd al-Salam Yasin of Morocco, Umr Abd al-Rahman of Egypt, and Sa'id Hawwa of Syria, who have gone beyond the view of Sayyid Qutb in his judgment that our times are a match for or worse than the *jahiliyya*, that is, the age of ignorance prior to the coming of Islam. They draw the implication that all "human government" is blasphemous, that piety requires revolution, and, in the

11. Saad Eddin Ibrahim, "Egypt's Islamic Activism in the 1980's," *Third World Quarterly*, 10:684 (1988).

12. Edmund Burke III, "Islam and Social Movements: Methodological Reflections," in *Islam, Politics and Social Movements*, ed. Edmund Burke III and Ira Lapidus (Berkeley: University of California Press, 1988), p. 26.

13. *New York Times*, 3 Jan. 1992.

14. *Chicago Tribune*, 18 Jan. 1992.

extreme, that present leaders can be deemed in the condition of apostasy.[15]

Islamic modernists, on the other hand, pressing for the opening and restructuring of their societies, demand greater political participation, reform through decentralization, broader economic liberalization, a priority upon social justice, and more pluralism and tolerance. Taking democratization or, in Islamic terms, *shura* or "consultation" as their chief demand, they seek to restore confidence in government after decades of discredited military regimes. Furthermore, they tend to regard themselves, being the leading proponents of this delicate transformation, as at least implicitly the most suitable candidates to effect its eventual realization.

WHICH ISLAM IS UNDERGOING A REVIVAL?

But it is important to note that neither of the variously shaded components of this movement draws pervasive or consistent support from the masses. In fact, the general perception among the rural poor has been that issues such as the veiling of women, interest-free banking, the banning of alcohol, the closing of nightclubs, and regular attendance at mosques, which preoccupy the urban Islamicists, are virtually irrelevant to them. Rather, as al-Sadiq al-Mahdi has cogently put it, "the masses have always regarded Islam as the basis of their identity [and] the source of their morality."[16] In their

view, it is the elite who have fallen prey to foreign acculturation and the West's corrupting models of development. If an Islamic revival is needed somewhere, it is not among those who have never fallen away from it in the first place.

Furthermore, the heavy emphasis of Islamicists on the refuting of the godless, alien, unjust, and immoral contents of so many modern "isms" points to another perceived deficiency of the movement, namely, its penchant for negativism. While it has proven capable of opposing programs and denying legitimacy to regimes, it has never succeeded in elaborating concrete and constructive alternatives upon which Islamic activists themselves could agree. In part, surely, this shortcoming stems from the unresolved contradictions within the movement itself. But looking from the bottom up, this inability may also be evidence of another sort of cleavage.

The use of Islam as a political discourse that brings together liberals and conservatives, radicals and reactionaries across regional and generational lines may itself be a key factor in the exclusion of the masses from this movement. Insofar as these activists have arrogated to themselves the symbols of Islam as indicative of the popular will, they presume to translate the aspirations of the lower classes into political force. On the other hand, the fact that the masses resist cooperation and seem largely unmoved or even alienated by these processes might also suggest that those for whom Islam has always been "the basis of their identity" do

15. Shireen T. Hunter, ed., *The Politics of Islamic Revivalism* (Bloomington: Indiana University Press, 1988).

16. Al-Sadiq al-Mahdi, "Islam—Society and Change," *Voices of Resurgent Islam*, ed. John L. Esposito (New York: Oxford University Press, 1983), p. 231.

not feel themselves summoned by the major themes of this revival. In this sense, the inability of Islamicists to clarify their message, whether it is the "corrupt" elite or the "backward" masses who have deserted Islam, stands as a primary liability on both fronts.

Since activists can effectively unify only around dissent, their ranks have frequently been broken by government moves that co-opt or suppress selected parts of the movement. But at the same time, by refusing to recognize the deeply felt legitimacy of popular Islam among those with an undisturbed assurance of their relative moral integrity, Islamicists distance themselves from the very population they claim to represent. In the end, therefore, in the eyes of "the rural majority in Islamic countries . . . revivalists are one segment of the elite doing battle with another segment of the elite, while unjustly condemning the masses as deficient religiously."[17]

But this general disinterest on the part of the masses in an essentially urban struggle against corruption and tyranny should not be taken for mere social stagnation or inertia. In fact, in addition to the massive rates of migration and dislocation affecting rural populations, life everywhere in the countryside is rapidly being drawn into an ever tighter web of economic interdependency, political centralization, and cultural syncretism. Popular Islam as a set of distinct practices and beliefs continues

17. Abdulwahab Saleh Babeair, "Contemporary Islamic Revivalism: A Movement of a Moment," *Journal of Arab Affairs*, 9:137 (1990).

therefore to change. The old ways marked by folkloric rituals with their aura of magic around localized devotional centers have long been giving way, albeit at times reluctantly, to patterns of observance more in conformity with the *sunna*.

But this considerable upgrading of Islamic expression may not indicate a comparable shift in the structure of societal relations. The corps of juroreligious scholars of old who functioned as intermediaries between multiple levels of a highly stratified society have, for all practical purposes, disappeared. In the nationalist vision of a society built on equality, the *'ulama'* has become superfluous as rational bureaucracies have replaced primary relationships of kinship and patronage.

In this sense, the emergence of a new and increasingly institutionalized Islamic voice occupying the moral and political space between the populace and the governing elite may offer an important clue as to how the current Islamic resurgence or revival is authentic in its own way. It is not necessarily doomed just because it has not incited the sudden arousal of popular Islam from its presumed fourteen centuries of slumber. Rather, its achievement has been the restoration, however incomplete and experimental, of a composite of self-consciously committed guardians, instructors, preachers, and arbiters who define their social responsibility in terms of their privileged relation to the *shari'a*. This reestablishment and reconfiguration of the *'ulama'*, in mixed clerical and lay garb, who assume the right, however disparate

their opinions, to speak authoritatively in the name of the *umma*, suggest that the current movement belongs as much to Islam's past as to its
future. But by the same token, it argues strongly for retaining the concept of popular Islam rather than dis-
carding it any time soon.

ANNALS, *AAPSS*, 524, November 1992

Militant Islam and the Politics of Redemption

By MARY-JANE DEEB

ABSTRACT: Militant Islam has emerged in the 1980s and 1990s as a major political force to be contended with in the Middle East. It is characterized by its readiness to use violence and by the challenge it constitutes to existing political institutions. This article looks at the conditions under which five militant Islamic movements in Algeria, Tunisia, Libya, Lebanon, and the Gaza Strip and on the West Bank have emerged as a political force, and the concepts they have used to mobilize public support and to create a mass base for themselves in order to challenge leaders or governments in power. The conditions include political stagnation and the weakening of central authority, economic stagnation leading to the decline in standards of living, deteriorating security conditions, pervasiveness of Western culture, and secular states and leaders perceived as antagonistic to Islamic movements. The leaders of these movements do not portray themselves as revolutionaries trying to create a new society but rather as saviors trying to rescue the old society from self-destruction. Their ideology is an ideology of redemption.

Mary-Jane Deeb is academic director of the Omani Program at the School of International Service at the American University, Washington, D.C. She received her Ph.D. in international relations from the School of Advanced International Studies, Johns Hopkins University, and is the author of Libya's Foreign Policy in North Africa, *and coauthor with M. K. Deeb of* Libya since the Revolution: Aspects of Social and Political Development.

MILITANT Islam has emerged in the 1980s and 1990s as a major political force to be contended with in the Middle East. It is characterized by its readiness to use violence and by the challenge it constitutes to existing political institutions. Although ideologically it may not differ greatly from the earlier and somewhat more moderate Islamic movements, it is more aggressive in propounding and attempting to implement its ideas. The overwhelming success of the Islamic Salvation Front (FIS) in December 1991 in the first free elections since independence in Algeria highlights the significance of this new trend. Iran has been a Shiite Islamic republic for more than a decade, and in the Sudan the first military-Islamic government in the modern history of the Middle East came to power in 1989 by means of a coup that overthrew a democratically elected government.

This article looks at the conditions under which five Arab militant Islamic movements have emerged as a political force and at the concepts they have used to mobilize public support and to create a mass base of support for themselves in order to challenge leaders or governments in power. The basic thesis is that militant Islamic movements emerge under certain specific conditions that enable them to capture a broad audience and they capitalize on those conditions to create an ideology of redemption wherewith all societal problems can be resolved through religion.[1]

1. The specific conditions under which Shiite militant movements emerge are discussed in Juan R. I. Cole and Nikki R. Keddie, eds.,

CONDITIONS FOR THE RISE OF MILITANT ISLAM

Militant Islam has emerged under five broad conditions: the first is political stagnation and the weakening of central authority. This could be due to a loss of legitimacy with a change of leadership, as in the case of Tunisia; the failure of the ruling party to fulfill its promises or to live up to the expectations of the people, as in Algeria; the regional and international isolation of the Libyan leadership; an inability to control the political events or prevent the breakdown of law and order, as in Lebanon; or the inability of the Palestine Liberation Organization (PLO) leaders to achieve any significant gain for Palestinians despite the enormous costs of the *intifada* for the Arab population of the West Bank and Gaza.

The second condition for the emergence of Islamic militancy has been economic stagnation and decline and/or a growing gap between the haves and the have-nots. In all five cases—in Algeria, Tunisia, Libya,

Shi'ism and Social Protest (New Haven, CT: Yale University Press, 1986). Others have looked at the conditions under which Islamic movements emerge in North Africa; see, for instance, Susan Walz, "Islamist Appeal in Tunisia," *Middle East Journal*, vol. 40 (1986); Jean-Claude Vatin, "Popular Puritanism versus State Reformism: Islam in Algeria," in *Islam in the Political Process*, ed. James P. Piscatori (New York: Cambridge University Press, 1983). Abdelkader Zghal sees the Islamicist phenomenon as "a component of the ideology and the dynamics of nationalist movements." Zghal, "The New Strategy of the Movement of the Islamic Way: Manipulation or Expression of Political Culture," in *Tunisia: The Political Economy of Reform*, ed. I. William Zartman (Boulder, CO: Lynne Rienner, 1991), p. 206.

Lebanon, and the West Bank and Gaza—life became harder, unemployment increased, as did inflation, while major shortages in commodities and housing occurred and even accessibility to good health care was severely reduced. Higher education was no longer a guarantee of employment, and even the number of jobs abroad declined as did remittances to families dependent on them for survival. In Lebanon the misery was compounded by a war that impoverished large sections of the population and destroyed houses and places of work. Militant Islamic movements emerged in the 1980s as a direct outcome of the war.

The third condition under which militant Islamic movements have thrived has been a deteriorating security situation that could be caused by external or internal factors or both. In Tunisia, Israelis attacked PLO headquarters twice, and Libya supported a very serious armed attack on Gafsa; Libya was bombed by the United States in 1986 and suffered a major military defeat by Chad in 1987; Algerian-Moroccan relations were tense throughout the 1980s over the Western Sahara; insecurity was prevalent in Gaza and on the West Bank, exacerbated by the *intifada* and the Israeli reaction to it. In Lebanon the civil war threatened everyone in the country, and the air raids by Israel culminating in the 1982 invasion of Lebanon were the ultimate security threat.

What was perceived as an even greater threat to the Muslim populations of the Middle East was the insidious invasion of the region by Western culture and values. Every night, Maghrebi television broadcast shows from Europe depicting a way of living that was different but fast becoming the model of the good life for North Africans. Western and Jewish culture were the dominant cultures in Israel, where Arab and Islamic cultures were disparaged. In Lebanon, the dominant culture by the mid-1970s in Beirut had become Western, with shops carrying the latest in fashion, music, books, and newspapers from the West; the restaurants, cafes, and nightclubs being similar to those on the other side of the Mediterranean; and the most prestigious academic institutions being American or French.

In every case, finally, the governments in power were perceived as encouraging this cultural change and as being themselves secular or paying only lip service to Islam. In Algeria, Libya, and Tunisia, the governments were seen as attempting to separate religion from politics and as harassing and persecuting Islamic organizations and their leaders. The PLO's leadership was always secular, with Christian and Muslim leaders sharing power and formulating policy for the rest of the movement. In Lebanon, the president was Christian, and the Muslim leaders came from traditional bourgeois and notable families who were westernized and secular.

It is under those conditions that strong militant Islamic movements emerged throughout the southern Mediterranean claiming to be able to save Muslims from the political, economic, social, and cultural problems they were facing in their bewildering and fast-changing societies.

THE POLITICS
OF REDEMPTION

There is nothing new in such movements. Max Weber, in "The Economic Ethic of the World Religions," noted:

The conception of the idea of redemption as such is very old, if one understands by it a liberation from distress, hunger, drought, sickness, and ultimately from suffering and death. Yet redemption attained a specific significance only where it expressed a systematic and rationalized "image of the world" and represented a stand in the face of the world.[2]

The militant Islamic movements that emerged in the region in the last decade and a half offered to save Muslims from those very conditions that had enabled them to mobilize public opinion in the first place. They did not portray themselves as revolutionaries trying to create a new society but rather as saviors trying to save the old society from self-destruction. This may explain why they look back to a golden age to which they wish to return, rather than forward to a new age that they want to create. In the final analysis, the two processes may be the same, and the retrospective movement may be as revolutionary as the forward-looking one, but, at the outset at least, the conception of what each is trying to achieve is different.

RELIGION AND
POLITICS IN ALGERIA

Although Islam became the religion of the state under the new Algerian Constitution after independence, the *shari'a*, or Islamic law, was not made an integral part of the legal system of the state, nor were Muslim jurists allowed to play an independent role in legislative matters on the national level. Instead, a minister of religious affairs was appointed by the Algerian leaders to head a bureaucratic organization that had the final authority to appoint or dismiss clergymen, review Friday sermons, administer religious endowments, control religious publications, and set up Islamic institutions of higher learning.[3]

In 1964, an Islamic militant group, al-Qiyam (Values), with links to the Algerian Muslim Brothers, emerged and became a precursor of the Islamic fundamentalists of the 1980s. It called for a more visible role for Muslim practices in society and opposed Western cultural manifestations in clothing and entertainment in Algeria.[4] One of its leaders, Muhammad Khider, was a founding member of the National Liberation Front (FLN), who had broken away from the party and set up the nucleus of an opposition to Ben Bella and

2. H. H. Gerth and C. Wright Mills, eds., *From Max Weber: Essays in Sociology* (London: Routledge & Kegan Paul, 1964), p. 280.

3. For a discussion of the role of Islam in Algerian society, see Jean-Claude Vatin, *L'Algérie politique: Histoire et société*, 2d ed. (Paris: Presses de la Fondation Nationale des Sciences Politiques, 1983); Christiane Souriau, ed., *Le Maghreb musulman en 1979* (Paris: Centre National de la Recherche Scientifique, 1981); Ali Merad, *Le réformisme musulman en Algérie de 1925 à 1940* (Paris: Mouton, 1967); Susan E. Marshall, "Islamic Revival in the Maghreb: The Utility of Tradition for Modernizing Elites," *Studies in Comparative International Development*, 14:95-108 (1979).

4. Raymond Vallin, "Muslim Socialism in Algeria," *Man, State and Society in the Contemporary Maghrib* (New York: Praeger, 1973), p. 56.

later to Boumedienne. The movement was eventually suppressed by the Boumedienne regime, and Khider was assassinated in 1967.

By the end of the 1970s, Ahl al-Da'wa (People of the Call), an autonomous Islamic movement with strong links to the original al-Qiyam movement, began to voice the dissatisfaction of many Algerians with state policies and with the direction they were taking the country.[5] But it was only after the death of Boumedienne in 1978 and the emergence of an Islamic republic in Iran the following year that the movement became organized and active.[6]

In the early 1980s, the members of al-Da'wa took over mosques that had been under government control for two decades, and when government security forces attempted to stop the takeover—in Laghouat, in 1981, for instance—bloody clashes erupted and resulted in a number of casualties. University campuses witnessed pitched battles between Muslim fundamentalists and left-wing students. These confrontations culminated in the death of a student on the Ben Aknoun campus of the University of Algiers in November 1982.[7]

5. For an analysis of Islam and the state at that juncture, see Jean Leca and Jean-Claude Vatin, L'Algérie politique, institutions et régime (Paris: Fondation Nationale des Sciences Politiques, 1975), pp. 304-31.

6. For an excellent discussion of the impact of Boumedienne's policy on the Islamic fundamentalist movement in Algeria, see Hugh Roberts, "Radicalism and the Dilemma of Algerian Nationalism: The Embattled Arians of Algiers," Third World Quarterly, vol. 10 (1988).

7. John P. Entelis, Algeria: The Revolution Institutionalized (Boulder, CO: Westview Press, 1986), p. 87.

This event led the government of Chadli Bendjedid, whose policy toward al-Da'wa activities had hitherto been rather tolerant, to clamp down. During the rest of the 1980s, the Algerian state began a systematic campaign to undermine the movement by arresting its leaders, conducting police raids on the homes of suspected members, and branding them in the mass media as "criminals" and "agitators."[8] Three of the leaders arrested were clergymen and founding members of the FIS.

In October 1988, riots broke out in the Bab al-Oued sector of Algiers over government austerity measures to cut state subsidies on some basic commodities. The riots spread quickly to the rest of the capital, to Oran, Constantine, Annaba, Blida, Tiarret, and Sinya, and beyond to Tizi-Ouzou in the Berber Kabylie region. Demonstrators were protesting the high unemployment, the shortage of basic consumer goods, and the unavailability of affordable housing in the cities. The armed forces brought in to quell the riots were unable to restore law and order for 10 days, at the end of which more than 150 people were reported dead, over a thousand injured, and an estimated 3000 arrested.[9]

Although the riots were not initiated by Islamic militants, these militants tried to exploit the disturbances to mobilize support for their views. Two days after the riots broke out, several thousand young Muslim

8. See Mary-Jane Deeb, "Algeria," in Religion in Politics: A World Guide, ed. Stuart Mews (Harlow, Essex: Longman Group, 1989), pp. 6-9.

9. Le Monde, 15 Oct. 1988.

fundamentalists demonstrated in the Belcourt District of Algiers, while the army attempted to keep them away from demonstrations in other sectors of the city. When the riots were over, President Bendjedid met with Muslim fundamentalist leaders. They condemned acts of violence and sabotage and submitted a number of proposals for economic and social reforms including a demand that Islam constitute the basis of all such reforms.

In February 1989, a new constitution was approved in Algeria. Among other things, it permitted the creation of "associations of a political character."[10] In March 1989, the first Algerian Islamic political party, the FIS, was proclaimed in Kouba, a suburb of Algiers, and was officially legalized in September 1989.[11] It had a consultative council, or *shura*, made up of 14 members, some of whom were very important Islamic leaders in Algeria. In June 1990, the first test of strength took place between the FLN and the FIS in local elections for the 1539 municipal councils and the 48 provincial assemblies. The Islamicists won 54 percent of the vote as compared to the FLN's 28 percent, giving them control of 850 municipalities, including those of major urban centers such Algiers, Constantine, and Oran. On 25 May 1991, on the eve of general legislative elections,

10. See the analysis in Robert Mortimer, "Islam and Multiparty Politics in Algeria," *Middle East Journal*, 45:578-79 (1991).

11. For an excellent analysis of Algerian politics at the end of the 1980s, see Robert A. Mortimer, "Algeria after the Explosion," *Current History*, 89(546):161-64, 180-82 (Apr. 1990).

the FIS called for an indefinite and nationwide strike and announced rallies and marches all over the country. The strike was called to protest the government's gerrymandering tactics to give rural districts a greater electoral representation, which would favor the ruling party. They also demanded that presidential elections be held simultaneously with the legislative elections.

After days of disturbances, the Algerian government took new measures to deal with these disturbances: it ordered the reestablishment of all public services and the arrest of those who were obstructing government officials from performing their duties. Clashes between demonstrators and the gendarmerie turned violent, and the security forces used firearms. Finally, on 5 June President Bendjedid ordered a state of siege for four months to restore public order. All gatherings, demonstrations, and marches were banned. A curfew was imposed between 11 p.m. and 3:30 a.m. in the provinces of Algiers, Blida, Tipasa, and Boumerdes, and the military began patrolling the capital in tanks. Legislative elections were postponed, and the government resigned.

After jailing both the leader of the FIS and his deputy and breaking off further negotiations with the Islamicists, the government set the date for legislative elections. On 26 December 1991, elections were held, and the FIS won a landslide victory, capturing 188 seats out of the National Assembly's 430, with 176 seats to be contested in a runoff election three weeks later. The FLN came in third, with only 15 seats. Bendjedid resigned on 11 January, leaving the door open to a confrontation between the army and the FIS. The army created a High Security Council, which canceled the runoff elections and effectively blocked the FIS from coming to power.[12]

Ideologically, the Algerian Muslim fundamentalists are among the most radical in North Africa. They advocate a complete restructuring of society "in an attempt to realize the City of God on Earth."[13] They have pushed for the application of Islamic law, *shari'a*, to replace the code of civil law of Algeria and for reforms based on Islamic principles such as a stricter dress code for women, more religious broadcasts on radio and television, and banning the consumption of alcohol in public places.

RELIGION AND POLITICS IN TUNISIA

The Islamicist movement in Tunisia has its roots in the Quranic Preservation Society, founded in 1970. The Tunisian government permitted its development to counterbalance a growing leftist movement on the campuses of the University of Tunis. Only in the late 1970s did a loose coalition of Islamicists, many of whom had links to the Quranic Preservation Society, emerge as an important element in Tunisian politics, voicing the economic, social, and political grievances of many Tunisians.[14] This coalition, which became known as the Islamic Tendency

Movement (MTI), set up organized committees primarily in urban centers of Tunisia and openly began criticizing the government and calling for economic and political reforms based on a return to the true principles of Islam.

One of the principal ideologues and leaders of the MTI, Rached Ghannouchi, describes the movement in his speeches and writings as one that would save the Islamic nation from domination by the West and by atheist or secular governments allied to the West. Westernization or what he calls "the Western plan" would destroy civilization, religion, morality, the nation, the family, and the tribe. The Islamic movement, on the other hand "would save human civilization from the domination of the Samaritans who worship the golden calf."[15] Ghannouchi, like the leaders of the other militant Islamic movements, believes in the use of force to achieve the ultimate Islamic state. Like others, he calls for *jihad* as a step in liberating the land of Islam, which he believes has been invaded by the West due in part to the weakness of the Islamic *umma* and the collaboration of regional governments with the West.[16] He sees the enormous wealth of the Islamic world as a sacred *waqf* ("Islamic religious endowment") that should be distributed equitably among Muslims and serve to resolve its economic problems.[17]

Realizing that the MTI was developing into a major opposition force,

12. *Washington Post*, 15 Jan. 1992.

13. Entelis, *Algeria*, p. 85.

14. On the origins of the movement, see Walz, "Islamist Appeal in Tunisia," pp. 652-54.

15. See Rached Ghannouchi, Speech at the First Islamic Congress on the Palestinian Question, Tehran, 4-6 Dec. 1990, pp. 5-6.

16. Ibid., pp. 15-16, 21.

17. Ibid., pp. 21-22.

the Tunisian government began to crack down on its members as early as 1979. By 1981, MTI members were being arrested in significant numbers and accused of various political crimes. The MTI tried unsuccessfully to gain acceptance as a political party within the constitutional framework of Tunisia throughout the 1980s and resorted to violence to pressure the government to legalize the movement.[18] In August 1987, four tourist hotels were bombed, and MTI members were accused of the crime. When they came to trial a few weeks later, large antigovernment demonstrations took place in protest, and the judge presiding over their trial was sprayed with hydrochloric acid. In September 1987, the State Security Court sentenced 7 of the 90 MTI members to death, Rached Ghannouchi to life imprisonment, and 67 members from two years to life in jail; 14 were acquitted. In October 1987, the first death sentences were carried out, and two MTI members were hanged. Later that month, two MTI leaders, Ali Laaridh and Fadel Beldi, were captured by the security forces, after having been sentenced to death and to hard labor, respectively, in absentia in September.

On the eve of the November 1987 ouster of Bourguiba, it was reported that the Tunisian President was planning on reopening the trials and extending the death penalty to other members of the MTI. Fear that such an action would lead to more violence and bloodshed was apparently behind the timing of the overthrow of

the ailing head of state.[19] In December 1987, the new Tunisian leader, Ben Ali, granted amnesty to 2487 prisoners, including 608 MTI members. He also commuted the death sentence of Ali Laaridh to hard labor and dropped charges against another 60 MTI members. In May 1988, he pardoned Rached Ghannouchi and set him free, and in July a number of MTI members who were imprisoned for crimes "against public rights" were released from jail. In September 1988, Ben Ali allowed the secretary-general of the MTI, Abd al-Fattah Mourou, to return to Tunisia after two years in exile.

In April 1989, the Tunisians went to the polls to elect their president as well as their deputies for parliament. Once again, the Islamicists were not allowed to run as Islamicists and so ran as independents under the banner of the Nahda, or Renaissance Party. They were well organized and able to mobilize significant support. There were reportedly 1200 Islamicist observers in Tunis alone to ensure fair elections. Although the Constitutional Rally, the government party, won all the seats, the Islamicists won 14 percent of the national votes and reportedly almost 30 percent in some urban centers.[20]

In mid-May 1991, the Tunisian government announced that it had

18. Mohammed Elbaki Hermassi, "La société tunisienne au miroir islamiste," *Maghreb-Machrek*, vol. 103 (1984).

19. Marion Boulby, "The Islamic Challenge: Tunisia since Independence," *Third World Quarterly*, 10:613 (1988).

20. For an analysis of the electoral results, see Habib Slim, "Réflections autour des résultats des élections législatives en Tunisie: Implications et perspectives" (Paper delivered at the Twenty-Third Annual Meeting of the Middle East Studies Association of North America, Toronto, Nov. 1989).

uncovered a plot by Islamic fundamentalists to overthrow the government of President Ben Ali. The Nahda Party was accused of having masterminded the plot. The alleged plot consisted of a long-term strategy to infiltrate the army, the security forces, and the customs service, and to destabilize the government by means of terrorist activities, protests, demonstrations, and the call to general strikes. The Tunisian government also made public the organizational structure of the Nahda which was shown to have not only a political wing but also a paramilitary wing trained for special operations.[21] Three hundred people were arrested, including one hundred military men and several officers sympathetic to the Nahda. Its leader, Rached Ghannouchi, denied that such a plot existed and accused the government of fabricating the story to crack down on the movement.[22]

MILITANTS AGAINST REFORMISTS IN LIBYA

Opposition to Qadhdhafi's regime has come from many sides. Islamic groups such as the Ikhwan al-Muslimin (Muslim Brothers) directly challenged many of Qadhdhafi's ideas and policies from the start. Those groups were influenced by their counterparts in Egypt and existed in Libya even before Qadhdhafi came to power.[23]

The Hizb al-Tahrir al-Islami (Islamic Liberation Party) is a major Islamic organization in Libya rooted in the Ikhwan movement. It appears to be linked to similar organizations in other parts of North Africa, in Egypt, and in Jordan, where the movement was originally founded in the 1950s. It has made deep inroads into the military and among students in universities in Tripoli and Benghazi and believes in the restoration of the original purity and morality of Islamic society at the time of the first four Muslim caliphs. It also believes in the use of violence to achieve its goals.

The National Front for the Salvation of Libya (NFSL), created in Khartoum in October 1981, is another movement opposed to the Qadhdhafi regime that has a strong Islamic tendency. It is headed by Mohammed Youssef al-Maqaryaf and includes a number of high-level government officials who have defected from Libya.[24] Some of its members belonged to the Islamic Association of Libya, which had ties to the Muslim Brothers. They publish a magazine called, appropriately enough, *al-Inqadh* (Salvation), which reports events in Libya and regularly calls for the overthrow of the government.[25] They also publish a series of

21. Tunisian Republic Radio Network, Tunis, 22 May 1991, in Foreign Broadcast Information Service, *FBIS—NES*, 23 May 1991, pp. 15-16.

22. Interview with Rached Ghannouchi, Paris Radio France International, 23 May 1991, in Foreign Broadcast Information Service, *FBIS—NES*, 23 May 1991, p. 16.

23. Mary-Jane Deeb, "Tunisia," in *Religion in Politics*, ed. Mews, pp. 268-69.

24. François Burgat, "Libye," *Annuaire de l'Afrique du Nord, 1983* (Paris: Editions du Centre National de la Recherche Scientifique, 1985), p. 771.

25. This group is discussed in the larger framework of opposition to the Qadhdhafi re-

pamphlets called Kul al-haqiqat lil-sha'b (The Whole Truth for the People), among which is one on Qadhdhafi's position on Islamic issues. They attack his position as heretical for trying to separate church and state; putting *shari'a*, or Islamic law, on a par with Roman law or the Napoleonic Code; taking the position that the *sunna*, or traditions of the Prophet Muhammad, are not sacred; changing the start of the Islamic calendar, and misunderstanding the concept of *jihad*, or holy war, as being one between believers and unbelievers and adding that Christians and Jews are believers.[26] The pamphlet thus shows how the NFSL views Islam and the relation between state and religion, the role of Islamic law in Libya, and the concept of holy war.

The NFSL, however, is a broad organization with both secular and Islamicist members, as well as a paramilitary wing. Like the other militant organizations discussed earlier in this article, it aims at overthrowing the government in power and has made a number of such attempts. The best known was the May 1984 attack on the Bab al-'Azizya barracks, Qadhdhafi's own headquarters, which was instigated at the behest of the Islamicists in the NFSL.[27]

In September 1986, 26 men were arrested, accused of being members of Jihad al-Islami (Islamic Jihad Organization), which the Libyan government had discovered only a few months earlier. In February 1987, 9 people arrested with them were hanged and their execution televised. They were accused of belonging to the Islamic Jihad Organization, of having carried out two assassinations, and of being involved in acts of sabotage.[28]

Qadhdhafi repressed these groups ruthlessly from the early 1970s through the 1980s, arresting their leaders, hanging their members, and discrediting their views.[29]

In January 1989, unrest spread throughout Tripoli, Benghazi, Ajdabiya, and al-Kufrah with Libyans protesting deteriorating economic conditions, lack of jobs for graduating students, and attacks on religious figures and institutions by government security forces. This unrest followed a raid on the mosque of al-Zurayraq bil-Sabri in Benghazi.[30] The teaching section of the mosque was also closed down because the imam had been publicly critical of Qadhdhafi's views on religion. In Tripoli, a number of mosques were raided in December 1988 and January 1989 during the time of prayer.[31]

Islamic opposition has become more outspoken and more organized. It does not want to compromise or

gime in Lisa Anderson, "Qadhdhafi and His Opposition," *Middle East Journal*, 40:232 (1986).

26. 'Abdallah al-Sadiq, *Tajribat al-Qadhdhafi fi itar al-mawazin al-Islamiyya*, 5th pamphlet in Kul al-haqiqat lil-sha'b (n.p., n.d.).

27. George Joffe, "Islamic Opposition in Libya," *Third World Quarterly*, 10:628 (1988).

28. Tripoli Television Service, 17 Feb. 1987, in Foreign Broadcast Information Service, *FBIS—NES*, 18 Feb. 1987, p. Q1.

29. Amnesty International, "Libya: Summary of Amnesty International's Prisoner Concerns," *Summary* (London), 26 Oct. 1987.

30. *Al-Inqadh*, 7(27):8-9 (Mar. 1989).

31. Mary-Jane Deeb, "New Thinking in Libya," *Current History*, 89(546):151 (Apr. 1990).

cooperate with a regime it perceives as evil.[32] It may become the most important opposition to the Qadhdhafi regime in the near future and prove to be the unifying force that until now has eluded the Libyan opposition domestically and externally.

MILITANCY IN THE OCCUPIED TERRITORIES

In the 1970s, several Islamic groups emerged in the Occupied Territories, encouraged by the Israeli government's eagerness to undermine the power of the PLO and other nationalists and leftist organizations. Among them were the Islamic Charitable League, led by Shaykh Ahmad Yassin, and the Islamic Society, whose founder was Khalil al-Qoqa. Both movements were part of the Muslim Brothers organization that had been active in the territories since the time of the Egyptian administration. Those organizations centered their efforts around educational institutions and mosques to provide youngsters with an Islamic awareness. They wanted to create an alternative to the PLO, whose leadership they believed was not representative of the Palestinians. Their goal was the establishment of a Muslim state in Palestine.

But it was the Islamic Jihad, which emerged in the mid 1980s in Gaza, that became the most militant Islamic movement in the area. One of the founding members was Imad al-

Saftawi, who rejected both the leadership of the PLO, which he saw as too willing to compromise with Israeli authorities, and the more conservative Islamic Charitable League, which he perceived as ritualistic and inactive on the nationalist front.[33] This movement believed in the use of force to achieve its goals and first became known in 1986 after it attacked Israeli recruits at a ceremony in Jerusalem. Throughout 1987, Islamic Jihad was very active against Israeli forces, which responded by imprisoning several of its members and deporting many of its leaders to Lebanon. In May 1987, al-Saftawi escaped from jail and was next heard of in Baghdad. Damascus also harbors a wing of Islamic Jihad that is often active in Lebanon, where it operates against Israeli forces there.

The Islamic Resistance Movement, Harakat al-Muqawama al-Islamiyya, better known by its Arabic acronym, Hamas, emerged in August 1988, a few months after the start of the *intifada*. It was founded by Shaykh Ahmad Yassin of the Islamic Charitable League and a member of the Ikhwan. Hamas was created in part to steal the thunder of the nationalist movement in the territories and eventually replace its leadership.[34] Like the other Islamic movements, it rejects the leadership of the PLO and believes that it is the duty of every Muslim to struggle for an Islamic state.

For Hamas, the Islamic Jihad, and other Islamic organizations on the West Bank and in Gaza, the political

32. See, for instance, an editorial in *al-Inqadh*, 2(9):7 (June 1984).

33. Ann M. Lesch, "Prelude to Uprising in the Gaza Strip," *Journal of Palestine Studies*, 20:10, 11 (1990).

34. See Lisa Taraki, "The Islamic Resistance Movement in the Palestinian Uprising," *Middle East Report*, p. 30 (1989).

entity they are fighting against and wish to replace is more complex than that of any opponents of the other organizations discussed here. Not only are the Palestinians fighting Israelis, whom they see as foreigners and infidels, but in addition they are up against a nationalist movement that also seeks to liberate the territories. Their weapon against the PLO or the Communist Party in Israel is religion. They see those organizations as secular or even as atheist and attribute their failure to their lack of faith. Hamas is, however, less vocally in opposition to the PLO than are the other organizations; nonetheless, it has asked that the PLO become ideologically more Islamic.[35]

THE PARTY OF
GOD IN LEBANON

Hizballah (the Party of God) was founded in the summer of 1982, the brainchild of Muhammad Hussain Fadhlallah, a Shiite clergyman whose family comes from southern Lebanon but who was born and studied in Najaf, Iraq. The leader and ideologue of the party, Fadhlallah was inspired by the Iranian revolution, which has since supported him politically, financially, and militarily, sending both men and arms to strengthen his movement.[36] His closest aides are also Shiite clergymen who studied theology in Najaf.

Like some of the other militant movements in the region, Hizballah has two wings: the political, which deals with the dissemination of information and the organization's planning and policymaking, and an underground paramilitary wing, which operates under the name "Islamic Jihad." The latter group undertakes all the major terrorist operations associated with the movement.

Ideologically, Hizballah is very close to the Islamic militancy of Khomeini's Iran. In his major political treatise, *al-Islam wa mantiq al-quwwa* (Islam and the logic of force),[37] Fadhlallah put forward the ideas that have become the main tenets of the movement. He believes it is the duty of Muslims to fight *al-dawla al-kafira* ("the heretical state").[38] Like other Islamic militants, he wants to help establish an Islamic republic in Lebanon as well as in other Muslim countries, although, according to him, they are not yet ready for such a state.[39] Like them also, he believes that the Islamic *shari'a* should be the law of the land, but he insists it should also be applicable to Christians living in the Islamic world.

Fadhlallah also believes in organizing Muslims to fight what he calls the unbelievers, whether they be parties or states. According to his writ-

35. Ibid., p. 32.
36. See Marius Deeb, "Shia Movements in Lebanon: Their Formation, Ideology, Social Basis, and Links with Iran and Syria," *Third World Quarterly*, 10:683-98 (1988).

37. Mohammed Hussain Fadhlallah, *al-Islam wa mantiq al-quwwa*, 2d ed. (Beirut: al-Muassasat al-Jami'iyya li-al-Dirasat Wa al-Nashr Wa al-Tawzi', 1981).
38. For an analysis of Hizballah and other Islamic groups in Lebanon, see Marius Deeb, *Militant Islamic Movements in Lebanon: Origins, Social Basis, and Ideology*, Occasional Paper Series (Washington, DC: Georgetown University, Center for Contemporary Arab Studies, Nov. 1986).
39. Malaf al-Shira', *al-Harakat al-Islamiyya fi Lubnan* (Beirut: Dar Sannin, 1984), p. 263.

ings, political forces fall into two categories: *hizballah* (God's party) that unites all believers and *hizb al-Shaytan* (the Devil's party) to which all others belong. This concept, taken from the Iranian revolution, is appealing because of its stark simplicity. There is a commitment that has to be made, as no one can be left on the periphery lest he fall into *hizb al-Shaytan*. Western governments and local governments that cooperate with the West fall within the latter category. Like its Iranian counterparts, Hizballah is profoundly suspicious of the West's intentions and motivations in the region.

Hizballah supports armed struggle to liberate Muslim land and establish an Islamic republic. It has encouraged a number of operations against Israeli forces in southern Lebanon and wants to liberate Jerusalem, arguing that the Palestinian struggle has been a failure until now because of its secular nature.[40]

The social basis of the movement is the poorer areas of Lebanon in the south, the Biqa' region, and the slum areas of Beirut. Hizballah as well as a number of other Islamic organizations have done what their counterparts have done elsewhere in the Middle East: they have provided health care, education, vocational training, and financial support at a time when the state has been incapable of providing that type of assistance.

CONCLUSION

Militant Islamic movements in the Arab world have emerged in the

40. *Al-Nahar* (Beirut), 5 June 1985.

1980s, but all derive from earlier movements that either were suppressed or agreed to play by the rules of the governments in power. Most of the Sunnite militant groups examined here were influenced by, or were offshoots of, organizations having links with the Muslim Brotherhood of Hasan al-Banna in Egypt, which emerged in 1928. The Shiite movements, on the other hand, have their roots in Iran or in the Iraqi holy cities of Shiism like Najaf and Karbala.

Ideologically, they are not very different from their predecessors. What differentiates them is their commitment to achieving their goals not in the distant future but in the present. They are much better organized than earlier movements; they are better financed, as they raise money from their members and from external sources and governments; and they have younger, better-educated, and more active leaders. Most are very secretive about their organizational structures and have separate wings with different names that perform different functions. All have a paramilitary arm for terrorist activities.

Militant Islamic movements are also much more outspoken than their predecessors in their criticisms of governments and leaders in power. They use the difficult economic conditions under which their fellow citizens live to support their allegations of corruption, mismanagement, and kowtowing to the West. They argue that those leaders have failed and that it is time for change, an idea appealing even to those who do not support them.

These movements are militant because they refuse to compromise with the powers that be. They all argue that there can be no compromise with the forces of evil. They are, however, pragmatic and ready, as in Algeria, to maneuver tactically to achieve their goals. The ultimate goal is an Islamic republic that would transcend national borders, but until that time they want to establish Islamic republics within national borders that would assist similar movements elsewhere. Another characteristic of these movements, therefore, is the close links they maintain with each other and the support they give one another.

Because of their unwillingness to compromise, their criticisms of governments in power, their use of force and violence, and their expressed goal of overthrowing ruling elites, they have all been suppressed and their leaders and followers imprisoned. Many have had harsh prison sentences, have suffered torture in captivity, and have been sent or have fled into exile. They have therefore been able to glean a great deal of support as the underdog organization that has stood up to the powerful and corrupt.

Conservative and Traditional Brotherhoods

By JOHN OBERT VOLL

ABSTRACT: The major Sufi brotherhoods have a significance in the development of political Islam in the modern era that is often underestimated. The traditional brotherhoods provided the basis for much of the militant opposition to European imperial expansion in the nineteenth century and, through these efforts, created symbols for Islamic authenticity that have remained important throughout the twentieth century. These brotherhoods also were major conservative forces, preserving a sense of an Islamic identity in times of rule by non-Muslims or secularizing and westernizing Muslim elites after independence. The long-term impact of this conservative force is to provide a foundation for popular support for political Islam at the end of the twentieth century. This popular support is a major factor in transforming political Islam from a radical force on the periphery of the political arena into the basic foundation of mainstream politics in many Islamic societies.

John Obert Voll is professor of history at the University of New Hampshire. He is the author of Islam: Continuity and Change in the Modern World *and other publications on Islam in the modern era. He is president-elect of the Middle East Studies Association of North America and serves on the editorial board of the* Encyclopedia of the Modern Islamic World.

POLITICAL Islam in the modern era reflects the influence of the great Sufi brotherhoods, for they play an important role in Islamic society and history. A major force in the life of personal and social Islamic piety, they have also helped shape the definition of Islam in the modern political arena. The position and significance of the brotherhoods have changed in recent years, but the traditional structures have shown a remarkable ability to adapt to the major social and political transformations of the present day.

During the past two centuries, the world historical context within which the Sufi brotherhoods operate has changed dramatically. In each of three phases of historical-political development, the brotherhoods in different areas have been able to respond in significant and usually effective ways. In the first era, that of Western imperialist conquest and establishment of Western dominance, the brotherhoods sometimes performed the active function of providing organization and inspiration for military resistance. Then, when foreign dominance was established, the brotherhoods often provided the means for communication between the rulers and the general Muslim populace, especially the nonliterate, nonelite segments of society.

In the second phase, however, when both foreign rulers and then Western-educated nationalist elites worked to create modern societies utilizing Western secular models, the brotherhoods were a significant conservative force. They provided means whereby traditional identities and modes of operation could be maintained while avoiding open social conflict. Often the brotherhoods became, in this way, the vehicle for expanding the modern awareness of important parts of the general population without creating a total disruption of societal continuity.

Recent years mark the beginning of what many see as a major third phase in this set of experiences and developments. The domination of the West, both in imperial forms and in the form of rule by local, culturally Western elites, has significantly declined. This does not mean that the modernizing transformation has stopped, but that it is assuming often radically new forms. The older liberal Westernist and radical Westernist approaches to modernization no longer represent the only or even the dominant perspective underlying policies and aspirations. In this dramatically changing context, the Sufi brotherhoods face challenges in the redefinition of their role and mission within Muslim societies.

Political establishments themselves, with important lines of continuity in maintaining the more Westernist perspectives, have significantly altered their roles as leaders of Islamic societies. Islamic conceptualizations play an increasingly important role in the politics of established regimes. At the same time, a new style of political Islam, affirmed in a form sometimes called "fundamentalist," reflects the rise of new types of popular and political organizations. As these newer organizations provide the leadership for the affirmation of the new political Islam, the more traditional brotherhoods appear to be more conservative and less openly visible in the political arena. Their impact is, however, still significant in the developing articulation of both the political Islam of political establishments and the new political Islam.

THE CONTINUING IMPACT OF NINETEENTH-CENTURY POLITICAL SUFISM

Political Islam in the nineteenth century was importantly identified with major brotherhoods and brotherhoodlike organizations. Even at the end of the twentieth century, this identification is important in the struggle to define and control the heritage of this activist political Islam. The nineteenth-century brotherhood leaders have been adopted by a variety of twentieth-century groups who claim to be their heirs. Sufi leaders in Algeria, Somalia, Libya, and elsewhere became, in twentieth-century terms, the "first nationalists." In the current Islamic resurgence, the symbolism of these early activists continues to have persuasive power.

In an era when the steady advance of European imperial control in Africa and Asia was a major feature of political history, the resistance movements organized by the Sufi brotherhoods were a significant force. Other major social institutions and structures seemed less well-equipped to provide this organization. The political and military establishments of the existing states were relatively weak and were undertaking major reforms utilizing Western models, thus only strengthening the picture of Western domination.

The 'ulama' were not organized in a way that would encourage military resistance. Their major actions in the political arena tended to be like those of the 'ulama' of Cairo who invited the Ottoman soldier Muhammad Ali to undertake the responsibilities of governing Egypt in order to avoid further invasion or internal disorder. The great schools like al-Azhar in Cairo or Kairouan in Tunisia could provide advice but not political leadership. Major ethnic and tribal groupings of the day could and did provide some resistance, but this was only in particular localities and did not have much of a large-scale impact. It was the major popular organizations of piety, the brotherhoods, that provided models of organization and leadership for the defense of society.

The traditional brotherhood organizational structure was relatively simple and effective. The key is the relationship between the spiritual guide, often called a "shaykh," and his disciples. The disciple is bound to the shaykh by an oath of absolute obedience. There is usually a hierarchy of followers, with designated representatives of the shaykh serving particular groups and in specific areas. After the death of the shaykh who established the group, succession to leadership is sometimes hereditary and sometimes by designation.

The core of the identity is the regulated life of personal and group piety utilizing special collections of prayers and recitations. These devotional materials are "the path," or the *tariqa*, and the brotherhoods are usually identified as being the *tariqa* of the particular individual who initiated the prayers and devotional tradition. The group gathers regularly to recite the prayers and engage in other acts of devotion. The gathering place of the order often becomes a major social center for the members, providing a concrete focus for the lives of the followers of the shaykh. Even at the end of the twentieth century, this type of organization continues to provide an effective foundation for socially and politically influential organizations. It is not as highly visible as the more purely political groups, but this is part of its strength as a continuing force within Muslim societies.

At the beginning of the nineteenth century, there was already an established tradition of Islamic political activism utilizing brotherhood organization in many parts of the Islamic world. In West Africa at the end of the eighteenth century, for example, Uthman dan Fodio began a militant movement of Islamic renewal that resulted in the creation of an important political system, with a sultanate centered in the present northern region of Nigeria. Dan Fodio's initial identification was with a major Sufi brotherhood, and it was as a scholar and a shaykh in this order that he began his movement of renewal. The state that was created by the West African Jihad movement of dan Fodio provided the political organization for northern Nigeria as it came under British control. After independence in 1960, the major Muslim political leaders in Nigeria had ties with the Jihad tradition.

The effort to control the office of sultan in the north, now formally outside of the Nigeria political system, continues to involve major political struggles. The succession of a relatively liberal Islamic modernist, Al-

haj Ibrahim Dasuki, as the sultan of Sokoto in 1988 was the cause for strong protests among the more activist Islamicist groups, who spoke of the "unholy alliance between the Sultanate and secularism."[1] The continuing political importance of the symbols created by the political Islam of the brotherhoods in the nineteenth century is a factor that must be kept in mind when evaluating the contemporary role of the traditional brotherhoods.

During the nineteenth century, many major movements of Islamic renewal and resistance to European expansion arose out of the traditions of the brotherhoods and their organizations. Some of these were *tariqa*s that remained basically traditional orders while performing major functions beyond those of individual and group piety. One important cluster of such brotherhoods was created by the followers of Ahmad ibn Idris (d. 1837). These orders were influential in varying ways from North Africa to the islands of Southeast Asia. The disciples of ibn Idris developed brotherhoods that "were relatively more centralized and less prone to fission than their predecessors; they introduced into the areas where they proselytized new forms of social organization, often based on autonomous agricultural communities, *zawiya* or *jama'a*; recruited *en masse*, and later were politically active."[2]

1. Ibraheem Sulaiman, "Caesar on a Sacred Throne," *Africa Events*, Dec. 1988, p. 13. See also Kenneth B. Noble, "A Sultan with His Feet Planted in Two Worlds," *New York Times*, 11 Mar. 1989, p. 4.

2. R. S. O'Fahey, *Enigmatic Saint: Ahmad Ibn Idris and the Idrisi Tradition* (London: Hurst, 1990), pp. 4-5.

Among the most important of these brotherhoods was the Sanusiyya, which was established in Libya in the nineteenth century, led the resistance to Italian control in the twentieth century, and provided the basis for the monarchy when Libya became independent in 1951. Another important brotherhood in this tradition was the Khatmiyya in the Sudan. Under the leadership of the Mirghani family, the order became an important political force in the twentieth century, first as a patron for an emerging nationalist movement and then as the basis for one of the major political parties in the postcolonial era. The Khatmiyya-supported political parties were influential forces in the politics of the parliamentary periods in 1956-58, 1964-69, and 1985-89. The traditional brotherhood structure continues to provide an effective basis for mobilization of political support in the context of parliamentary party politics.

There were many other brotherhood-based movements of political Islam in the nineteenth century, and their traditions continue to have an impact on the development of political Islam in the late twentieth century. In the republics of the former Soviet Union in the Caucasus region, for example, there continue to be reflections of the Naqshabandiyya-led resistance to Russian imperial expansion. The Imam Shamil was able to maintain a holy war against the Russians for almost a quarter of a century before his final defeat in 1859. In Somalia, Muhammad Abdallah Hasan (1864-1921) was the leader of the Salihiyya who led a major holy war of resistance to expanding British imperial control. The so-called Mad Mulla became a symbol for later Somali nationalism, and the recent disintegration of independent Somalia shows the importance of having a supratribal principle of political unification in that country.

While the brotherhoods were not the only source of political Islamic activism in the nineteenth century, they did provide important foundations for continuing political Islam in many areas. In concrete terms, the orders were able to provide a structure through which actual military resistance to European imperial expansion organized. Their campaigns helped to define the specific boundaries of the resisting societies. Thus the Qadiriyya resistance to the French led by the Amir Abd al-Qadir helped to provide a historical foundation for the Algerian identity. The Sanusiyya provided a similar basis for Libya, and the Salihiyya for Somalia. The brotherhoods therefore made contributions to the nationalist mode of political Islam as it emerged during the twentieth century.

THE CONSERVATIVE ROLE OF THE BROTHERHOODS

The great brotherhoods also played, and continue to play, an important conservative role in Muslim societies. It is mistaken to identify radical Islamic revolutionism as a "conservative" force in the normal meaning of that term. In broader political discussions, conservatives are people who attempt to preserve the general outlines of the existing social order. They are protectors of the status quo. Modern and premodern fundamentalists, in contrast, are radically dissatisfied with the existing conditions. Some brotherhoods, like the renewalist movement in West Africa led by Uthman dan Fodio, were not conservative. But, within Islamic societies in the modern era, many brotherhoods have served as a profoundly conservative force. Even in their militant opposition to Western imperial expansion, they were primarily working to preserve society as it existed.

Once European imperial control was established in many areas, the brotherhoods were often important vehicles for helping the system operate. Working within the system of imperialist control, the brotherhoods were an important source for maintaining the Muslim identity of the peoples. As the educated elites became increasingly westernized in their thinking and daily lives, the brotherhoods provided an alternative arena within which even the Western educated elite could continue to function as visibly believing Muslims. In some cases, the brotherhoods provided some of the most effective means for preserving an Islamic identity and even spreading Islam beyond previous limits in the context of non-Muslim and sometimes anti-Islamic rulers.

Highly visible examples of this conservative role of the brotherhoods can be found in Africa and in Central Asia. In West Africa, both the militant and the more quietist orders of the nineteenth century were important forces in the territories ruled by the French and the British. As imperial rulers established more stable governing systems, the leaders of the brotherhoods provided "leaders of public opinion" who could be consulted and who could influence the local populations. In the Sudan, the Mirghani family provided an important intermediary between large numbers of people in the northern Sudan and the British rulers. Leaders of these more staid *tariqa*s were thought to be a force that could prevent the resurgence of militant Islamic activism in the country.[3] In Algeria, the French worked with the Sufi organizations; in northern Nigeria, the heirs of Uthman dan Fodio became the Native Administration of British indirect rule.

This role has been criticized by later nationalists and secular radicals because it involved collaboration with the imperial rulers. It provided, however, a vehicle for conservative preservation of the fundamental Islamic identity when militant resistance seemed impossible. Beyond this, in Africa, the "modern state in its colonial form established an institutional framework which allowed the *tariqa* new possibilities of expansion."[4] New means of communication and more open trade patterns were elements in this. In this colonial context, the boundaries of the Islamic world expanded considerably beyond

3. See, for example, the discussions in Gabriel Warburg, "Religious Policy in the Northern Sudan: Ulama and Sufism, 1914-1945," *Asian and African Studies*, 7:163-78 (1971); John O. Voll, "The British, the Ulama, and Popular Islam in the Early Anglo-Egyptian Sudan," *International Journal of Middle East Studies*, 2:212-18 (1971).

4. Donal B. Cruise O'Brien, "Islam and Power in Black Africa," in *Islam and Power*, ed. Alexander S. Cudsi and Ali E. H. Dessouki (Baltimore, MD: Johns Hopkins University Press, 1981), p. 160.

where they had been at the time of the eighteenth-century revivalist holy wars. It was the conservative gradualism of the orders that helped to expand Islam in the twentieth century, making it the most rapidly expanding religion on the African continent.

An even more dramatic case reflecting the power of the conservative brotherhoods can be seen in the Muslim societies of Central Asia. Russian imperial expansion under the czars began a process that continued after the Communist revolution. Both regimes actively sought to discourage adherence to Islam, either through Russification or, under the Communists, through vigorous anti-religion campaigns. Initially, there had been active resistance, much of which was led by Sufi leaders and involved the brotherhoods. There was the Naqshabandiyya resistance in the Caucasus during the nineteenth century, and in the Basmachi revolts following World War I, brotherhood leaders also played an important role. This resistance was crushed, however, and Central Asian Muslims faced the problems of living under non-Muslim and frequently actively anti-Islamic rule.

Soviet leaders engaged in both a frontal assault on the ideas and institutions of religion and a direct attempt to institutionalize and control what Islamic activity could survive the assault. As a result, a government establishment was created that was to regulate Muslim life. There was a structure of councils and directorates with the major regions and republics having muftis and directors appointed. In this way, a Muslim governmental institution came into existence as a structure for bringing the Communist regime and the Muslim peoples more closely together. This religious establishment had some resources available to it but had little control or influence over most of the lives of the majority of Central Asian Muslims.

Under Soviet rule, formal, visible Muslim organizations other than those of the religious establishment were suppressed, and most such groupings disappeared. But the Sufi brotherhoods, based as they are on the private devotional lives of the believers, had the means to maintain an underground religious tradition. Such a phenomenon would reflect great diversity because it would usually be highly localized in structure and following. As these groupings developed, Soviet analysts began to speak of an unofficial, unregulated "parallel Islam," with leaders drawn to a remarkable degree from the Sufi brotherhoods.[5]

The leaders of parallel Islam maintained many of the older social and religious traditions and rituals and, in this way, performed a profoundly conservative function that, in the context of Soviet rule, could have revolutionary implications. After the wars of the 1920s, however, there were few major revolts that had any impact on the direction of Soviet rule. Instead, the Sufi-based parallel Islam simply resisted the ideological expansion of communism in its athe-

5. Alexandre Bennigsen and S. Enders Wimbush, *Mystics and Commissars: Sufism in the Soviet Union* (Berkeley: University of California Press, 1985), p. 86. In many ways, this book is the standard source on Sufism in the former Soviet Union.

istic form and provided a continuing distinctive basis for Central Asian sociocultural identities. Before the collapse of the Soviet Union, Alexandre Bennigsen wrote, "Although Soviet dogma has insisted for nearly seventy years that Islam must be eliminated in the course of producing the 'New Soviet Man,' all evidence points to just the opposite having happened: Islam has strengthened and Marxism-Leninism has failed to inspire and to satisfy."[6]

The continued existence and growing strength of Islam were not the products of fundamentalist activism over the decades. They were primarily the products of the patient and quiet maintenance of Islamic customs and identity, in other words, the products of a strong conservative force, and this force is primarily identified with the traditional Sufi brotherhoods. With the sudden collapse of the Soviet Union at the beginning of the 1990s, the conservative contribution of the brotherhoods has immense significance, regardless of whether or not the brotherhoods will emerge as visible political forces within the Central Asian republics. It may be that the era of necessarily conservative approaches is past, but, if so, the passing is itself the product of the brotherhoods' work.

The general conservative role of the traditional brotherhoods throughout the Muslim world has had significance. It allowed conquered populations to adjust to non-Muslim rulers without losing their own religiocultural identity. Indeed, these brother-

6. Alexandre Bennigsen, "Unrest in the World of Soviet Islam," *Third World Quarterly*, 10:786 (1988).

hoods, at least at times, were the agents for the expansion of Islam and the turning back of the challenges of non-Islamic forces. In contrast to the tradition of the nineteenth-century activist brotherhoods, however, the twentieth-century conservative efforts of the orders were less militant and overcame opposition more by patient and quiet diligence than by violent resistance. The major contribution of these conservative orders is that when non-Muslim rule was withdrawn, there remained a core of Islamic community and identity on which independent Muslim leaders could and can build.

INDEPENDENCE AND THE TRADITIONAL BROTHERHOODS

In most Muslim societies, the era of independence from imperial control was not initially a time of establishment of clearly Islamic regimes. Most of the leaders of the new states were themselves strongly influenced by Western conceptualizations of the nature and needs of political development in the modern world. The great competition was frequently between liberal and radical Western-style approaches to nation building, and more explicitly Islamic approaches to fundamental issues of political order and development were viewed with suspicion.

In the years following World War II, as growing numbers of Muslim societies became independent states, much effort was given to the establishment of liberal parliamentary regimes. When those failed, they were replaced by military governments who often looked more to the example of Mustafa Kemal Ataturk, the secularist reformer of Turkey following World War I, than to more explicitly Islamic models.[7] Later, more explicitly radical programs were developed by leaders in major Muslim countries like Egypt, Syria, and Algeria, and even more traditional monarchs articulated their programs in the terminology of Western concepts of development.

In this context, political Islam was a concept and force that tended to run counter to the political mainstream in most Muslim societies. The more secular leaders made an effort not to appear anti-Islamic and often used Islamic forms and slogans in their programs and pronouncements. The groups that directly advocated programs of Islamization of state and society were, however, actively suppressed or shunted to the periphery of politics by the 1960s. Most leaders of the Muslim Brotherhood in Egypt, for example, were imprisoned by President Nasser, and other branches of this organization or groups inspired by its message had similar experiences in other parts of the Arab world. The activist followers of Mulla Kashani in Iran also had political difficulty, as did groups like the Dar ul-Islam movement in Indonesia.

The traditional brotherhoods were not usually a direct part of this more revolutionary style of political Islam. At least some of the emerging Islamicist movements had had contact with Sufi orders in their early days. The founder of the Muslim Brotherhood in Egypt, Hasan al-Banna, for example, was strongly influenced by the Hasafiyya *tariqa* and had been involved with this particular order for twenty years and "with Sufism in a special way for most of his life."[8] Groups like the Muslim Brotherhood were not and are not, however, Sufi brotherhoods. They represent a new form of popular Islamic activism, even though they often interact with and resemble the more revivalist brotherhoods of the eighteenth and nineteenth centuries.

The position of the traditional brotherhoods under national rulers with relatively secular perspectives tended to be similar to that adopted under imperial rule. There was a quiet cooperation and an underlying persistent devotion to the older piety. In other words, the response of the traditional orders to both radical and liberal westernizers tended to be conservative rather than militant. Egypt during the 1960s provides an instructive example. While the militant Islamicists of the Muslim Brotherhood were being suppressed, many of the traditional Sufi orders were flourishing. The Rifa'iyya *tariqa*, as just one example, regularly brought significant numbers of people to the Rifa'i mosque for devotional exercises, and a respected philosopher at the University of Cairo, who was a member, was highly regarded by both government officials controlling cultural affairs and teachers at al-Azhar

7. See, for example, the comments in Anwar al-Sadat, *In Search of Identity: An Autobiography* (New York: Harper & Row, 1977), chap. 1.

8. Richard P. Mitchell, *The Society of the Muslim Brothers* (London: Oxford University Press, 1969), p. 2. For Banna's observations on the Hasafiyya and Sufism, see *Memoirs of Hasan Al Banna Shaheed*, trans. M. N. Shaikh (Karachi: International Islamic Publishers, 1981), pp. 67-76.

University.[9] Although people like this scholar were eager to maintain a clearly Islamic tradition in a relatively conservative manner, they were not interested in advocating a program of political activism and were not necessarily concerned with the formal Islamization of the state structures of the day.

The primary role of the traditional *tariqa*s in the context of the liberal and radical modernizers was conservative. This represents a style of political Islam but one that is different from that of the activists like the Muslim Brothers. However, the long-term significance of this conservatism may be great because it helped to maintain the popular sense of the long continuities of the identity of the Islamic community. Just as the early fundamentalist writers and activists, like Hasan al-Banna and Sayyid Qutb in Egypt or Abu al-A'la al-Mawdudi in South Asia, may have laid the conceptual foundations for the Islamic resurgence of the late twentieth century, the conservative persistence of the traditional brotherhoods may have preserved and even created the mass audience for the fundamentalists' message.

9. Based on observations of *dhikr* ceremonies at the Rifa'i mosque during 1960-61 by the author and also on interviews with officials at the Ministry of Awqaf and the Islamic administration of al-Azhar at the time. The professor mentioned was Dr. Muhammad Mustafa Hilmi, who was the author, for example, of a popular booklet published by the Ministry of Culture and National Guidance on Sufism: *al-Hubb al-ilahi fi al-tasawwuf al-Islami*, al-Maktaba al-Thiqafiyya no. 24 (Cairo: Wizara al-Thiqafa wa al-Irshad al-Qawmi, 1970). Comments on Professor Hilmi's views are based on a series of interviews with him during 1960-61.

THE CURRENT RESURGENCE AND TRADITIONAL BROTHERHOODS

In many parts of the Muslim world, there is an increasing sense of affirmation of Islam in an active mode. Political Islam in an activist sense is emerging as a vital part of the politics of Muslim societies. This Islamic resurgence has received much attention, but the role of the traditional brotherhoods has been relatively ignored despite their potential importance. In addition to having preserved a popular audience for emerging Islamicist tendencies, these orders have other roles. They may provide mass support at key moments of crisis and stable continuity in times when the sense of crisis or mission is less acute. The experience of the Sudan in recent years can provide an important example of how these roles can function in the context of the contemporary world.

In the Sudan during the 1980s, the more traditional and conservative brotherhoods played a significant but usually indirect role in the developing Islamization of state and society. A group of younger military officers led by Ja'far Numayri took control of the government in 1969, and the regime of the May Revolution went through many different phases. It began as a relatively radical and secular regime, strongly influenced by the Sudan Communist Party. When the Communists in the military leadership attempted to overthrow Numayri in 1971, he began a shift in his orientation. Eventually, he became fully committed to an activist program of Islamization of state and society in the Sudan, culminating in

1983 in what are now known as the September Laws.[10]

The traditional brotherhoods played some important roles in this process of the transformation of the basic orientation of Numayri and his political system. The most visible of the older orders was the Khatmiyya, which continued to play the political role that had been defined earlier by the Mirghani family. They provided patronage and leadership for one of the major political parties that had been active in the eras of party politics and parliaments. The Khatmiyya-supported party, called the Democratic Unionist Party since the late 1960s, was a major part of the alliance of forces opposed to the Numayri regime during the 1970s. Within the alliance, it was a conservative force countering both the activist Islamicists and the leftist groups.

Traditional brotherhoods also had a more direct impact on the increasingly Islamic orientation of Numayri. Many of the Sudanese brotherhoods had not taken a direct role in the politics of anti-imperialism or the politics of the parliamentary periods. Instead, they had continued to function as local centers of devotional piety and social life. In the times of major social change, they had provided a more conservative focus in the lives of many people, especially in the smaller towns and villages. Often the local leaders of these orders were seen as obstacles to development, as they might oppose expansion of the modern education system or the extension of certain modern services. By the early 1970s, however, at least some of the local leadership became more active in these types of activities. They also were viewed as a balance to the influence of Islamic leaders like the Mirghani family and so were increasingly consulted by government officials. The evolution of the social and political role of the leader of the local order centered in Um Dubban is a good example of this transition, which involved increasing interaction with government officials. "The close links between state senior policy-makers and religious leaders of *turuq* have provided the latter with immense influence over government officials working in their areas. That has in turn given the religious leaders leverage over local political and social organizations."[11]

In the early 1980s, Numayri began to articulate policies in a more explicitly Islamic mode, and he drew on a number of sources for this. He had initiated a "national reconciliation" in the late 1970s that drew the Sudanese Muslim Brotherhood into the regime. Hasan al-Turabi, the leader of the brotherhood, served in a number of high-level posts and was assigned the task of leading a special committee for the Islamization of Sudanese law. As a result, the emerging Islamization program was strongly

10. For Numayri's public account of the early stages of this reorientation, see Ja'far Muhammad Numayri, *al-Nahj al-Islami li-madha?* (Cairo: al-Maktab al-Masri al-Hadith, 1980).

11. Idris Salim El Hassan, "On Ideology: The Case of Religion in Northern Sudan" (Ph.D. diss, University of Connecticut, 1980), p. 185. This is a thorough study of the development of a local *tariqa* center, Um Dubban, in the modern era.

influenced by the more activist Islamicist forces in the Sudan.

At the same time, Numayri had developed a strong personal relationship with some leaders of the more traditional and conservative brotherhoods. These people were not organized as a cohesive political faction but were able to encourage the official reaffirmation of Islam by the revolutionary regime. As Numayri moved in the direction of direct and rapid Islamization, he distanced himself somewhat from the leadership of the Muslim Brotherhood and turned to more conservative and directly loyal people from the smaller *tariqas*. By the time of the actual announcement of the implementation of a direct Islamization program, the effort was managed by two younger men, Nayal Abu Groon and Awad el Geed Mohamed Ahmed, who were drawn from smaller orders. The more traditional Sufi tone was emphasized by the initial importance of the oath of allegiance to Numayri that Abu Groon and Awad el Geed defined.[12]

In the Sudan in recent years, the traditional brotherhoods have in these ways provided strong support for the main trends of the Islamic resurgence even though they have not been the most visible forces within those trends. They have had special influence by working in the arena of personal piety to provide personal spiritual comfort as well as political support for a leader like Numayri. This personal dimension of

political Islam is often ignored, but it may be the arena of the most significant contributions of the traditional orders to political Islam in the long run. In the emerging Central Asian republics, for example, leaders long nurtured by the parallel Islam of the orders may be the shapers of political Islam in that region.

The political Islam of the 1990s already may be reflecting the broader influence of the more traditional and conservative Sufi brotherhoods.[13] As the concept and ideal of explicit Islamization of society spreads from the radical fringes of the political system into the mainstream, political Islam becomes a more complex force. This normalization of the original more revolutionary impulse of Islamic resurgence[14] is distinctly influenced by conservatism of the type shown throughout Islamic history by at least some of the traditional Sufi brotherhoods. The contribution of the traditional and conservative brotherhoods to contemporary political Islam is their traditionalism and conservatism, which provide a strong sense of continuity in personal and

13. Relatively little has been published about the continuing and probably growing popular influence of the more traditional brotherhoods. However, works of scholars like Valerie J. Hoffman-Ladd and Albrecht Hofheinz on orders like the Burhaniyya in Egypt and the Majdhubiyya in the Sudan will be making significant contributions as conference papers become published as articles and monographs.

14. For a more complete discussion of this process of normalization in the context of Egypt, see John O. Voll, "Fundamentalism in the Sunni Arab World: Egypt and the Sudan," in *Fundamentalisms Observed*, ed. Martin E. Marty and R. Scott Appleby (Chicago: University of Chicago Press, 1991), pp. 384-90.

12. John Obert Voll, *The Political Impact of Islam in Sudan: Numayri's Islamization Program*, INR/LAR 1722-420140 (Washington, DC: Department of State, 1984), pp. 89-91.

public life. It is not an antimodern force so much as a force that reminds both leaders and the general public that there are devotional and spiritual resources available within the Islamic cumulative tradition for coping with the great problems and issues of the contemporary world.

ANNALS, *AAPSS*, **524**, November 1992

State Islam and Communal Plurality

By NAZIH N. AYUBI

ABSTRACT: The historical Islamic state developed interesting methods of quasi-consociational and semi-corporatist aggregation of communities. From quite early on, Sunnism became the religion of the ruling elite and of the state as well as part of the state's legal and cultural system. Subsequently, the geographical distribution and the political economy of the Islamic sects and of the religious minorities manifested quite distinct features that were mainly a function of their relationship to the state. Whereas the Islamic sects did not come to terms ideologically and organizationally with the state, the religious minorities, on the whole, adjusted themselves mentally and behaviorally to its requirements. By comparison, the contemporary Middle Eastern state, both the secular and the Islamic, is achieving less success in dealing with its communal problem. Certain groups are excluded in the former type in spite of the secularist slogans, and certain groups are excluded in the latter because of the ideological or religious nature of the state. Improvisation is needed, and Muslim statesmen and intellectuals may need to go beyond, and even outside, conventional Islamic jurisprudence in order to deal with this issue.

Nazih N. Ayubi is a reader in politics and director of the Middle East Politics Program at the University of Exeter, United Kingdom. He holds a Jean Monnet Fellowship at the European University Institute in Florence, Italy (1991-92) and will be a Hallsworth Fellow at Manchester University in 1992-93. A graduate of Cairo University, he obtained his doctorate from Oxford University. He is the author of Bureaucracy and Politics in Contemporary Egypt; Political Islam: Religion and Politics in the Arab World; *and* The State and Public Policies in Egypt since Sadat.

M OST contemporary countries with Muslim majorities declare in their constitutions that Islam is the religion of the state, and many of them have increasingly incorporated a further clause to the effect that *shari'a* is a major, or sometimes the major, source of legislation. In so doing, modern politicians are trying to impart to the contemporary state some of the legitimacy that the historical Islamic state used to derive from being perceived as the "guardian of the faith." In that capacity, activist opposition to the historical Islamic state, as for example by the Kharijites ("deviants," "exiters"), or disgruntled withdrawal from public affairs, as for example by the Sufis ("mystics," "gnostics"), were both dealt with severely by the state as being heresies against the religion itself.

Much of Islamic jurisprudence, especially that of the mainstream Sunnite tradition, was consequently related to a doctrine of civil obedience. The *'ulama'* (religious scholars) often taught that the caliph, or in reality anyone in effective possession of political power, had to be obeyed since an unjust ruler was still better for the community than civil strife. Yet the historical Islamic state was not as monolithic a polity as some maintain. Not only did *fiqh* ("jurisprudence") develop into a multiplicity of schools, but the state also developed interesting methods of quasi-consociational and semi-corporatist aggregation of communities that were quite advanced and sophisticated in their time and that should provide the comparativist scholar with very rich material for study and analysis.

The purpose of this article is (1) to illustrate the ways in which Sunnism has developed, historically, as state Islam; (2) to examine the ways in which the Sunnite establishment dealt, historically, with the communal diversity of society, that is, with the existence of Islamic sects and non-Muslim minorities; and (3) to consider the ways in which the modern territorial state in the Middle East has tried to grapple with the contradiction between the principle of state Islam and the reality of communal plurality.

SUNNITE CENTRALIZATION AND SECTARIAN AUTONOMY

From quite early on, Sunnism developed to become the religion of the ruling elite and of the state and to be part and parcel of the state's legal and cultural system. Sunnism developed in close alliance with, and through adjustment to, the requirements of the central state, whereas "sects" (*firaq, nihal, tawa'if*) emerged and developed as ideologies of groups opposed to the central state and concerned with their own cultural and social group autonomy. Sunnism developed historically as *the* religion (*al-din*) and described its doctrine as being that of the entire group or collectivity (*al-jama'a*), whereas sects were variously described as deviationist (*khawarij*), extremist (*ghulat*), or rejectionist (*bughat, rawafid*), and their followers were regarded as discordant "parties" (*ahzab*). It is therefore fairly understandable why Sunnite scholars are to be found, even to this day, classifying Kharijism and its offshoots—for example, Azariqa,

Ibadiyya, and so on—and Shiism and its offshoots—such as Isma'iliyya, Druze, and the like—as "political sects."[1]

Over time, the Sunnites absorbed the accumulated religious heritage and incorporated it more thoroughly with politics, whereas the Shiites—who originally came mostly from the underprivileged groups and tended to extol the virtues of austerity, meekness, and simplicity—had for a long time been excluded from political power. Whereas the Sunnites, usually in government, emphasized agreement and consensus (ijma') and strove to turn religion into "public policy," the Shiites, who were usually subservient, lamented injustice and complained about the arbitrariness of government. Whereas the Sunnites did things publicly and openly, the sects were more inclined to concepts such as al-batin (the inner, hidden truth) and to devices like taqiyya (concealment of real beliefs).[2] Whereas the Sunnites expanded the scope of their authoritative leadership, their religious sources, and their juridical schools, the sects confined these to a few selected leaders, sources, and schools. Whereas the Sunnites have tended, to this day, to admit most people to their mosques, the Shiites confine mosques to their own. Sunnite men often marry Christian or Jewish women; Shiites seldom do. Sunnites eat food slaughtered or prepared by Christians or Jews; Shiites have traditionally regarded this as najas, polluted and impure.[3] In short, the Sunnites have tended to be both expansionist and assimilationist; the sects have tended to be withdrawn and exclusivist.

The Sunnites' dominance over the state has meant their control over the city as well and their preponderance in official and administrative affairs, even in societies where the Sunnites coexist with other important sects, such as in Iraq, Yemen, and Morocco. The sects, which have long maintained their fighting spirit, tend—with the tribes—to be more strongly represented in the military forces: the Zaidis (Zuyud) in Yemen, the Berbers in Morocco, and various minority groups in Syria, Lebanon, and Oman. This is particularly true when the solidarity of sect is reinforced by a solidarity of tribe, as with the Ibadis of Oman, the Zuyud of Yemen, the Druze and Alawites of Syria and Lebanon, and the Yazidis of Iraq.

When the solidarity of sect coincided with the solidarity of tribe, the group was more often capable of achieving an element of political autonomy, especially in times of weakness of the central Islamic state, as happened in the second Abbasid era and in some periods of the Ottoman era and, of course, during the colonial and modern eras. Thus, for example, the settlement of a Kharijite branch, the Ibadis, in Oman toward the end of the second century A.H. (eighth

1. See Muhammad Ahmad Abu Zahra, al-Madhahib al-Islamiyya [Islamic sects] (Cairo: Maktabat al-Adab, n.d.), pp. 29-130; Manna' al-Qattan, al-Tashri' wa al-fiqh al-Islami [Islamic legislation and jurisprudence] (Cairo: Wahba, 1979), pp. 280 ff.

2. Fu'ad al-Khuri, Imamat al-shahid wa imamat al-batal [Leadership of the martyr and leadership of the hero] (Beirut: Markaz Dar al-Jami'a, 1988), pp. 29-48, 132.

3. Fouad Ajami, The Vanished Imam: Musa al-Sadr and the Shia of Lebanon (Ithaca, NY: Cornell University Press, 1986), p. 133.

century A.D.) gave the country the distinct political character that it has retained ever since. The settlement of a certain Shiite branch, the Zuyud, in northern and eastern Yemen toward the end of the third century A.H. (ninth century A.D.) has also given that country a certain distinct political personality. In Lebanon, too, the emergence from the beginning of the seventeenth century A.D. of the Ma'ni and Shihabi emirates—the first Druze, the second Maronite, but tribally related—contributed to the development of a certain Lebanese distinctiveness. In modern times, the appearance of new religious sects or movements has also been influential in imparting a certain political character to a particular country, as with the Wahhabis in Arabia during the eighteenth century and the Sanusi in Libya during the nineteenth century.[4]

There has also been a geographical map and a political economy of Muslim sectarianism in the Arab world. The Sunnites, who dominated the state and the city, also dominated the fertile plains and prairies of the whole of the Arab world. Even where they do not form the overwhelming majority of the population, they are to be found in the fertile regions of Lebanon, Oman, Yemen, Iraq, and Bahrain. In most cases, Sunnites have owned the land, whereas Shiites and other sects have tilled it; this applies to Iraq, Syria, Bahrain, Saudi Arabia, and elsewhere. Historically, of course, landownership was an ex-

tension of state power, where the urban Sunnites were already dominant.

In Iraq, the Sunnite-Shiite dichotomy has been geographical—the former in the middle and north, the latter in the south—but it also overlapped until the interwar period with class divisions. Thus the most influential landlords of the province of Basrah were Sunnites, while the cultivators of their palm groves were overwhelmingly Shiites. Sunnites were also highly represented among the affluent landowners or merchants of all other southern areas except for the Shiite holy cities of Najaf and Karbala. In Baghdad, too, where the two sects enjoyed almost numerical parity, the socially dominant families were, with some exceptions, Sunnite. In the Iraqi army of the 1930s, the officers were Sunnite but the rank and file was mostly Shiite.[5] The Shiite south had for a long time been more culturally and economically tied to Iran, whereas the Sunnite north had been more culturally and economically tied to Syria and Turkey. From the interwar period, and especially after World War II, the Shiites went through a period of accelerated social mobility, not least in the matter of wealth, which they managed to accumulate through commerce. The Sunnites, however, continued to be more preponderant in holding state offices, both civilian and military.[6]

Smaller sects tend to reside in peripheral and mountainous territo-

4. Al-Khuri, *Imamat al-shahid*, pp. 53-65; Iliya Harik, "The Origins of the Arab State System," in *The Foundations of the Arab State*, ed. Ghassan Salamé (London: Croom Helm, 1987), pp. 25-30.

5. Hanna Batatu, *The Old Social Classes and the Revolutionary Movements of Iraq* (Princeton, NJ: Princeton University Press, 1982), pp. 44-45.

6. Ibid., pp. 47-49.

ries: the Alawites, an offshoot of the Shiites, in the mountainous Latakia region of northwest Syria; the Druze, an offshoot of the Isma'ilis, in Jabal al-Duruz and in Wadi al-Tim in Syria and Lebanon; the Ibadis, a branch of the Kharijites, in the interior of Jabal Oman and in mountainous or oasis areas in Libya, Tunisia, and Algeria; the Zuyud in the mountainous regions of northeast Yemen; and the Yazidis on the Sinjar mountains in northern Iraq. The sects tend to be highly concentrated in their regions; thus 68 percent of the Alawites, 82 percent of the Syrian Druze, and 68 percent of the Ibadis live in their own territory. Similarly, 68 percent of the Lebanese Shiites and 91 percent of the Saudi Arabian Shiites all live within their own region, namely, southern Lebanon and eastern Arabia. Most sects also represent the statistically predominant religious denomination within their own region —for example, over 87 percent of the inhabitants of southern Iraq are Shiites. These sects have not only developed their own religious symbols and constructions in their territories but also tend to possess a fairly comprehensive economy of their own, based on diversified agriculture, local crafts, and small towns. Landownership is often extensively spread among members of the community and so are things such as the ownership of palm trees—the community is obviously striving for economic self-sufficiency in grains and other basic foods, as well as in crafts and small industries. The religious symbols and the self-contained economy reinforce the sense of psychological and cultural distinctiveness from the surrounding society.[7]

SUNNITE-SHIITE DISTINCTIONS

The social and cultural differences between the Sunnites and the other Islamic sects are all reflected in the political realm. The Sunnites tend to look to the state as the organizer of their religious affairs. In their traditional theory, the ruler is the implementer of the Word of God; and in this capacity obedience is due to him from every believer. And that Word of God is specifically translated, by the jurists, into law, the shari'a. Little space is allowed for disagreement: consensus (ijma') is a cardinal principle, based on the decisions of those who "bind and loosen" (ahl al-hal wa al-'aqd), who are mainly the caliph and the 'ulama'. The culture is assimilationist in spite of social diversity, giving an impression of unity and harmony to be derived from the comprehensive translation of religion into public policies. Opposition to the state is therefore almost tantamount to abandoning the faith; it is not only to be condemned by the society but is also to be prevented by the state.[8]

By contrast, the Shiites are not etatists but imamites—their imam or spiritual leader (a term they prefer to the term "caliph," which is more familiar to the Sunnites) is the peak of their religiosity and pious emotions; he is an example to be followed and an inspiration to be striven after. His

7. Al-Khuri, Imamat al-shahid, pp. 71-92.
8. See Nazih Ayubi, Political Islam: Religion and Politics in the Arab World (London: Routledge, 1991), chap. 1.

is an internal spiritual authority, whereas that of the Sunnite caliph is more of an external political control. Whereas the Sunnites have tended to believe that government is legitimate and just as long as it follows the *shari'a*, the Shiites have on the whole maintained that government can never be legitimate and just as long as the Imam remained absent or "hidden." Their attitude toward government has therefore tended to oscillate between the concealment of their real feelings (*taqiyya*) and the mobilization of forces against the existing illegitimate order. A sense of permanent revolution has thus tended to be part of their ideological and psychological outlook, always kept alive by the memory of their martyrs and by their own readiness to emulate their example. Their rites and rituals are often intense and collective, maintaining group cohesiveness and a certain sense of distinctiveness and moral superiority.[9]

The Sunnite state controls its jurists and clerics tightly. Originally the restricting of juridical schools to four in number—Hanafi, Maliki, Shafi'i, and Hanbali—was a political decision; the Ja'fari school might also have been recognized by al-Mutawakkil (A.H. 232-47) had it not been for the Shiite disturbances during his time. Although the original writings of the jurists of the four Sunnite schools might to some extent have mirrored the environment in which each of them had lived—for example, Abu Hanifa, a liberal, might have reflected the more complex and more advanced Iraqi society in which he functioned, whereas

Malik, a conservative, might have been more representative of the harsher Arabian society—what is more important is the way in which teachings of the various schools were acclimatized in various societies. Thus, with the passing of time, certain countries came to be more favorable to a certain school than others; for example, Malikism was favored in North Africa; Shafi'ism in Egypt, Syria, and Lebanon; Hanafism in Iraq, Turkey, and the Caucasus; and Hanbalism in the Arabian Peninsula.[10]

A rather distinctive feature in Arabia and the Persian Gulf is the greater emphasis attached there to people's *madhhab*, that is, their juridical "sect" or "school"; indeed, in Yemen the Sunnites are commonly known by their juridical sect as *shawafi'*. Apparently, tribal and familial groupings try to distinguish themselves by following a specific *madhhab*. Thus, in Bahrain, for example, tribal lineages would follow the Maliki school; al-Hawla—Sunnite Arabs of Iranian background—the Hanbali; and urban and rural Shiites, the Ja'fari.[11] In other societies, the following of a particular *madhhab* may indicate some professional or social difference. Thus, in Tunisia and other parts of North Africa, most Hanafi families are of Turkish and/or a princely or official background. For that matter, too, Hanafism remains a favorite school among the *'ulama'* in Egypt; sanctioned as the state's official *madhhab*

9. Al-Khuri, *Imamat al-shahid*, pp. 156-63.

10. Hasan Sadiq, *Judhur al-fitna fi al-firaq al-Islamiyya* [Roots of discord in the Islamic sects] (Cairo: Madbuli, 1988), pp. 227-43.

11. Al-Khuri, *Imamat al-shahid*, pp. 222-23.

by the Ottomans, it remains to this day the official juridical school of *ifta'* ("counseling") and *qada'* ("the judiciary"), even though the majority of the population, especially in the rural areas, are non-Hanafis. In northern Lebanon, whereas the distinguished families of merchants and landowners are often Shafi'is, the families of artisans and craftsmen are overwhelmingly Maliki.[12]

The *'ulama'* are an integral part of the state establishment in Sunnite countries, fitting very often within the contours of its administrative organization. They are frequently employed by the government as judges, preachers, and teachers. As state functionaries, they often dissociate themselves from the more ritualistic functions in which less educated and more popular types engage in the countryside, such as circumcision, burial, and chanting. Among the Shiites, on the other hand, the role of the clergy who are directly involved—in a more voluntary way—in the social and cultural affairs of their local communities is much more profound. Religious services and ceremonies are very extensive at the grass-roots levels, with an abundance of festivals to commemorate all kinds of religious occasions, both sad and joyful. The Shiite clergy are also more likely than their Sunnite counterparts to adjudicate in sensitive family conflicts involving adultery, sodomy, violence, or black magic, since on the whole the Shiite clerics are much more socially intimate with their congregations.[13] Among Shiite communities there is a higher percentage of

clergy to attend to all such functions than there is among communities of Sunnites; for instance, there is about one cleric to every 2000 of the population in predominately Sunnite Syria compared to about one to every 300 of the population in predominately Shiite Iran. The intensity of the Shiite rituals is also more remarkable, as for example in the Karbala commemorations, where the public believes that the status of the *mulla* is to be measured by his ability to inspire weeping, agony, and torment in his audience.

This does not mean that the clergy in Shiism do not cooperate with the state, for indeed many of them do. These are the ones whom Ayatollah Khomeini designated as the "jurists of the Sultans" (*fuqaha' al-salatin*), for they interpret religion to suit the requirements of the government even at times when the Imam remains absent and politics therefore continue to be unjust. Their standing, however, is never considered to be as noble as the status of those who work for the autonomy of the religious society, away from government and the central authority, in preparation for and in expectation of the arrival of the just Imam. It should be remembered as well that the political economy of the Shiite establishment is also different. For apart from the religious judges who may work for the state, most Shiite scholars derive their incomes from private popular sources and various tithes and donations or else from religious endowments subject to their direct control. All this gives the Shiite clergy a certain measure of autonomy vis-à-vis the state and enables them in many

12. Sadiq, *Judhur al-fitna*, pp. 229-31.
13. Al-Khuri, *Imamat al-shahid*, pp. 224-52.

instances to voice their protest against government.

To speak about the social, economic, and political distinctiveness of the Muslim sects is not to suggest, however, that such characteristics are permanent or eternal. In the same way in which many of the original aspects of distinction were accentuated by various economic, political, and cultural developments, changes in these latter factors can in turn induce significant changes in the general outlook of the sects. To illustrate this point, two examples concerning the political outlook of the Shiite community in Iraq and in Lebanon can be cited.

The conventional view on the position of the Shiites in Iraq maintains that the traditional supremacy of the Sunnites, inherited from Ottoman and pre-Ottoman times, has been continued in independent Iraq, royal and republican. Because the Shiites were politically disenfranchised, the conventional argument runs, they have come to represent on the whole an oppositional community. While Sunnites have identified with Arab nationalism—the other Arab states are predominantly Sunnite—those Shiites who have adopted modern political ideologies have tended toward leftist orientations, notably the Communist Party. Yet as Sami Zubaida rightly illustrates, the political orientations of the Shiites are diverse, and this diversity is as much the product of political institutions and processes and of class and economic factors as it is of communal solidarity.[14]

Under the monarchy, southern Shiite shaykh-landlords were a predominant part of the political establishment. Different factions of the 'ulama' had different associates: peasants and merchants, conservatives and progressives, domestic patrons and foreign agencies. In due course, Nasserism and Ba'thism did attract many Shiites. Equally, at various points in its history, the Communist Party included many Sunnite Arabs in its leadership. The presence of the Shiites was notable, but their numerical representation was no higher, and perhaps even a little lower, than their representation in the population at large. The remarkable fact about Iraqi Shiites is the extent to which they have been predominant in politics generally: rather than saying that they have a propensity toward communism, it would be more accurate to say that they have a propensity for politics. Moreover, the directions in which this propensity is expressed change often, with yet another shift occurring after the Iranian Revolution, which has politicized the Iraqi Shiites even further.[15]

Another interesting example may be observed with regard to the Lebanese Shiites. For centuries, this community appeared to accept its marginal and downtrodden status. Ritualistic ceremony could provide psychological consolation, but little more. In the collective memory of the Shiites, the seventh-century story of

14. Sami Zubaida, "Class and Community in Urban Politics," in *Urban Crises and Social Movements in the Middle East*, ed. Kenneth Brown et al. (Paris: Editions l'Harmattan, 1989), pp. 63 ff.

15. Ibid., pp. 63-66; see also Tawfiq al-Shaikh, 'An al-'Iraq wa al-haraka al-Islamiyya [On Iraq and the Islamicist movement] (London: al-Safa, 1988), pp. 60-67.

Husain's martyrdom appeared to have a permanent, sad, and lonely relevance: "Every day is Ashura, and every place is Karbala" was the teaching of Shiite history. This ritualistic reminder of the Shiites' solitude and defeat, however, could also be transformed into a celebration of defiance and moral superiority—both Ayatollah Khomeini in Iran and Musa al-Sadr in Lebanon have managed to turn it in that direction. With the victory of clerics in Iran,

the once embarrassing symbols of [Shiite] Islam were exalted. Men no longer awaited the millennium; they proclaimed that in Iran they had an answer for the ailments of the Muslim world.... A political tradition of submission gave way to a messianic movement; [Shiite] clerics who once summoned men to worship, who monitored ritual, were summoning men to arms.[16]

From its inception, Shiite thought did not see the acquisition of power as a prerequisite for a good and pious life. Now, however, in the thinking of the Lebanese Shiite Muhammad Hussain Fadhlallah, as in that of Khomeini himself, there is a new, "curiously [Sunnite] orientation—the sense that taqiyya, dissimulation, should be abandoned, that men should create a Muslim order and defend it."[17]

It is also important to note that the recent politicization of the Shiites has taken different forms, depending on the distinct political conjunctures pertaining in various Arab countries. The contrast between Iraq and Lebanon is again illustrative in this regard, refuting as it does the claim

that communal entities have a permanent, essentialist character. In spite of their exclusion from authority and in spite of the opportunity for rebellion provided for them by the prolonged Iran-Iraq war—the majority of the soldiers being Shiites—the Iraqi Shiites have not opted for a purely Shiite solution, as through secession or segregation, or even for a separate political organization for their community. Exclusively Shiite political parties have always been weak, from the Nahda party in the 1920s to the Da'wa party in the 1980s. The Shiites of Lebanon, on the other hand, have either accepted the confessional framework of Lebanon and tried to enlarge their share within its confines as a community, as Amal has done, or else have rebelled against the entire territorial-state paradigm and declared their identification with the Islamic revolution of Iran, claiming that religion has no geography. The latter is the course chosen by Hizballah.[18]

The idea to be deduced from the previous analysis is that the ideological and political import of religious communal identification does not have an essential, unchanging nature but is contingent upon the sociohistorical environment and on the political conjunctures in which these communities function. It is only with such an idea in mind that one can understand how the Shiite doctrine has been turned, with such people as Khomeini, Sadr, and Fadhlallah, from a doctrine of political quiet-

16. Ajami, Vanished Imam, pp. 141-52, 191.
17. Ibid., pp. 214-15.

18. Ghassan Salama, al-Mujtama' wa al-dawla fi al-Mashriq al-'arabi [Society and state in the Arab Levant] (Beirut: Centre for Arab Unity Studies, 1987), pp. 85-98.

ism and resignation into a doctrine of political action and struggle. This is also how one may understand the way in which the presumably statist Sunnite doctrine, which has been built into the entire tissue of the state in countries such as Saudi Arabia and Morocco, has been able to generate oppositional religiopolitical movements, such as al-Jihad, al-Takfir wa al-Hijra, and Hizb al-Tahrir al-Islami.[19]

THE RELIGIOUS MINORITIES

Following the precepts of the Quran and *hadith*, those *ahl al-kitab* ("People of the Book"—mainly Jews and Christians) who lived within the Islamic dominion (*dar al-Islam*) were normally accorded their freedom of belief and security of life and possessions in return for paying a sort of poll tax (*jizya*). A juridical disagreement eventually emerged as to whether the *jizya* was to be levied as a means of pressure to induce more people to convert to Islam or whether it was enforced in return for the non-Muslims' not being required—owing to their sensitive position—to participate in the activities of war, that is, whether it was a payment in return for their being protected and exempted from the military duties of *jihad*. Christians and Jews, as well as Sabaeans and Magi, were subsequently categorized by the jurists as *ahl al-dhimma* or *dhimmi*s, implying that they were, by accord (*'ahd*), under the protection of the Muslims. Their conditions varied from ruler to ruler, but they were on the whole—given the standards of the day—treated with tolerance, and

many of them did assume fairly influential posts as administrators, accountants, physicians, and the like in the service of the state. Historically, they were also on occasion exempt from paying the *jizya* if the state failed to protect them or if they were recruited for military service.[20]

The Ottomans institutionalized the Islamic tradition with regard to the position of non-Muslims, under the label of the *millet* system, and accorded them a considerable degree of cultural, social, and legal autonomy. Consequently, a Christian or a Jew did not enjoy as an individual whatever rights he had; rather, he enjoyed them as a member of his community. If he deserted his church, for example, he lost his legal status and the rights and duties that went with it. The religious communities represented, therefore, part of the general pattern of unity in diversity, as the historical Islamic state was perhaps almost as much corporatist as it was integrative.[21]

Nonetheless, the religious minorities have developed their lives in close proximity to the Muslim state and have adjusted their perspectives and attitudes to its requirements. Many of the Eastern churches—the Copts as well as the Nestorians,

19. For details, see Ayubi, *Political Islam*.

20. See Radwan al-Sayyid, *Mafahim al-jama'at fi al-Islam* [The concept of groups in Islam] (Beirut: Dar al-Tanwir, 1984), pp. 115-30; Victor Sahhab, *Darurat al-turath* [The necessity of the heritage] (Beirut: al-'Ilm li-al-Malayin, 1984), pp. 169-70; Muhammad Hamdi al-Manawi, *al-Wizara wa al-wuzara' fi al-'asr al-Fatimi* [The vizarate and vizirs in the Fatimid era] (Cairo: Dar al-Ma'arif, 1970), pp. 38-39, 133 ff.

21. Cf. al-Sayyid, *Mafahim al-jama'at*, pp. 134-40.

Jacobites, and Maronites, which sprang from the Syriac tradition— had originally emerged by way of a kind of national reaction and self-assertion vis-à-vis the Byzantine establishment. Most of them had welcomed the Muslim conquerors as saviors from Byzantine persecution and subsequently learned to adjust themselves to the ideology and institutions of the Islamic state and to play a complementary economic role within it.

As a result, the religious minorities, unlike the Islamic sects, have tended to be geographically dispersed and doctrinally diverse. Thus, among the Christians of the Middle East, there are Orthodox churches known as Coptic, Syriac, Greek, Armenian, Nestorian, Chaldean, and so on as well as the more recent Catholic and Protestant offshoots of the older orthodox churches. The organizational diversity of the religious minorities was partly a function of their residence in the cities and their direct relationship with the central state, which, dominated as it was by the assimilationist Sunnites, was prepared to accept them socially but only as weak, scattered entities deprived of any clear manifestations of cultural distinction.[22] Whereas the Islamic sects opposed the dominant ideology and the central power and existed only by way of resisting or deceiving it, the religious minorities accepted the ideology of the government, however reluctantly, and conformed to its expectations of them; their survival is not as much a func-

tion of their resistance as it is of the tolerance of the Muslims.

The Maronites were almost unique among the religious minorities in their resistance to the *dhimmi* status, an attitude that eventually culminated in their refusal to join the *millet* council organized by the Ottomans in the nineteenth century. Such an attitude, derived as it is from their distinctive history as well as from their collective mythology, makes them different from other religious minorities—to the extent that Fu'ad al-Khuri classifies them, functionally speaking, among the sects (*tawa'if*) and not among the minorities (*aqalliyyat*).[23] Like the sects, the Maronites have historically inhabited the mountains and developed their own semi-autonomous political economy. Their sense of distinctiveness has been reinforced by the fact that they probably originated as a tribe rather than as a church. Indeed, their bishops were, conventionally, representatives of the various sublineages of the tribe and not of various geographic parishes, as is the case with other churches, Eastern and Western.[24]

The specificity of the Maronites becomes all the more obvious when one compares them to the other major Christian communities of the Levant, the Greek Orthodox. From the beginning, the Orthodox adjusted themselves to the requirements of the Byzantine and then the Islamic state. They have always prayed in

22. Waddah Sharara, *Isti'naf al-bad'* [Resuming the start] (Beirut: Dar al-Hadatha, 1981), pp. 170-71.

23. Al-Khuri, *Imamat al-shahid*, pp. 13, 109.

24. Salama, *al-Mujtama' wa al-dawla*, p. 109, n. 28 and references; Harik, "Arab State System," pp. 31-33.

their Mass for the ruler of the day and asked God for victory over "the enemy of the land." It is little wonder that the Arabs were to call them the "royalists" (al-Mulukiyyun). Their assimilation into the Arabic culture has been extensive, and their commercial activities have often been complementary to those of the Sunnite Muslim merchants. Many among them have been members of, and even leaders in, the modern and contemporary Arab nationalist movements; examples include Michel 'Aflaq and George Habash.

Within the Islamic state, the religious minorities, while they do not possess their own economy as the Islamic sects do, are often professionally distinct from the majority of Muslims. There has been a certain element of ethnoreligious division of labor in the Muslim state since its early days. The situation continued for many centuries, and some features of it can be detected to this day. Not only do non-Muslims often engage in activities prohibited by Islam, such as the practice of usury and the making of wines, but they have tended historically to be highly represented in professions carrying lower social status, such as tanning, tailoring, smithing, carpentry, jewelry making, and entertainment.

The ethnoreligious division of labor was eventually to be somewhat reversed and to work for the benefit of the religious minorities when, from the eighteenth century but especially from the nineteenth, European colonialism was opening up the Ottoman empire, Egypt, and North Africa to the world capitalist market. Christians and Jews were preferred as commercial agents, possibly because of religious affinity with the Europeans but more importantly because of their commercial and financial expertise as well as their greater proficiency in foreign languages. A new type of ethnoreligious division of labor was to develop, and, indeed, until the interwar period and in some cases until later, an exceptionally high percentage of all people involved in business, commerce, and finance in Turkey and most parts of the Arab world were normally from among the non-Muslim communities. This, in turn, sometimes led to a Muslim backlash against the minorities once national independence had been gained, even though the Christians, in particular, had played a prominent role in the nationalist movements of several countries, including Egypt, Syria, and Palestine.

PROSPECTS FOR THE TERRITORIAL STATE

I have argued here that partly as a result of religious doctrine and partly as a result of the political precedence of the historical Islamic state, Islamic sects and religious minorities have conventionally developed certain distinct characteristics. The geographic distribution as well as the political economy of the sects and of the minorities manifest in reality quite different features, which are in the main a function of their relationship to the state. Whereas the Islamic sects—in varying degrees, of course—have not come to terms ideologically or organizationally with the state, the religious minorities have on the whole—with the possible exception of the Maronites—

adjusted themselves mentally and behaviorally to the requirements of the state.

The modern Middle Eastern state has largely ignored the communal problem, pretending as much as possible that it does not exist. The Islamicists, on the other hand, have remained in this regard the prisoners of early juridical interpretations and political precedents, which are not capable of offering effective solutions to today's problems. If anything, the contemporary Islamicists seem to be less imaginative and innovative than their earlier predecessors. Even the *sahifa* ("constitution") of Medina, prescribed by the Prophet Muhammad himself, was to include the Jews in the definition of the *umma* ("nation"). Yet there is no effective solution to the communal problem in the contemporary state that can be derived literally and ready-made from the conventional jurisprudence of the early Islamic state. The *ahl al-dhimma* formula that was so noble and progressive ten centuries ago is hardly suitable after the centuries of human and constitutional progress that has affected all societies. One can quite understand the alarm with which the Christians of Egypt, for example, receive the incessant calls for a full application of the *shari'a*, which is often taken to mean conventional jurisprudence. Nor is there any provision in the conventional jurisprudence for the position of other Muslim sects within an Islamic state.

Improvisation and innovation are therefore required, and it is thus refreshing to observe a few attempts by contemporary Islamic writers to address such issues in an enlightened way. Islamic sympathizers such as Tariq al-Bishri, Muhammad 'Imara, and 'Adil Husain have produced some interesting improvisations with regard to the position of non-Muslims in a modern Islamic state.[25] Most explicit, however, has been Fahmi Huwaidi, who has put forth a persuasive case for the full citizenship of non-Muslims in a contemporary Islamic state. He derives his argument from Islam's humanitarian inclination, from the shared monotheism of the three major Middle Eastern religions, from the Medina Constitution, and from Muhammad's ruling about *ahl al-kitab*: "To them what is due to us, and from them what is due on us."[26]

25. Tariq al-Bishri, *al-Muslimun wa al-Aqbat* [Muslims and Copts] (Cairo: Hai'at al-Kitab, 1980); Muhammad 'Imara, *al-Islam wa al-sulta al-diniyya* [Islam and religious authority] (Cairo: Dar al-thaqafa al-jadida, 1979); 'Adil Husain, *Nahwa fikr 'arabi jadid* [Toward a new Arab thought] (Cairo: Dar al-Mustaqbal al-'Arabi, 1985).

26. Fahmi Huwaidi, *Muwatinun la dhimiyyun* [Citizens, not protected subjects] (Beirut: Dar al-Shuruq, 1985), pp. 128-45.

ANNALS, *AAPSS*, 524, November 1992

The Clergy's Concepts
of Rule in Egypt and Iran

By SHAHROUGH AKHAVI

ABSTRACT: In the wake of the current cycle of Islamic resurgence, which began at the time of the June 1967 Arab-Israeli war, the question of rule has been at the center of clerical discourse. This article analyzes this question in the debates of the Egyptian and Iranian *'ulama'*. While they agree upon the perception of Islam as both religion and state and upon the need to base public law upon the *shari'a* (the holy law of Islam), they differ on the role of secular rulers, the relevance of *jihad*, identifying apostates, calling for rebellion, authorizing the *'ulama'* to rule society, and endowing Islamic states with extraordinary powers. The debate will continue to focus on these issues in the future, as Islamic groups press the case for full implementation of the *shari'a* in all areas of life, not only in Egypt and Iran but in all Muslim societies.

Shahrough Akhavi is professor of government and international studies, University of South Carolina. He is editor of the Middle East Series of the State University of New York Press and an editor of Oxford University Press's forthcoming Encyclopedia of the Modern Islamic World. *He has published widely on Egyptian and Iranian politics.*

NOTE: Part of the research for this article was undertaken by the author as a Fulbright Research Scholar in Cairo during the autumn of 1991. The author would like to thank the Fulbright Commission of Egypt for its support.

AS in earlier cycles of Islamic resurgence during the modern period, the current one highlights the question of rule. In Islamic discourse, the term "rule" is usually rendered "imamate" or "caliphate," and the theory pertaining to it was elaborated in the medieval era. Those contributing to the theory had to grapple with the fact that, although the doctrine held that, after the Prophet's death, rule should devolve upon the most learned, just, pious, and capable leader of the community, in fact, it was increasingly appropriated by the strongest prince. The Muslim jurists rationalized these arrant seizures of power by tribal chiefs on the grounds that the continued existence of the Islamic community depended upon the acceptance of these actions, as long as the chiefs upheld the basic pillars of the faith. However, current activists—termed here Islamicists—reject such compromises with power holders and insist that they are responsible, in great measure, for the difficulties Muslims face today.

There is consensus that the current Islamic resurgence has its roots in the disastrous Arab defeat in the June 1967 Arab-Israeli war.[1] This suggests that it antedates the Iranian revolution, although it certainly received a major impetus from that shattering event. This article focuses upon the clergy's discourse on the question of rule in Egypt and Iran, where the debates have probably had the greatest impact in the Islamic world.

THE EGYPTIAN 'ULAMA'

In Egypt, the 'ulama' ("clergy") of al-Azhar, the most famous mosque and Islamic theological college in the world, have been generally supportive of the state over the generations. Those clergymen who have opposed the government's policies have gravitated to the Sunnite Islamic world's most important social movement, the nonviolent Muslim Brotherhood, which was established in 1928. It is predominantly a lay organization of religiously minded Muslims. The most radical clergymen, younger in age and committed to violent opposition, have affiliated with splinter organizations that have split from the Muslim Brotherhood.

The Shaykh al-Azhar owes his post to the government and supports the latter on issues of moment. The Ministry of Religious Endowments and al-Azhar Affairs is another government body that exercises authority in the religious field. Within the ministry is the Supreme Council on Religious Affairs, on which sit, inter alia, the Shaykh al-Azhar, the Minister of Religious Endowments and al-Azhar Affairs, and the Mufti of Egypt, who is the country's chief Islamic jurist.

Despite the differences between the state religious institutions, the Muslim Brotherhood, and the radical

---

1. Husayn Ahmad Amin, "al-Tayyarat al-Islamiyya fi Misr khilal al-sab'inat" [Islamic trends in Egypt during the 1970s], in al-Islam fi 'alam mutaghayyir wa maqalat Islamiyya ukhra [Islam in a changing world and other Islamic essays] (Cairo: Maktaba Madbuli, 1989), p. 169; Hasan Hanafi, "Ahadith fi al-harakat al-diniyya al-Mu'asira" [Comments about contemporary religious movements] in al-Din wa al-dawla fi Misr [Religion and state in Egypt], vol. 6, al-Usuliyya al-Islamiyya [Islamic fundamentalism] (Cairo: Maktaba Madbuli, 1989), p. 320.

Islamic groups, all three support the idea of making the holy law—the *shari'a*—the source of law in Egypt. They also agree that Islam is both a religious and a political system: *Islam din wa dawla* ("Islam is religion and state"), according to this view.[2] There may be differences between them as to whether the *shari'a* should be the only source of public law or just the major source, but in any case their position contrasts with that of the regime, which has temporized and failed so far to take a final decision on this crucial matter. However, the regime has accepted the parliament's 1985 amendment to the Personal Status Law, which changed the more liberal version of 1979 on questions of divorce and custody of children by making it more difficult for women to initiate divorce or to have custody over children.

Generally speaking, al-Azhar, the Ministry of Religious Endowments, and the Mufti do not get involved directly in central public policy issues. Occasionally, however, they are implicated in the hurly-burly of what we may term, for lack of a better phrase, religious politics. Between 1979 and 1981, clashes broke out between Copts (Christians) and Muslims in Egypt over the issue of land and religious activity, and Egyptian President Sadat, the official Islamic bodies, the Muslim Brotherhood, and the militant Islamicists all criticized the Coptic leadership and community.[3]

THE ARGUMENT OF *THE ABSENT PRECEPT*

But perhaps the most interesting intervention by the official Egyptian clergy on a political matter occurred in the aftermath of President Anwar al-Sadat's assassination in October 1981 by radical Islamicists of the Tanzim al-Jihad (Jihad Organization). In this case, the then Mufti (currently Shaykh al-Azhar), Shaykh Jadd al-Haqq 'Ali Jadd al-Haqq, issued a *fatwa* (an authoritative opinion), rejecting arguments made in a pamphlet that apparently was the inspiration of the assassins. This pamphlet, known as *The Absent Precept* (*al-Farida al-gha'iba*), was a 54-page text written by an engineer, Muhammad 'Abd al-Salam Faraj. Because of its importance, it will be discussed in some detail, as will the Mufti's *fatwa* refuting its contents.[4] Although Faraj was not a member of the *'ulama'* stra-

2. This is not a unanimous view, but it certainly is the overwhelmingly majority position of the contemporary clergy. See, for example, Shaykh Muhammad al-Ghazali, *Min huna na'lam* [From here we know], 5th ed. (Cairo: Dar al-Kutub al-Haditha, 1965 [originally published in 1950]); Shaykh 'Umar al-Tilimsani, *Dhikrayat, la mudhakkarat* [Remembrances, not reminders] (Cairo: Dar al-Taba'a wa al-Nashr al Islamiyya, 1985), p. 274; Khalid Muhammad Khalid, *al-Dawla fi al-Islam* [The state in Islam] (Cairo: Dar Thabit, 1981). Interestingly, Khalid had, in 1950, concluded the contrary.

3. Hamied Ansari, "Sectarian Conflict in Egypt and the Political Expediency of Religion," *Middle East Journal*, 38:397-418 (1984); idem, "The Islamic Militants in Egyptian Politics," *International Journal of Middle East Studies*, 16:123-44 (1984); Sa'd Eddine Ibrahim, "The Anatomy of Egypt's Militant Islamic Groups," *International Journal of Middle East Studies*, 12(4):423-53 (Dec. 1980).

4. For an English translation of Faraj's pamphlet and an analysis of al-Haqq's *fatwa*, see J.G.G. Jansen, *The Neglected Duty* (New York: Macmillan, 1986).

tum, some leaders of his organization were clergymen, and, on the whole, this pamphlet represents the thinking of younger-generation militant *'ulama'* who feel betrayed by the formal religious bodies and also by the Muslim Brotherhood.

Faraj's argument was that Muslims had neglected the categorical imperative of *jihad* ("struggle for the faith") at their peril. He noted that the principle of *jihad* was one of the collective obligations of the Muslims, and their abandonment of it had led them to their current difficulties.[5] Faraj insisted that the establishment of an Islamic state was mandated by the Quran and the Prophet.[6] He also held that Muslims must rule according to what Allah has revealed. This is a reference to the so-called *hakimiyya* or sovereignty/rulership verses of the Quran, to which the Pakistani Muslim Abu al-A'la al-Mawdudi (d. 1971) and the Egyptian thinker Sayyid Qutb (d. 1966)—under Mawdudi's influence—had attached such major importance.

Other points made by Faraj included the idea that the current rulers of Islamic countries were like the Mongols at the time of Genghis Khan's invasion of the Middle East in the thirteenth century. Like the Mongols, he argued, the current rulers do not rule according to Islamic

laws but according to secular laws into which have been suffused elements of Islamic legislation.[7]

As a consequence, Faraj pointed out, the current rulers of Islamic countries are in a state of apostasy with respect to the faith, even though they preserve some of the outward manifestations of belief, such as upholding prayer and fasting during Ramadan. Apostates are more dangerous than unbelievers who never committed themselves to Islam, and hence it is imperative to pronounce *takfir* (formally stating that they have turned to unbelief) against these rulers. Not only that, but the Islamic law on apostasy sanctions capital punishment.[8]

Faraj argued that the violent overthrow of existing regimes is the only path that could guarantee the establishment of a truly Islamic state. This is more effective than, for example, trying to retake Jerusalem from the Israelis on grounds that, at first, one fights the enemy who is near at hand, for only after defeating him can one move to defeat the opponent who is further afield.[9]

He then cited the sword verse of the Quran (9:5), which proclaims that after the lapse of the months during which no fighting is allowed between the Muslims and their enemies, "slay the idolaters wherever you find them, and take them captive or besiege them, and lie in wait for them at every likely place." In Faraj's opinion, this verse superseded all the 124 verses of the Quran that counsel

5. Muhammad 'Abd al-Salam Faraj, *al-Farida al-gha'iba* [The absent precept], reprinted in Jumhuriyya Misr al-'Arabiyya, Wizara al-Awqaf, al-Majlis al-A'la li al-Shu'un al-Islamiyya, *Al-Fatawa al-Islamiyya min dar al-ifta' al-Islamiyya* [Islamic fatwas from the office of the Mufti] (Cairo: al-Majlis al-A'la li al-Shu'un al-Islamiyya, 1403 H.Q./1984), 10: 3762; 3780 ff.

6. Ibid., pp. 3763-64.

7. Ibid., pp. 3765-66; comparisons with the Mongols continue, pp. 3767-71.

8. Ibid., p. 3766.

9. Ibid., pp. 3775-76.

patience or abjuring armed conflict with the non-Muslims in a spirit of peaceful persuasion.[10]

His last major point is that it would be wrong to suggest that there are stages of *jihad* and to hold that the current stage is simply one of *jihad al-nafs*, or struggling inwardly to purify oneself for the sake of Allah. In fact, such individual cleansing goes hand in hand, in his view, with *al-jihad al-akbar*, or struggling at the community level for the sake of Allah against the enemies of Islam. To say that Muslims are still at the preliminary point of self-*jihad* is to rationalize inaction at a time when the community is in great danger from without. This sort of individualist *jihad* must be simultaneously accompanied by *jihad* at the community level against Islam's enemies, identified as neo-Crusaders, imperialism, and Zionism.[11]

AL-AZHAR'S RESPONSE

In his *fatwa*, the Mufti of Egypt considers first the question of who is a Muslim. He cites the Prophet as having declared that the Muslim is the one who recites the credo "I attest that there is no god but Allah and Muhammad is his prophet" and also commits himself to the remaining four pillars: prayer, alms, fasting, and pilgrimage.[12] When, then, may a

person be said to have abandoned Islam? The Mufti replies by citing the Quran (4:116): "Allah does not forgive one who associates others with Himself; otherwise, He forgives whom He wants." Then, he cites a tradition of the Prophet, who is said to have declared, "The archangel Gabriel came to me and said: 'He of your community who has died but not in any way associated others with Allah will enter paradise.' I said: 'Even if he has committed adultery and theft?' He said: 'Even if he has committed adultery and theft.' "[13] In other words, only arrant polytheists may be apostates, according to the Shaykh.

Consequently, Shaykh al-Haqq concludes that a person who genuinely believes in Islam but can be objectively shown to have violated even a core religious tenet has done no more than commit a sin. While sinning is reprehensible, it does not cause the believer to have renounced his belief in Islam. Thus, although it is true that our actions are the warrants of our beliefs, only Allah, not mere mortals, can punish a sinner.[14]

The Mufti cautions that false accusations of unbelief against Muslims are themselves cause for the most serious breach of Allah's laws. He declares that the Quran commands Muslims to submit disputes among themselves to Allah—that is, to the Quran—and to the Prophet (4:59) and orders the faithful to "ask the keepers of the scripture" when in doubt over a matter of faith (21:7). The Prophet, hearing Muslims dis-

10. Ibid., pp. 3777-78.

11. Ibid., p. 3780.

12. Shaykh Jadd al-Haqq 'Ali Jadd al-Haqq, "al-Mawdu' (1326) Katib al-farida al-gha'iba wa al-radd 'alayhi" [The problem (1326) The absent precept pamphlet and a riposte to it], in Jumhuriyya Misr al-'Arabiyya, Wizara al-Awqaf, al-Majlis al-A'la li al-Shu'un al-Islamiyya, *al-Fatawa al-Islamiyya min dar*

al-ifta' al-Islamiyya [Islamic fatwas from the office of the Mufti], 10:3730.

13. Ibid., pp. 3731-32.

14. Ibid.

puting over verses of the Quran, warned that in the past those who had disputed over Allah's words had perished, and he enjoined them to "say what you know about it [the Quran] and of that about which you are ignorant, assign it to the person who knows."[15]

For the Mufti, not surprisingly, the *'ulama'* are the ones to whom the Quran and the Prophet are referring. Religiosity is the province of all Muslims, he notes, but the clarification of Islam's ordinances and of what is permitted and prohibited is for the specialists—the *'ulama'*—to decide.[16]

As for *jihad*, Shaykh al-Haqq reasons that the law prescribes *jihad* in times of peace and also in times of war. During times of peace, *jihad* is characterized by the individual's struggle to purify his or her soul and distance himself or herself from Satan. In times of war, *jihad* devolves upon the community to fight those who repudiate the oneness of Allah and the prophecy of His messenger.

It is true that *jihad* was the obligation of every individual (*fard 'ayn*) at the time of the Prophet, but after him, it devolved upon the community if necessity called for it. Such necessity existed when the land of the Muslims was occupied by non-Muslims, but even then it would be conducted not only by armed conflict but by means of wealth, words, and heart, in accordance with the saying attributed to the Prophet: "Fight the polytheists by means of your wealth, your hands, and your tongues."[17]

The Mufti acknowledges the sword verse but rejects the view that it supersedes all others counseling patience, dialogue, and persuasion. The latter are more representative, the Mufti opines; examples include the following: "There is no compulsion in matters of religion" (2:256); "call them to the path of your Lord with wisdom and words of good advice, and reason with them in the best way possible" (16:125). As for the *hakimiyya* verses (especially 5:44, 45, and 47: "And those who do not rule[18] according to Allah's revelation are unbelievers/oppressors/dissolutes"), Shaykh al-Haqq counters that, first of all, only he who irrevocably abandons Allah's ordinances is an unbeliever; someone who incidentally and casually happens to have done so is not. Second, given the verses immediately preceding these, it is clear that the antecedent noun of the pronoun "those" are the "people of the book"—in this particular case, the Jews, since it is they who, by worshipping the golden calf, had abandoned the Torah and thus come to be unbelievers. The reference, then, is not to the Muslims.[19]

18. "*Wa man lam yahkum....*" Faraj, as with al-Mawdudi and Qutb before him, has rendered the verb *yahkum* as "rule," rather than the traditional "judge." It is interesting that in rebutting Faraj's interpretation of this verse, the Shaykh does not pronounce this newer interpretation to be *bid'a* ("reprehensible innovation") but rather contents himself with reproving him for taking it out of context.

19. Al-Haqq, "al-Mawdu'," pp. 3742-43. The alert reader will have noted a contradiction here. First, the Mufti is saying that only Muslims who totally break with Allah's ordinances may be considered unbelievers, and then he says the verse refers to the Jews who abandoned the Torah.

15. Ibid., p. 3735.
16. Ibid.
17. Ibid., pp. 3736-37.

The Mufti holds that Egypt, more-over, is not the abode of unbelief but rather the abode of Islam, since prayer, alms, pilgrimage to Mecca, and many other aspects of the faith are observed there. The only exceptions pertain to the Islamic punishments, usury, and the like, where positive law has been enacted and implemented. These exceptions do not warrant the conclusion that the rulers and people who accept such a state of affairs are apostates. To the contrary, Shaykh al-Haqq insists, both rulers and ruled believe in the abolition of usury, prostitution, theft, and so on, even though those phenomena occur in Egypt. The people of Egypt want Allah's dispensation and His law, and they implement it "within the limits of their capability." As justification for this less than categorical commitment, the Mufti cites the verse, "So fear Allah as much as you can" (64:16).[20]

The Mufti goes as far as to argue that, according to several sayings attributed to the Prophet, no insurrection against a Muslim ruler is allowed, even if the only religious prescription that such a ruler upholds is prayer. When the Muslims differ with their ruler, they must counsel him and peacefully try to bring him to their way of thinking, says Shaykh al-Haqq.[21]

The analogy of current Muslim rulers as modern-day versions of Genghis Khan will not wash, argues the Mufti, since such rulers have not made the mosques stables for their animals, nor have they destroyed mosques or shredded the Quran. Ibn

Taymiyya's *fatwa* authorizing *jihad* against the Mongols was due to such behavior and to the fact that, under their aegis, prayer was haphazard, muezzins and imams were missing from the mosques that had not been destroyed, the rulers absconded with the people's wealth, destroyed their villages, and promoted the view that Genghis Khan was the son of Allah.[22]

Shaykh al-Haqq also declares that Faraj's pamphlet is out of touch with the Quran's political tenets. Consultation is the basis of rule in Islam, he alleges, citing four different verses (3:159, 42:38, 88:22, and 50:45): "And consult them in affairs"; "their affairs are a matter of counsel"; "you are not a warden over them"; "it is not for you to compel them." These verses, he maintains, make clear that the ruler in Islam is a mere agent of the people, who elect and dismiss him. Accordingly, the community is the source of authority in Islam. The implication is that a self-styled group within the community may not, on its own, decide the fate of rulership. Furthermore, the early Islamic method of appointing leaders is not necessarily the model for today. Since succession is a worldly matter, it is subject to change over time, and it is up to the community to decide the best procedure to adopt concerning it.[23]

The important thing is not to have a caliph per se, given the fragmentation of the *umma* into separate states. The important thing, the Mufti holds, is that the ruler in such states be a Muslim and that he tend to the affairs of the Muslims. As for the oath of allegiance to the ruler—

20. Ibid., pp. 3743-44.
21. Ibid., pp. 3744-45.

22. Ibid., pp. 3747-49.
23. Ibid., pp. 3749-51.

the *bay'a*—elections in modern times take its place.[24]

In conclusion, Shaykh al-Haqq contends that if there is a summons to do battle in defense of religion and the country, Muslims will respond, but the army, rather than a self-designated group of private individuals, is their instrument. But there is also *jihad* against oneself and Satan, and this is a continuous type of *jihad* incumbent on every individual Muslim. This allows the Muslim to improve himself or herself to do good works, to be pious, to be true to agreements, and to avoid evil. As one can therefore see, argues the Mufti, *jihad* is hardly an "absent precept." What should be "made absent" is the view that *jihad* entails pronouncing unbelief upon Muslims or violently attacking their community and leaders. Finally, *jihad* is not implemented by interpreting texts in a way that those texts will not bear. For if this were to be allowed, then there would be perversions in the meanings of phrases and concepts—something prohibited by Allah.[25]

SHIISM AND THE
THEORY OF RULE

The theory of *vilayat-i faqih* (the authority of the Imam as exercised by the leading jurist), propounded by Ayatollah Ruhollah Khomeini (d. 1989), is a reconsideration of the classic Shiite theory of rule. Although it would be wrong to intimate that any theory is once and for all set in concrete at its inception, it is nonetheless the case that Khomeini's per-

spectives on the imamate constitute a radical departure from the views of mainstream Shiism. In looking at the constituent elements of Khomeini's theory of rule, we must stress the following factors: (1) the role of the Imams and the nature of their authority; (2) the significance of the oath of allegiance (*bay'a*); (3) the principle of deputyship; and (4) the role of the clergy. According to Shiism, only the Imam is entitled to rule the Islamic community. The Imams were 'Ali, the cousin of the Prophet, and 'Ali's descendants through his wife, Fatima, the Prophet's daughter. Shiites differ in their interpretation of how many Imams there were, but the dominant view is known as the twelver. According to this view, the twelfth Imam disappeared on Allah's commands, but the faithful believe he will return as the messiah, thereby ushering in the Day of Judgment.

The Imams were all considered "the proofs of Allah" in that the community had always to be led by one of their number as evidence of Allah's existence. The Imams were deemed to be the incarnations of Allah's light and were judged to have special abilities, such as foreknowledge of events to come, immunity from error, and the like. If there were no Imam leading the community, then the religious injunctions would lapse and Muslims would be in a state of ignorance, incapable of carrying out Allah's commands.

It is true that the disappearance of the twelfth Imam left the community without a leader, but the religious injunctions were considered to be still intact because the disappearance was at Allah's command. For

24. Ibid., pp. 3750-51.
25. Ibid., p. 3761.

him to have remained would have subjected him to murder by his opponents, thereby extinguishing the line of Imams forever. For the Imam was a young lad at the time of his disappearance and had no progeny to succeed him.

During his occultation, the obligation of Shiites to give the Imam their oaths of allegiance was considered to be in abeyance. This crucial fact made it possible for them to tolerate rule by secular leaders—provided that such leaders were just, consulted the people, and heeded the advice of the clergy.

According to the standard view of the doctrine of rule, while the Imam was in occlusion, he was in touch with his community through a series of agents, considered as the Imam's deputies. This period of contact lasted from about A.D. 874 to 940. After the death of the fourth of these agents, the Imam was considered to have entered the period of the greater occultation, which is to last until the end of time. During this period, the clergy are viewed collectively to be the general agents of the Imam.

Neither the four special agents nor the clergy in their capacity as the general agents were ever considered by the doctrine to be entitled to exercise the Imam's full authority on his behalf, however. The authority they wielded was residual in nature and limited them to such things as superintending the care of orphans, widows, the infirm, and the destitute.

What this suggests is that the doctrine did not permit the clergy to exercise substantial authority in the sense of sovereign rule over the community. Khomeini's achievement was

to mount a theoretical argument that empowered precisely the clergy to take over executive power and rule on the Imam's behalf until his return.

In his reasoning, Khomeini tried to adduce evidence from the classic sources of Islamic law. This proved difficult, since the Quran contains no references to the Imams and only vaguely refers to the obligation of Muslims to follow the commands of "those in authority among you" (4:59). Nor could Khomeini find any support for his radical view in the traditions (*sunna*) about the Prophet's behavior and statements.

On the other hand, he claimed to have found a sound tradition relating to the statement of the sixth Imam, Ja'far (d. 765), that allegedly empowered judges to rule the Shiite community should the Imam not be available. On closer inspection, however, it would appear that the tradition in question authorizes the clergy not to exercise sovereign rule but simply to give a ruling in technical disputes over inheritance or debts.[26] Nonetheless, Khomeini invoked reason as a source of law and maintained that, since the sources contained many references to the clergy as the "fortresses of Islam" and the like, they were the logical referents when the sacred texts made mention of leaders of the community after the Prophet's death.

The term *vilayat-i faqih* refers to the leading jurist as the one to carry out the authority of the Imam. At the time of the Iranian revolution and

26. Joseph Eliash, "Misconceptions Regarding the Juridical Status of the Iranian 'Ulama'," *International Journal of Middle East Studies*, 10:9-25 (1979).

during the next decade, this jurist was considered by many to be Khomeini himself, the author of the doctrine. This was so even though, on traditional grounds, other jurists could be said to have been his senior in learning and other qualities normally considered important in designating leaders among the jurists. Some eminent jurists actively disputed Khomeini's concept of *vilayat-i faqih*, but their objections were silenced by the revolutionaries, and the Constitution of 1979 contains several references to Khomeini by name as the *faqih*.

In lionizing Khomeini's role as *faqih* during the years 1979-89, his supporters went to extraordinary lengths. This may be seen, for example, in the following two citations from senior members of the regime, Ayatollah Rabbani 'Amlashi and Ayatollah Mu'min:

"Obedience to *vilayat-i faqih* is an incumbent duty . . . like the daily prayer and fasting, and disobeying it is like disobeying the Islamic sacred law."

"The legitimacy and legality of whatever is done and whatever institutions exist is due to the fact that they are buttressed by *vilayat-i faqih*. As the *vali-yi faqih* is at the head of all affairs and main guarantor of the current laws of the country, it is the *divinely ordained duty of all the people* to follow every law which is passed and given to the Islamic government for execution. Disobeying such a law is as forbidden as drinking wine is forbidden by Islam."[27]

Such sentiments found their practical crystallization in two *fatwas* issued by Khomeini in late 1987 and early 1988 dealing with the hegemonic power of the state. In defending the state's power to impose sanctions on those refusing to obey the laws, Khomeini wrote that the state could even abrogate one of the five pillars of Islam if it saw that this was necessary for the safeguarding of the 1979 revolution. In his reasoning, the Iranian state and the revolution that had spawned it were tantamount to Islam itself.[28]

Upon Khomeini's death, however, a crisis arose, as no individual could be found within the regime who had his stature. Whereas Khomeini both had been a *marja' al-taqlid* (a term referring to the most distinguished jurists of the age) and had been given unprecedented political powers in the 1979 Constitution as the *faqih*, his successor was not even an ayatollah. Therefore, at the time of the constitutional reforms of July 1989—a month after Khomeini's demise—official sources began to use the religiously neutral term *rahbar* ("leader") rather than *faqih* to refer to Khomeini's successor, Sayyid 'Ali Khamanah'i. It is true that this term had also been used to refer to Khomeini, but that did not detract from his towering stature in the eyes of his followers as *vali-yi faqih*.

Moreover, it has been argued that there is no longer a necessity for the leader to be a *marja' al-taqlid* on grounds that learnedness in the religious law does not guarantee "great

27. Cited in Said Arjomand, *The Turban for the Crown* (New York: Oxford University Press, 1988), p. 182. Emphasis added.

28. "The state, which has the full delegated authority of the Prophet . . . takes precedence over other Islamic regulations, even prayer and pilgrimage," asserted Khomeini. *Iran Times* (Washington, DC), 4 Day 1366 H. Sh.; ibid., 25 Day 1366 H. Sh.

capability in management" or "strong political and social perspicacity in regard to the social affairs of the moment." Since the latter qualities are deemed more important, the qualification that the leader be a *marja' al-taqlid* lapses "since it is seen as a superfluous requirement."[29]

CONCLUSION

One dimension of the question of rule that unites the Islamic *'ulama'* is the belief that Islam is both religion and politics. Although one may be able to identify religiously minded lay thinkers today who believe the contrary,[30] almost all *'ulama'* insist on the integration of religion and politics. The one reputable contempo-

rary *'alim* ("clergyman") who believed in the necessity of separating religion and state in Islam—Shaykh Khalid Muhammad Khalid—suddenly recanted his views in 1981, after thirty years.[31]

A second dimension of the question of rule upon which the Islamic *'ulama'* have created a consensus is the issue of applying the *shari'a* in public life rather than only in personal matters. The current constitutions of Middle Eastern states are found wanting because they are based on Western models that rule out the possibility for the Quran and the Prophet's traditions to be the source of law.

29. See the comments of Shaykh 'Abdullah Nuri, the Minister of the Interior of the Islamic Republic of Iran, as cited in *Iran Times*, 3 Shahrivar 1368 H. Sh.

30. For example, Muhammad 'Amara, *al-Dawla al-Islamiyya bayn al-'Almaniyya wa al-Sulta al-Diniyya* [The Islamic state between secularism and religious authority] (Cairo: Dar al-Shuruq, 1988), pp. 31-82.

31. It was Shaykh Khalid Muhammad Khalid who argued for their separation in his landmark polemic *Min huna nabda'u* [From here we begin] (Cairo: Dar al-Nil li al-Taba'a, 1950). For two interpretations of why he did so, see Emanual Sivan, *Radical Islam* (New Haven, CT: Yale University Press, 1985), p. 132; Leonard Binder, *Islamic Liberalism: A Critique of Development Ideologies* (Chicago: University of Chicago Press, 1988), pp. 158-61.

ANNALS, *AAPSS*, 524, November 1992

Monarchs, Mullas, and Marshals: Islamic Regimes?

By IBRAHIM A. KARAWAN

ABSTRACT: This article examines three regime types that assert that they represent "Islam in power." They are the conservative dynastic regime of Saudi Arabia, the populist clerical regime of Iran, and the authoritarian military regimes of the Sudan and Pakistan. These regimes articulate different interpretations of Islam that reflect the interests and ideology of those who control the state machinery, the influence of society's historical legacy, and specific characteristics of the immediate situational setting. The Islamic legitimization of all three types has been contested on religiopolitical grounds by domestic rivals for power and external rivals for leadership in the Muslim world. The most effective challenges to regime legitimacy have been manifested in the Islamized military regimes. The predicament of "the Islam of the marshals" is due to several factors: their lack of the political capital available in the Saudi type of "the Islam of wealth," or the legitimacy generated by revolutionary change under charismatic leadership known in the Iranian type of "the Islam of revolution," and their antipolitical character, manifested in their distrust of political movements that supported their Islamization programs and whose leaders aspired to play the roles of its theoreticians and organizers.

Ibrahim A. Karawan teaches Middle Eastern politics at the University of Utah. He has also been a research associate in the Center for Political and Strategic Studies in Cairo. His publications include Beyond Desert Storm: The Middle East after the Gulf War, *coedited with Peter von Sivers (forthcoming) and* Israeli Settlement Policy, *coauthored with Ali Dessouki and K. Qassimiya. He has contributed chapters to a number of volumes including* The Middle East and the Western Alliance *and* Defense Planning in Less-Industrialized States. *His articles have appeared in the* Journal of Arab Affairs; Contention; al-Siyassa al-dawliya; *and* al-Tali'a.

NOTE: I am grateful to Tim Sullivan, F. Gregory Gause, Nikki Keddie, Peter Diamond, and Donald Hanson for offering helpful comments, and to Janessa and Suhayla Karawan for their unlimited support.

IRONICALLY enough, Islamic political movements assessed by modernization theorists as destined to become relics of the past have been presented lately as the most potent sociopolitical force, perhaps even the wave of the future, in many Muslim countries. Instead of the earlier failure to see any sustained political significance for Islamic movements, many commentators now seem to have great difficulty seeing anything else.[1] One possible explanation of such a reversal may be the fact that political action under the banner of Islam has become a widespread phenomenon shared by many actors in Muslim societies. The extensive use of Islamic political discourse by avowed Arab nationalists since the eruption of the gulf conflict in 1990-91 is one clear illustration; for example, many of them described Iraq's battle as a "rage for God" against the "infidel evildoers" and as a "holy war" of "faith" against "atheism." Even the Marxist Left is no exception. In the words of one prominent Arab Marxist addressing fellow leftists, "No political party can ignore the Islamic issue and not use it in the political struggle without suffering a tremendous loss by being isolated from the broad masses . . . as long as religious forces are dominant in the street. . . . Otherwise, you have to import another nonreligious people to help launch the desired revolution!"[2]

During the 1970s and 1980s, political regimes that were increasingly challenged or threatened by Islamic opposition made frequent attempts to check that threat by finding an Islamic garb or justification for their policies.[3] These attempts included utilizing Islamic symbolism, portraying political leaders as pious adherents of the Islamic faith and regular practitioners of its rituals, interrupting radio and television programs to broadcast the call to prayer, banning alcoholic beverages on national airlines, and forming *lijan muraja'at al-qawanin li-tatamasha ma'a ahkam al-shari'a al-Islamiyya* ("committees to revise the legal system to be in accordance with the rules of Islamic law").

The regime types addressed in this article, however, go beyond the usual resort to religious symbolism. These regimes do not merely suggest that one or another of their policies is congruent with Islamic principles. Their explicit point of departure, as far as legitimacy is concerned, is *la hukma wa la siyada illa li-allah* ("rule and sovereignty belong only to God"). They make an assertion, the essence

1. For more on this sharp reversal, see Ali E. Hillal Dessouki, "Islamic Resurgence," in his *Islamic Resurgence in the Arab World* (New York: Praeger, 1982), pp. 2-9; Gilles Kepel, "God Strikes Back: Movements of Re-Islamization in Contemporary History," *Contention*, 2:151-59 (Fall 1992); Ibrahim Karawan, " 'Reislamization Movements' according to Kepel: On Striking Back and Striking Out," ibid., pp. 161-79.

2. The statement was made by Lutfi al-Kholi in *Nadwat al-tataruf al-siyasi al-dini fi Misr* [The workshop on religiopolitical extremism in Egypt], *Fikr li-al-dirasat wa al-abhath* (Cairo), p. 100 (Dec. 1985).

3. See the perceptive analysis by Ali E. Hillal Dessouki, "Official Islam and Political Legitimation in the Arab Countries," in *The Islamic Impulse*, ed. Barbara Stowasser (London: Croom Helm, 1986), pp. 135-41; Sadek Belaid, "Role of Religious Institutions in Support of the State," in *Beyond Coercion*, ed. Adeed Dawisha and I. William Zartman (London: Croom Helm, 1988), pp. 147-63.

of which is that they represent "Islam in power." Such regimes elevate the objective of defending the faith and implementing the totality of the *shari'a* to the level of their very political raison d'être. By striving to approximate a certain image of Islam's founding period or golden age, they claim also to provide other Muslims with an example of how to proceed toward building a genuine Islamic state and society.[4]

My objective in this article is to address the following question: Is there a model of Islamic governance that reveals certain common characteristics among regimes proclaiming themselves to be Islamic? The argument I advance here is that an analytical perspective focusing on diversity of types rather than their unity, historical and societal variety rather than coherent pronouncements on the ideational level, and the multiplicity rather than the oneness of political legitimation patterns may enable us to gain a better understanding of Islamic regimes. Such an understanding should cover the various ways and the broad settings in which they get to power, their formulas for seeking legitimization, and the challenges with which they have to contend.

A consensus already exists among students of Islamic resurgence that what is known as popular Islam has diverse manifestations and components. It includes movements that pursue divergent objectives such as promoting individual religiosity, introducing social reform, and the fundamental restructuring of state-society relations in the image of Islam's founding period. It should come as no surprise that among those self-proclaimed Islamic regimes, diversity is an unmistakable feature of their domestic and foreign policies. After all, each has its historical specificity, varied societal characteristics, and particular attributes of its political leadership. Although all these regimes identify themselves as based on Islam, as Nazih Ayubi has put it, "Islam means different things to different people, and this applies to politics as it applies to other areas of social life. To some, Islam may serve as means for legitimizing . . . the status quo, while for others it may provide . . . a spearhead for revolution."[5]

It may suffice to recall here that both Saudi Arabia's monarchical, conservative, and pro-Western regime and Iran's republican, populist, and anti-Western regime based their political legitimacy on quite different interpretations of Islam. During the 1980s, each of them refused to recognize the Islamic "credentials" of the other and saw in such recognition a challenge to, and perhaps a negation of, its own legitimacy. In fact, each identified the other as posing the greatest danger to "the true Islamic call and movement." Accordingly, Saudi Arabia was both willing and able during most of the decade to ally itself with Iraq's secular pan-Arabist regime, in light of their shared hostil-

---

4. See Mohammed Arkoun, "The Concept of Authority in Islamic Thought," in *Islam: State and Society*, ed. Klaus Ferdinand and Mehdi Mozaffari (London: Curzon Press, 1988), pp. 53-73.

5. Nazih Ayubi, "The Politics of Militant Islamic Movements in the Middle East," *Journal of International Affairs*, 36:271 (Fall-Winter 1982-83).

ity toward the Iranian system after the Islamic revolution.

As William Quandt has accurately pointed out, what worried the Saudi regime most "about the Iranian revolution was not the personal fate of the Shah, but the specter of a mass-based revolution bringing about the downfall of a conservative monarchy." In daily Arabic radio broadcasts directed at Saudi Arabia, Iran's leaders emphasized that "monarchy and Islam are mutually exclusive" and called "for the overthrow of the Saudi dynasty in the name of Islam."[6] The political-ideological confrontation between the two Islamic protagonists continued to escalate. On the one hand, Saudi Arabia denounced the Iranian leadership for launching deliberate campaigns of subversion and political agitation, particularly around the holy places during the pilgrimage (*hajj*) and within the Shiite minority in the oil-rich Eastern Province of the kingdom. These campaigns, according to Saudi rulers, were not merely misguided acts per-

petrated by Iranian militants; rather, they reflected a state ideology that equated the Islamic call with fomenting discord, extremism, terrorism, and bloodshed as a prelude to Iranian regional hegemony.

On the other hand, Khomeini accused the House of Saud of being unfit for the custodianship of Islam's holiest shrines, "which belong to all Muslims," and of attempting to reduce the *hajj* to a "dry ritual" devoid of any political meaning or responsibility. According to him, the Saudi regime, which he often referred to with disdain as the "government of the Hijaz," was guilty of massacring defenseless Iranian pilgrims, desecrating God's Two Houses, and serving as a surrogate of the "Black House" of the "Great Satan" (read: the White House of the United States). The Islam to which Saudi leaders actually adhered was, in Khomeini's words, "the Islam of money and power . . . deception, compromise, and captivity, the Islam of the sovereignty of capital and capitalists over the oppressed . . . in a word the American Islam."[7]

Islamic regimes not only face external challenges to their legitimacy mounted by other contenders for leadership in the Muslim world; they also have to contend with domestic Islamic opposition groups. Many of these groups call into question the authenticity of the regimes' Islamic claims and denounce the contrast between lofty ideological formulations and concrete realities of social corruption, political repression, and

6. William Quandt, "Saudi Views of the Iranian Revolution," in *Iran since the Revolution*, ed. Barry Rosen (Boulder, CO: Social Science Monographs, 1985), pp. 53-57; Jacob Goldberg, "Saudi Arabia and the Iranian Revolution: The Religious Dimension," in *The Iranian Revolution and the Muslim World*, ed. David Menashri (Boulder, CO: Westview Press, 1990), pp. 155-70. See also Hermann F. Eilts, "Saudi Arabia: Traditionalism versus Modernism—A Royal Dilemma," in *Ideology and Power in the Middle East*, ed. Peter Chelkowski and Robert Pranger (Durham, NC: Duke University Press, 1988), pp. 78-81; David Long, "The Impact of the Iranian Revolution on the Arabian Peninsula and the Gulf States," in *The Iranian Revolution*, ed. John Esposito (Miami: Florida International University Press, 1990), pp. 100-115.

7. "Imam Khumayni's Message on the First Anniversary of the Makkah Massacre," in *al-Tawhid*, 6:83-91 (1988).

moral alienation. The historical experience has shown that opposing a certain regime on grounds that it is rigid in its understanding of Islam is not usually very efficacious from the opposition's perspective when compared with alternative strategies, such as criticizing the regime for its *nifaq* ("hypocrisy"), for *tahrif al-shari'a* ("distortion of Islamic law"), or for lacking Islamic resolve and decisiveness.

I shall address the diversity of self-proclaimed Islamic regimes along the aforementioned lines under three subcategories: the conservative dynastic regime of Saudi Arabia; the populist clerical regime of Iran; and Islamized military regimes of the Sudan and Pakistan.

LEGITIMIZING DYNASTIC CONSERVATISM: SAUDI ARABIA

One of the two countries in the Muslim world most identified with Islamic governance is Saudi Arabia. Historically, Saudi Arabia was based on a tribal dynasty, that of the Saudi family, which adopted a religious call, the Wahhabi *Da'wa*. The *Da'wa* was advocated by Muhammad ibn 'Abd al-Wahhab, who was inspired by the strict Hanbali school of Islamic jurisprudence. He called for a return to "true Islam" and condemned any lax or partial implementation of the rules of the *shari'a*. It is in that sense that Wahhabism has been referred to as the first revivalist movement in modern Sunnite Islamic history. Contemporary Saudi rulers emphasize that the country's constitution is the "Book of God and the sayings of His Prophet."[8] Its flag represents more than a national symbol since it has the Islamic *shahada* ("There is no God but Allah and Muhammad is his Prophet") inscribed on it. The state implements the *hudud* ("penalties") on those who violate the rules of Islam. A religious police or a public morality squad of sorts, known as the Organization for the Enforcing of Good and Forbidding of Evil, is assigned the task of ensuring the performance of daily prayers, the observance of fasting during the month of Ramadan, and the ongoing public segregation of the sexes.

Moreover, Saudi Arabia is associated with the holiest birthplaces of Islam, Mecca and Medina, and with one of the pillars of that religion, the *hajj*, which it assumes the responsibility of supervising. Every year Saudi rulers symbolize their commitment to Islam by assisting in the cleaning of its holiest shrine, al-Ka'ba. In October 1986, King Fahd requested that he no longer be addressed as "Majesty" but as *Khadim al-Haramayn al-Sharifayn* (custodian of the two revered sacred places in Mecca and Medina). The kingdom sponsors a host of pan-Islamic organizations such as the Islamic Conference Organization and the Muslim World League. It provides large sums of money to support the activities of Muslim groups, associations, and publications. Since the riyal is Saudi Arabia's currency, some commentators refer to this policy as "riyal-politik"! In short, Islam is proclaimed as the country's sole legitimate ideology; the pivotal foundation of its political system; the exclusive regulator of social, economic, and cultural life;

8. King Fahd's statement in *Middle East Report*, 14 Mar. 1992, p. 2.

the only source of legislation; and the most important factor in shaping Saudi international behavior.

In assessing how Islamic the Saudi regime is, however, three important qualifications must be added to the foregoing characterization. First, the relative influence of Shaykh ibn 'Abd al-Wahhab and his descendants regarding major policymaking issues has tended generally and gradually to decline. This should not be understood as implying that the role of the 'ulama' has become irrelevant. Their role remains important regarding specific issue areas—namely, judicial, educational, and religious matters—and under particular and rather exceptional conditions, such as a serious and open rift in the royal family. On the whole, however, it is not difficult to recognize an "actual imbalance in the joint venture" between the ruling dynasty's political power and the religious establishment's ideological influence.[9] While the Saudi regime, as Lisa Anderson has aptly put it, has been "more solicitous of religious sentiment than most . . . it is the . . . 'ulama' who are closely supervised by the government rather than the reverse."[10]

Second, the logic and requirements of state-building, consolidation, and development prompted Saudi leaders to form international alliances—such as the alliance of King 'Abd al-'Aziz with Britain—and to pursue domestic policies, such as the education of women, which were not, at least initially, deemed acceptable on purely religious grounds as understood by segments of the 'ulama'. More recently, some of the consequences of the massive inflow of oil wealth, such as greater exposure to Western influences, have periodically strained the relationship between the regime and the men of religion. The latter became critical of the erosion of traditional, austere, and conservative Wahhabi values as a result of that exposure. But such enormous oil-based fortunes also provided the regime with the means of co-opting many of the 'ulama' as salaried employees of the state. For example, the government appointed the members of Dar al-Da'wa wa al-Ifta (the Board of Islamic Research) as well as the Council of the Grand 'Ulama', who issue authoritative religious and legal opinions or judgments.

Third, as an outcome of the 'ulama''s structural dependency, their role in ideological and political legitimation has become conditioned primarily by the interests of what is known as al-dawla ("the state") or al-mulk ("reign" or "rulership"). In fact, this is how that relationship was perceived by Juhayman al-'Utaybi, the leader of the Ikhwan, the group that occupied the Ka'ba at the dawn of the first day of the fifteenth century according to the Islamic calendar (20 November 1979).

9. Ghassan Salamé, "Islam and Politics in Saudi Arabia," Arab Studies Quarterly, 9:310 (1987). For other assessments, see Joseph Kechichian, "The Role of the Ulama in the Politics of an Islamic State: The Case of Saudi Arabia," International Journal of Middle East Studies, 18:62-66 (1986); William Ochsenwald, "Saudi Arabia," in The Politics of Islamic Revivalism, ed. Shireen Hunter (Bloomington: Indiana University Press, 1988), pp. 109-13.

10. Lisa Anderson, "Absolutism and the Resilience of Monarchy in the Middle East," Political Science Quarterly, 106:10 (1991).

The leaders of the Saudi regime, as seen by the group's founder, had been morally corrupt and guilty of consorting and collaborating with the infidels; for example, concerning the Saudi leaders, al-'Utaybi asked, "How can we preach Islam while we take Christians as professors?" The majority of the 'ulama' tended to be "court clerics," who were subservient to and apologetic for the corrupt rulers. Al-'Utaybi concluded that "if the devil had a state, he would have 'ulama' . . . working for him as long as he gave them an academic degree, a scholarly title, and a salary" and that the shari'a "could not be learned in government controlled institutions."[11]

Al-'Utaybi would have been the last person to be surprised that when the regime needed a religious fatwa in support of using force to regain control of the most sacred sanctuary in Islam, where fighting is explicitly prohibited, the 'ulama' complied with the king's request and authorized the use of force to end the occupation of the Ka'ba. In authorizing the resort to force, they characterized the Ikhwan's action as sedition, insurrection, encroachment on the sacredness of the holy place of God, and utter perversion of Islam committed by mufsidun fi al-ard ("those who corrupt on earth") and a clique of religious deviants against rulers who actually apply the shari'a.

In August 1990, the Saudi regime needed an Islamic legitimization of the massive deployment of American, European, and other non-Muslim troops to the kingdom in the aftermath of the Iraqi invasion of Kuwait. The stationing of these troops in Saudi Arabia was condemned by a variety of groups in the Muslim world as a violation of the sanctity of the territory where the Ka'ba and the Prophet's mosque are located. Shaykh 'Abd al-'Aziz Bin Baz and other senior religious authorities approved of the king's decision. They concluded that he was authorized, according to the rules of the shari'a, to "seek the help of whoever has the power that enables them to perform the task" of defending Muslim land and resisting aggression. Once again, on 18 January 1991, the top Saudi religious authorities issued another fatwa in which they described Iraq's President Saddam Hussein as "the enemy of God" and identified the battle that had just been launched against his army in Kuwait and Iraq as a jihad ("holy war").[12]

11. Salamé, "Islam and Politics," p. 315; Ayman al-Yassini, Religion and State in the Kingdom of Saudi Arabia (Boulder, CO: Westview Press, 1985), pp. 124-29; "Islamic Revival and National Development in the Arab World," Journal of Asian and African Studies, 11:105-9 (1986); James Buchan, "Secular and Religious Opposition in Saudi Arabia," in State, Society and Economy in Saudi Arabia, ed. Tim Niblock (London: Croom Helm, 1982), pp. 120-23. See also Rif'at Sayyid Ahmad, Rasa'il Juhayman al-'Utaybi [The letters of Juhayman al-'Utaybi] (Cairo: Madbuli, 1988), pp. 11-52.

12. Quoted in James Piscatori, "Religion and Realpolitik: Islamic Responses to the Gulf War," in Islamic Fundamentalisms and the Gulf Crisis, ed. James Piscatori (Chicago: American Academy of Arts and Sciences, 1991), p. 9. For examples of sharp religious denunciation of the 'ulama''s fatwa by Safar al-Hawali, dean of Islamic studies at Umm al-Qura University in Mecca, see his "Infidels Without, and Within," New Perspectives Quarterly, 8:50-51 (1991); Mamoun Fandy, "The Hawali Tapes," New York Times, 24 Nov. 1990; "An Open Letter to al-Shaykh 'Abd al-'Aziz Bin Baz," al-Gazira al-'arabiyya [The Arabian pen-

LEGITIMIZING REVOLUTION AND MULLASTROIKA: IRAN

If the Saudi system has been associated with religious and political conservatism, Iran's Islamic Republic has usually been identified as an embodiment of a radical, anti-monarchical, antidynastic, and anti-Western type of Islamic activism. In Saudi Arabia, the dynastic "protectors of the holy places" managed to co-opt or subordinate the religious establishment, while in Iran's case the clerical "custodians of the Islamic revolution" led the overthrow of a westernizing dynasty. According to this clerical elite, the only legitimate government is Islamic government, and the sole way to remove the *taghut* ("arrogant, tyrannical earthly power") and establish an Islamic state is through launching an Islamic revolution. Much has been written about the political efficacy with which Khomeini used the "Karbala paradigm," with its evocative symbols and emotive imagery grounded in Shiite traditions, to delegitimize the Shah by describing him as the "Yazid of our time" and to inspire the demonstrators against his regime during a critical stage of the revolution to emulate the courage and martyrdom of Imam Hussein in resisting tyranny.[13]

In addition, the ideology of the movement manifested an Islamic populist emphasis on the theme of social justice. It attacked those living in opulence who lead a life of luxury and moral decadence (*mutrafun*). At the same time, it was presented as backing the dispossessed (*mahrumun*) and the oppressed on earth (*mustaz'afun*), who were politically excluded and socioeconomically marginalized under the Shah; these are the poor urban workers, lower middle classes of the bazaar, and small peasants. Despite repeated denials of being a class-based movement, this populist identification with the disadvantaged or the underprivileged has created a supportive constituency for the Islamic activists during, and in the aftermath of, the Iranian revolution. Leading clerics stressed in their Friday sermons in Tehran that this identification with the downtrodden and disinherited in pursuit of social justice (*'adl*) was a common characteristic of both the Islamic revolution in Iran and the Muhammadan revolution in seventh-century Arabia.[14]

---

insula] (Feb. 1991). For a biting critique of the role of establishmentarian Islam during the crisis, see Magdi Hussein, *Azmat al-khalij bayn ahkam al-Qur'an wa fatawi al-sultan* [The gulf crisis between Quranic rules and sultanic stipulations] (Cairo: Dar al-Sharq al-Awssat, 1990).

13. Said Amir Arjomand, *The Turban for the Crown* (New York: Oxford University Press, 1988), pp. 99-100; Nikki Keddie, "Shi'ism and Revolution," in *Religion, Rebellion, Revolution*,

ed. Bruce Lincoln (New York: St. Martin's Press, 1985), pp. 172-75; Haggy Ram, " 'The Government Myth' of Early Islam: The Legitimation of the Islamic Government in Iran" (Paper delivered at the annual conference of the Middle East Studies Association, Washington, DC, Nov. 1991), pp. 4-6. According to Ram, the sermons delivered at the Friday prayers in Tehran described the victory of Iran's Islamic revolution as "reminiscent of the victory of the Noble Prophet over the infidels." Ibid, pp. 11-13.

14. Ervand Abrahamian, "Structural Causes of the Iranian Revolution," *MERIP Reports*, no. 87, pp. 24-25 (May 1980); Afsaneh Najmabadi, "Iran's Turn to Islam," *Middle East Journal*, 41:213-14 (1987); Ram, " 'Government Myth,' " pp. 13-15. In practice, however, the initial nar-

In less than three years, some fundamental changes have taken place in Iran, particularly regarding the background characteristics of the political elite.[15] The broad coalition that combined its political resources to launch the revolution has disintegrated. The clerical leadership managed to capture the state and control the political society after undermining, even crushing, any effective, organized existence of its national, liberal, leftist, and Islamic rivals. The legitimization of the ideological and political hegemony of the clerical elite, as reflected in the constitution, was based on Khomeini's doctrine of *vilayat-i faqih*, the guardianship of the jurisprudent or the mandate of the Islamic Jurist. In essence, he argued that since any duality of religious and political authority or separation of the spiritual and temporal realms is un-Islamic, and since the main obligation of the Islamic government is the full implementation of the Sacred Law, none other than a fully qualified Islamic jurist, who has the two essential qualities of profound concern with justice and comprehensive knowledge of the *shari'a*, is entitled to be in charge of such government.[16] During the absence of

the "Glorious Lord of the Age," the Islamic jurist, as the representative of the infallible imams, has to be the only authoritative interpreter of God's laws.[17]

Once in power, the Islamic regime presented the revolution itself as model for all Muslims. It called for an immediate overthrow of all the remaining functional equivalents of the Shah and lackeys of "satanical powers" in the Muslim world, particularly in the Persian Gulf area. The triumph of Iran's Islamic revolution seems to have bestowed on its leaders a strong sense of obligation to "make the world safe for Islam," by performing a universal mission that would not be deemed complete until all Muslim communities had undergone revolutionary transformations similar in essence to those witnessed by Iran.[18]

38-40; Marvin Zonis, "The Rule of the Clerics in the Islamic Republic of Iran," *The Annals* of the American Academy of Political and Social Science, 482:85-108 (1985); Mehdi Mozaffari, *Authority in Islam* (London: Sharp, 1987), pp. 49-51.

17. For a discussion of objections as well as amendments to the doctrine expressed by a number of Iranian Shiite religious authorities, see Arjomand, *Turban for the Crown*, pp. 155-60; Ahmad K. Moussavi, "New Interpretation of the Theory of Vilayat-i Faqih," *Middle Eastern Studies*, 28:101-7 (1992).

18. R. K. Ramazani, "Khumayni's Islam in Iran's Foreign Policy," in *Islam in Foreign Policy*, ed. Adeed Dawisha (New York: Cambridge University Press, 1983), pp. 16-23; idem, "Iran's Export of Revolution: Politics, Ends, and Means," in *Iranian Revolution*, ed. Esposito, pp. 40-62. For competing explanations of the resilience of Arab and particularly Persian Gulf regimes characterized by Khomeini as "un-Islamic," see Emmanuel Sivan, "Sunni Radicalism in the Middle East and the Iranian Revolution," *International Journal of Middle East Studies*, 21:1-30 (1989); F. Gregory Gause,

rowing of the income gap between the top and bottom segments in society was ultimately halted in the urban centers and reversed in the countryside. See Sohrab Behdad, "Winners and Losers of the Iranian Revolution," *International Journal of Middle East Studies*, 21:327-58 (1989).

15. Richard Cottam, "Inside Revolutionary Iran," in *Iran's Revolution*, ed. R. K. Ramazani (Bloomington: Indiana University Press, 1990), pp. 3-26; idem, "Charting Iran's New Course," *Current History*, 90:21-24 (1991).

16. Shaul Bakhash, *The Reign of the Ayatollahs* (New York: Basic Books, 1984), pp.

However, the current realities of Iran suggest that although the Islamic regime remains in control and presumably follows the imam's line, the self-righteous revolutionary zeal has been gradually losing ground to a more calculating pragmatic trend. The ascendant pragmatists favor a policy package known as Baz-Sazi (Rebuilding), which includes further liberalization of the economy, enhancing the powers of the presidency, incremental opening to the international economic system by encouraging foreign investment, and normalizing diplomatic relations with the outside world including the Arab regimes that supported Iraq during the first gulf war as well as Western countries.[19] They have been attempting to legitimize this restructuring, or mullastroika, under the banner of what may be described as "Islam in one country." By focusing on the economic development and welfare of Iran, they aspire to consolidate the Islamic Republic and export its revolution by other means, namely, by building a societal model worthy of importation by other Muslims. The outcome of the parliamentary elections of April 1992 indicates that the pragmatists have been gaining

influence at the expense of the ideologues.[20]

The increasing weight of the pragmatic trend cannot be adequately understood by focusing only on the personal characteristics of Khomeini's successors without taking into consideration the impact of the war fatigue stemming from the protracted military confrontation with Iraq and the extremely costly reconstruction of Iran's economy—estimates range from $350 to $600 billion.[21] In other words, the clerical accommodation with reality did not start exactly after June 1989, following Khomeini's death. The antecedents of some of the aforementioned policy reorientation go back to the mid-1980s. Moreover, it was Khomeini who finally decided on 18 July 1988 to accept, without conditions, an end to the war with Iraq as an overriding necessity to safeguard, as he put it, "the interests of the revolution and the system."[22]

"Revolutionary Fevers and Regional Contagion," *Journal of South Asian and Middle Eastern Studies*, 14:1-23 (1991).

19. Hooshang Amirahmadi, *Revolution and Economic Transition: The Iranian Experience* (Albany: State University of New York Press, 1990), pp. 119-24; Judith Miller, "Islamic Radicals Lose Their Tight Grip on Iran," *New York Times*, 8 Apr. 1991. For the radicals' critique of this policy shift as a betrayal of the "line of the imam," see Fahmi Huweidi, "The Mother of All Electoral Battles in Iran," *al-Majalla*, 18-24 Mar. 1992, pp. 22-31.

20. *Al-Majalla* (London), 15-21 Apr. 1992, pp. 24-25. On the significance of the April 1992 elections, see Elaine Sciolino, "For Iran Chief, a Mandate and a Test," *New York Times*, 14 Apr. 1992; Claude van England, "Iran Picks up the Pace of Reform," *Christian Science Monitor*, 17 Apr. 1992.

21. Hooshang Amirahmadi, "War Damage and Reconstruction in the Islamic Republic of Iran," in *Post-Revolutionary Islam*, ed. Hooshang Amirahmadi and Manoucher Parvin (Boulder, CO: Westview Press, 1988), pp. 126-49; G. Hossein Razi, "An Alternative Paradigm to State Rationality in Foreign Policy: The Iran-Iraq War," *Western Political Quarterly*, 41:700-701 (1988).

22. "Imam Khumayni's Message," pp. 99-102. Interestingly enough, two years earlier, Islamic modernists affiliated with the Liberation Movement of Iran led by Mehdi Bazargan argued that the regime's continuation of the war against Iraq and its rejection of peace proposals were "contrary to God's will, the tra-

Even during the early 1980s, Iran's leadership demonstrated that it had enough selective pragmatism to establish a de facto alliance with a secular regime like that of Syria on the basis of common interest and political expediency, regardless of that regime's pan-Arabist ideology or its ruthless suppression of Islamicists.

Needless to say, even more pragmatism was displayed in the early 1990s by the current leadership regarding the second gulf crisis, which exploded after the Iraqi invasion of Kuwait. Calls to join Iraq in a *jihad* against the United States and later to join Iraq's Shiites in another holy war against Saddam's army were made by some in the Iranian leadership.[23] However, Iran did neither. Its

behavior was actually more influenced by the raison d'état than by the ideology of the revolution. The formulation of Iran's policy during the various states of the crisis was, as Arjomand succinctly put it, the outcome of a "sober calculation of its interests as a regional power."[24]

ISLAMIZING MILITARY REGIMES: THE SUDAN AND PAKISTAN

Saudi Arabia and Iran are not the only cases to be studied under the category of Islamic regimes. Claims to have transformed particular regimes along the path of Islamization have been made in the Sudan and Pakistan. Obviously, the Saudi and Iranian regimes exercised and continue to exercise much greater influence within the Islamic world than did Numayri's Sudan or Zia's Pakistan. The latter two lacked the equivalent of the Saudi *tharwa* ("wealth") or the Iranian *thawra* ("revolution"). Moreover, the Sudan's and Pakistan's experiments in Islamization were introduced by military regimes as a means of arresting further erosion of their legitimacy.

Islamization in such cases had a certain instrumental quality best illustrated by the televised scenes of former Sudanese President Numayri pouring bottles of whiskey into the Nile or receiving the *bay'a* ("pledge of allegiance") from army officers as the commander of the faithful.[25] As one

ditions of the Prophet, and the record of the Imams." In their open letter to Khomeini, they argued, on the basis of *fiqh* (jurisprudence) sources, that "during the occultation of the Twelfth Imam all offensive wars were unlawful." H. E. Chehabi, *Iranian Politics and Religious Modernism* (Ithaca, NY: Cornell University Press, 1990), pp. 299-300.

23. "Calls for Jihad against U.S.," Radio Tehran, in Persian, Foreign Broadcast Information Service, 13 Sept. 1990, pp. 52-53. Sadeq Khalkhali advocated a military alliance with Iraq in order to "turn the Persian Gulf and Saudi Arabia into graveyards for American soldiers." See ibid., p. 57. Though Shiite holy places in Karbala and Najaf were under fire in March and April 1991 and fellow Shiites were being crushed by Saddam's Republican Guards, Iran's actual support of the Shiite uprising was quite measured. Iran's restraint reflected its leaders' concern that any overt and massive intervention on their part might have increased and prolonged the U.S. presence in the area or led to a large-scale Iranian military confrontation with Iraq, or both. Iran's interests were not going to be served by either outcome. Derek J. Harvey, "Determinants of Iranian Foreign Policy during the Gulf Crisis" (Manuscript, Middle East Center, University of Utah, Aug. 1991), pp. 17-37.

24. Said Amir Arjomand, "A Victory for the Pragmatists: The Islamic Fundamentalist Reaction in Iran," in *Islamic Fundamentalisms and the Gulf Crisis*, ed. Piscatori, pp. 52-69.

25. Gabriel Warburg, "The Shari'a in Sudan: Implementation and Repercussions,

astute Sudanese writer pointed out, the application of the *shari'a* or "the legislative coup d'etat of September 1983" by Numayri was "a natural continuation of [his] politics of sudden new initiatives and shifting alliances with various political factions . . . [and a means of legitimizing] his claim to the absolute powers" of a caliph. Although "Numayri's Islamization program" benefited from a growing Islamic resurgence in the Sudan, it was launched as a palace coup through a set of hastily formulated, poorly drafted, and erratically implemented presidential decrees.

Numayri's declaration, in September 1983, that the Sudan had become an Islamic republic was motivated primarily by considerations of political expediency in a societal setting characterized by a mounting politicization of socioeconomic grievances, frequent outbreaks of food riots in urban centers, resumption of ethnic conflicts in the south, and growing opposition activities in the ranks of army officers. Faced with such challenges and capitalizing on religious sentiments among Sudanese Muslims, the state-controlled media endlessly repeated Numayri's pronouncements about the Sudan's "Islamic revolution," the implementation of the Islamic legal code, replacing the state income tax with the *zakat*, and a plan to turn all banks into interest-free financial institutions.

Despite its initial popularity, Numayri's brand of Islamization was met with growing resistance, mostly by professional associations—such as those of judges, doctors, and aca-

demics—and a coalition of opposition forces. Prominent political figures, such as Sadiq al-Mahdi, the leader of the Umma Party, saw Numayri's Islamization as opportunistic. They called for reforming an unjust socioeconomic system, fighting endemic and planned corruption in high circles, as well as expanding the narrow scope of political participation prior to, or simultaneously with, the implementation of the Islamic *hudud*. They pointed out that ethnic conflict and economic crisis had escalated further in the Sudan after the implementation of the Islamization program. The religious pretensions of Marshal Numayri, who claimed to have become the imam of the *umma* —after years of identifying himself either as an Arab nationalist or a Sudanese socialist—were also criticized as a mask for dictatorship. This criticism became particularly more credible after Numayri, in response to this opposition, declared a state of emergency in April 1984 and proposed a set of constitutional amendments that would have allowed the president-imam to hold office for life. Even the usually tame parliament managed to resist Numayri's pressures to ratify these amendments immediately.

As the Islamization of the Sudanese regime was introduced from above by presidential decrees, it was suspended mostly through subsequent presidential decrees. Instead of gaining the president more political support, enhancing the regime's viability, and making the Sudan more governable, Numayri's initial introduction and later suspension of his Islamization program ultimately

1983-1989," *Middle East Journal*, 44:624-37 (1990).

weakened his regime's credibility and undermined its domestic political alliances. They were also among the factors that led to his overthrow in April 1985.[26]

Four years of political confusion and policy immobilism were followed, in June 1989, by a military coup led by General al-Bashir, who allied himself with al-Turabi's National Islamic Front to establish another Islamic government. The new military-Islamic regime imposed a state of emergency, suspended the constitution, dissolved the Constituent Assembly, and banned political parties. In al-Turabi's words, "Muslims themselves sometimes don't even know how to go about their Islam. They have no recent precedent of an Islamic government."[27] After the Sudan's second Islamic revolution in less than six years, however, its eco-

nomic crisis has worsened, and the deeply indebted government's response to it owed much more to International Monetary Fund orthodoxy than to Islamic teachings.[28] The sociopolitical dilemma facing the regime has been compounded further by a prolonged and severe drought, an escalating civil war, a taxing refugee problem, and a sharp decline in Arab and Western aid after the Sudan sided with Iraq during the gulf conflict/crisis in 1990-1991. As of this writing, the protracted and multidimensional crisis of the al-Bashir and al-Turabi regime continues to worsen. To the extent that the regime's performance and political legitimacy are interdependent, the challenges to its very survival are likely to increase.[29]

The case of Islamization in Pakistan is different from the Sudanese case in terms of historical evolution. The very rationale for the emergence of Pakistan as a separate political entity, as stated in its constitution, was to provide an independent homeland for Muslims on the Indian subcontinent. Thus the political identity of the community and the political function of the state were closely tied to Islam. Islamic identity and national self-determination became closely intertwined or, as articulated by the Jama'at-i Islami, "Pakistan came into being in the name of Islam,

26. Abdullahi Ahmad An-Na'im, "Constitutionalism and Islamization in the Sudan," *Africa Today*, 36:11-28 (1989); Nelson Kasfir, "One Full Revolution: The Politics of Sudanese Military Government," in *The Military in African Politics*, ed. John Harbeson (New York: Praeger, 1987), pp. 141-62; John Esposito, "Sudan," in *Politics of Islamic Revivalism*, ed. Hunter, pp. 193-201; Carolyn Fluehr-Lobban, "Islamization in Sudan," *Middle East Journal*, 44: 618-23 (1990); Farag Fouda, *Qabla al-suqut* [Before the fall] (Cairo: n.p., 1985), pp. 121-41; Ann M. Lesch, "The Fall of Numeiri" (Report no. 9, Universities Field Staff International, Indianapolis, 1985). See also Mansour Khalid, *al-Fajr al-kadhib* [The false dawn] (Cairo: Dar al-Hillal, 1986). Khalid is former foreign minister of the Sudan.

27. *Economist*, 18 Apr. 1992, pp. 41-42. For an earlier and more elaborate presentation of his critique of Western notions of popular sovereignty, political pluralism, and competitive politics, see Hassan al-Turabi, "al-Shura wa al-dimuqratiyya" [Shura and democracy], *al-Mustaqbal al-'arabi* [The Arab future], 7:4-22 (1985).

28. See Benaiah Yongo-Bure, "Sudan's Deepening Crisis," *Middle East Report*, pp. 9-13 (Sept.-Oct. 1991); John Voll, "Political Crisis in Sudan," *Current History*, 89:153-56, 178-80 (1990).

29. John Voll has concluded that the "issue may in fact have changed from who will rule Sudan to whether or not Sudan will be able to survive in any meaningful fashion." See Voll, "Political Crisis in Sudan," p. 179.

and it could exist in the name of Islam alone." The Objectives Resolution, approved by the country's first Constituent Assembly, centered around the notion that the very raison d'être of the state in Pakistan was to play an activist, interventionist role in bringing about a social and political order based on Islamic principles.[30] Given this historical legacy of "Pakistan's Islamic mandate," all of that country's successive regimes have sought to legitimize their power and their policies, as well as to contain or weaken their political opponents, on Islamic grounds.

As is to be expected, though, Pakistan's regimes differed in terms of their policy orientation and their interpretation of "Islamic ideology." Zulfikar Ali Bhutto's regime and his Pakistan People's Party (PPP), for example, adopted a populist interpretation of Islam. Under the banner of "Islamic socialism," the PPP pursued policies of socioeconomic redistribution at home and nonalignment abroad. The regime's reformist political discourse emphasized *musawat* ("equality") and social justice as basic Islamic principles and fundamental features of Muslim society and polity under the Prophet Muhammad.[31] Faced with growing urban restlessness in the mid-1970s, the party's platform for the March 1977 elections called for Islamic educational and social reforms and greater recognition of the role of the *'ulama'* and the mosques in society. Bhutto's re-

gime was already in retreat, however, and conservative Islamic organizations, under the umbrella of the Pakistan National Alliance, were increasing their appeal, influence, and protest. The regime was finally overthrown by the military coup of July 1977.

The new regime, under General Zia ul-Haq, was decidedly more conservative socioeconomically, more authoritarian politically, clearly pro-Western, and particularly pro-American in its foreign policy orientation. Divine guidance was invoked by the general regarding the origin of his Islamization program known as *nizam-i mustafa* ("order of the Prophet or the Chosen One"). As he put it, " 'I have a mission, given by God, to bring Islamic order to Pakistan.' "[32] The day selected for introducing the Islamization program was that of the Prophet's birthday. In the economic sphere, the program promised to safeguard private property rights and to abolish bank interest through the establishment of Islamic financial institutions. In the educational sphere, it placed greater emphasis on the Islamic content of textbooks and the expansion of *shari'a* training institutes. Regarding the social sphere, it called for a stricter enforcement of Islamic moral code and the prohibition of gambling and alcohol consumption. As to the legal sphere, Zia's program included the implementation of the *hudud* ordinances, the appointment of *muhtasib-i a'la* (a sort of Islamic ombudsman), and the es-

30. Mumtaz Ahmad, "Pakistan," in *Politics of Islamic Revivalism*, ed. Hunter, pp. 229-32.

31. Gerald Heeger, "Socialism in Pakistan," in *Socialism in the Third World*, ed. Helen Desfosses and Jacques Levesque (New York: Praeger, 1975), pp. 291-309.

32. Interview with the British Broadcasting Corporation, 15 Apr. 1978, as quoted in Omar Noman, *The Political Economy of Pakistan* (London: KPI, 1988), p. 141.

tablishment of a judicial review process by *shari'a* judges to decide whether all laws were in accordance with Islam.[33]

Among the major exceptions regarding the scope of such judicial review were various martial law ordinances. As Mumtaz Ahmad put it, Zia's government insisted on linking "the destiny of both Islam and Pakistan with the continuity of the military regime . . . [consequently] any deviation from the official interpre-

tation . . . becomes both a religious heresy and treason against the state . . . political rebellion and religious dissent become indistinguishable." The regime's main objective in pursuing this linkage was to gain legitimacy particularly among the lower middle classes and in the ranks of the *'ulama'*, as well as among conservative religious political parties. Another major objective of such linkage was to discredit leftist and liberal opposition forces and to portray them to the public as un-Islamic and thus unacceptable alternatives to an Islamic regime. In fact, the interim constitution of March 1981 empowered the President to dissolve any political party "operating in a manner prejudicial to Islamic ideology."[34]

As in the case of the Sudan, the call for Islamization in Pakistan gained what appeared at first to be a significant measure of support. But it also raised popular expectations regarding the prospects of more just and more livable conditions in Pakistan; however, the living conditions of many continued to deteriorate. No *shura* ("consultation") was seriously contemplated by the military-Islamic regime. On the contrary, freedom of expression was subjected to serious restrictions, opposition publications were banned, defiant writers jailed, and uncooperative newsmen flogged.[35]

Once again, as in the Sudanese case, most of the Islamization was concentrated on turning bank inter-

33. See Riaz Hassan, "Islamization: An Analysis of Religious, Political and Social Change in Pakistan," *Middle East Studies*, 21: 263-84 (1985); Charles Kennedy, "Islamization and Legal Reform in Pakistan, 1979-1989," *Pacific Affairs*, 63:62-77 (1990); idem, "Islamization in Pakistan," *Asian Survey*, 28:307-16 (1988). It is interesting to note that while General Zia's Islamization program won the endorsement and support of Saudi Arabia (see Noman, *Political Economy of Pakistan*, p. 150), Iran's media characterized it as " 'the exact antithesis of Islam' " and concluded that Zia " 'could much more readily be likened to the ex-Shah.' " Quoted in Roger Savory, "Ex Oriente Nebula: An Inquiry into the Nature of Khomeini's Ideology," in *Ideology and Power in the Middle East*, ed. Chelkowski and Pranger, p. 352. Iran's leaders, however, opted for a cautious policy toward Pakistan to ensure continued assistance to pro-Iranian groups in the Afghan resistance against the Soviets. See Zalmay Khalilzad, "The Iranian Revolution and the Afghan Resistance," in *Shi'ism, Resistance, and Revolution* (Boulder, CO: Westview Press, 1987), pp. 257-73. However, the Iranian leadership adopted a critical position toward "Numayri's Islamization," which they perceived as lacking credibility in light of his regime's alignment during the 1980s with the United States, Saudi Arabia, and Iraq. The Sudanese President even claimed that the Islamic Republic of Iran attempted to destabilize his regime. See Gehad Auda, "The Foreign Policy of a Fragmented Polity: The Case of Sudan," in *The Foreign Policies of Arab States*, by Bahgat Korany and Ali Dessouki (Boulder, CO: Westview Press, 1991), p. 368.

34. Ahmad, "Pakistan," pp. 231-33; Hassan, "Islamization," p. 269.

35. James Napoli, "Benazir Bhutto and the Issues of Press Freedom in Pakistan," *Journal of South Asian and Middle Eastern Studies*, 14:64 (1991).

est into profits, setting up the *shari'a* courts, and implementing the *hudud*. The initial popular support has gradually given way to disillusionment and cynicism. The political outcome of all this was captured by Hamza Alavi when he concluded that the "regime's strident rhetoric about the Islamic basis of Pakistan's ideology has failed to give it the basis of legitimacy that it has sought . . . its rhetoric has compounded its problems by raising the hopes . . . of Islamic fundamentalists."[36] The regime was in no position to fulfill these hopes, and in February 1984 it had to intervene and curtail a cycle of violence and assassinations that involved the Islamic Society of Students, which was an earlier collaborator with General Zia's regime in suppressing supporters of the PPP, and its leftist opponents on university campuses.[37] The 1988 national elections, which were held after Zia's death in a mysterious airplane crash, brought the PPP back to power in a coalition government led

36. Hamza Alavi, "Ethnicity, Muslim Society, and the Pakistan Ideology," in *Islamic Reassertion in Pakistan*, ed. Anita Weiss (Syracuse, NY: Syracuse University Press, 1986), pp. 45-46. For more on the growth of popular dissatisfaction with Zia's program, see Richard Kurin, "Islamization in Pakistan: A View from the Countryside," *Asian Survey*, 25:852-62 (1985); Hassan, "Islamization," pp. 279-80. On the organized opposition by women to particular draft "Islamic ordinances," see Khawar Mumtaz and Farida Shaheed, eds., *Women of Pakistan: Two Steps Forward, One Step Back?* (London: Zed Books, 1987), pp. 123-42.

37. On student political activism during that period, including a reference to the lives of 80 students lost in this wave of violence, see Seyyed Vali Reza Nasr, "Students, Islam, and Politics," *Middle East Journal*, 46:67-68 (1992).

by Benazir Bhutto. Other changes have occurred since then, but the nature of the regime is no longer what it was under Zia.

CONCLUSION

The core argument of this article can be restated briefly as follows: The diversity characterizing popular and oppositional Islamic movements is also evident in the regimes that base their very identity and legitimacy on Islamic grounds. In pursuing this path, Islamic regimes articulate different interpretations of Islam that reflect the interests and ideology of those who control the state machinery—for example, conservative, reformist, or revolutionary; the influence of society's historical legacy and traditions, such as identity formation, evolution of authority patterns, or crucial formative experiences; and specific characteristics of the immediate situational setting, such as crisis situations. I have examined three types of Islamic regimes, led by monarchs, mullas, and marshals, to illustrate and compare the Islamic legitimation of diverse domestic and foreign policy outcomes. The three are the conservative dynastic regime of Saudi Arabia, the populist clerical regime of Iran, and the military authoritarian regimes of the Sudan and Pakistan.

In all three regime types, the Islamic legitimization of their rule did not proceed uncontested. It has been frequently challenged on religiopolitical grounds by domestic rivals for power and external rivals for leadership in the Muslim world. Among the cases covered in this article, the most effective challenges to regime legitimacy have been manifested in the Islamized military regimes of the Sudan and Pakistan. Their predicament can be attributed to the fact that in addition to presiding over societies deeply divided along ethnic and linguistic lines, these regimes lacked the political capital provided by huge oil revenues available in the Saudi case of *al-Islam al-tharawi* ("the Islam of wealth," or, as described by one writer, "petro-Islam").[38] They also lacked the legitimacy generated by revolutionary change under charismatic leadership known in the Iranian case of *al-Islam al-thawri* ("revolutionary Islam").

Whether the Islamization of these military regimes followed a palace coup, as in the Sudan in 1983, or a full-blown army takeover, as in Pakistan in 1977, it did not alter their fundamentally discipline-centered, antipolitical character. This character has been manifested not only in their attempts to silence any opposition to their rule but also in their distrust of the political movements that supported their Islamization programs and whose leaders aspired to play the roles of its theoreticians and organizers; such movements include the Muslim Brotherhood in the Sudan and the Jama'at-i Islami in Pakistan. It is no wonder, then, that these regimes have lost, rather quickly, most of the popular support generated by the promise of Islamization. Whether Saudi Arabia and Iran provide alternative models of Islamic governance worthy of emulation by other Muslim communities is a subject of contention and debate. The Saudi monarchs and Iranian mullas have, however, managed with some degree of success to use available economic, political, and cultural resources in dealing with their diverse challenges. The same cannot be said for the Islam of the marshals.

38. See Fouad Zakariya, *al-Haqiqa wa al-wahm fi al-haraka al-Islamiyya al-mu'asira* [Reality and myth in the contemporary Islamic movement] (Cairo: Dar al-Fikr, 1986), pp. 23-26. On Saudi responses to the challenges posed by socioeconomic change under conditions of the oil boom and oil glut, see Kirin Chaudhry, "The Price of Wealth," *International Organization*, 43:108-19, 123-30, 135-42 (Winter 1989); David Long, "Stability in Saudi Arabia," *Current History*, 90:9-13 (1991).

Islamicist Utopia and Democracy

By LAHOUARI ADDI

ABSTRACT: This article addresses democratic construction in Islamic societies throughout the Algerian experience. Its main conclusions can be summarized as follows. First, in all Muslim societies, there exists an Islamicist utopia that stands as an obstacle not only to democracy but also to political modernity. Until now, this utopia has been contained only by repression that finally impedes the democratization. Second, Islam presents itself as a public religion that participates in the legitimization of political power. The democratic ideology, however, is compatible with religion to the extent that it is lived as a private concern. Finally, the Islamicist utopia and the public aspect of Islam aim at maintaining society's communal structures. They refuse to make the singularity of the political arena independent and reject differentiation through politics within a society that claims to be fraternal.

Lahouari Addi is professor of political sociology at Oran University, Algeria. He holds a degree from Université des Sciences Sociales de Grenoble and a doctorat d'état from École des Hautes Études en Sciences Sociales de Paris (France). He has written four books: De L'Algerie pre-coloniale à l'Algerie coloniale *(1985);* Approche methodologique du pouvoir et de l'état dans les sociétés du Tiers-Monde *(1990);* L'impasse du populisme *(1991); and* L'Algerie, l'économie et la question du politique, *edited by Bouchene Alger (1992). During the year 1991-92, he was a visiting fellow in the Near Eastern Studies Department, Princeton University.*

IN the years following the independence of much of the Third World in the 1950s and 1960s, political sociology examined developing polities through the concepts of nation building and state building. The object of this examination focused on the emergence of a political center or central power that structured its periphery in order to create a homogeneous nation and a developed economy. The accent was placed on the autonomy of central power vis-à-vis the exterior world and on its will and capacity to create a national society through the process of modernization and industrial development.

The record of the decades since independence, however, has shown that this approach overestimated the capacity of the political center to develop a modern economy and to begin the creation of a society, in the sense of Ferdinand Tönnies. Scholars realized that the central power, itself belonging to the historical reality it sought to transform, came to be governed by the dominant political logic. Setting itself up as a self-contained end, it created an obstacle to its proclaimed objectives. In the process, modernization called into question the dominant ideological interests and social structures, and the central power followed its own interests and entered into the collective image in order to ensure its own survival.

The concepts of modernization and of nation building—after Apter and Abdelmalek—remained incomplete because they were developed separately from the question of power, which is the basic question of political science and therefore the essential element in political analysis.

After noting that the political center is privatized, that is, considered to be a private patrimony and thus creating the notion of neopatrimonialism, political sociology leapt over the problem by focusing on the concept of democracy building. In order to understand what was going on, all that the analyst had to do was emerge from the neopatrimonial logic, face the question of pluralism, and introduce the laws of free competition and free enterprise. But the analyst forgot that neopatrimonialism was the political effect of a historic situation where the central power was privatized for ideopolitical reasons, making the central power the object of public competition. Deprivatizing it will be possible only if the ideopolitical factors lose their relevance and dominance.

POLITICAL CITIZENSHIP AND PUBLIC RELIGION

The example of Algeria shows that democratization was conceived as an operation to justify the disengagement of the state from the economy. But democratization is above all a political and ideological struggle; it implies the emergence of citizenship, with liberty. Without a central power to protect public liberty and the exercise of citizenship, there is no democracy. But in Algeria the team in power, delegitimized by the economic and social failures for which it was responsible, could not impose the authority of the state over the dominant ideological interests and the logic of the collective image that refused individual autonomy and its juridical political expression as a subject of law. The citizen is a legal subject of law who obeys civil laws born out of reasoned public debate. If the individual were to obey only other individuals, depend on the whim of the prince, submit to laws handed down from time immemorial, there would be no citizenship. The citizen is a free person vis-à-vis his or her peers, living and dead. This liberty is no caprice destined to diminish the citizen's human dignity, culture, religion, or history. Indeed, it permits the development, expansion, and liberation of all the potentialities within the human being.

In a society confronted with the process of modernization, the emergence of citizenship arouses suspicion among the religious. However, religious faith is true and sincere only when it is lived in a free social milieu. If the exterior appearances of faith were imposed by social constraint, there would be an unimaginable number of hypocrites among sincere believers. Religious awareness will accept political citizenship only after historical experience shows that citizenship does not diminish religion in the strict sense. Social constraint does not come from religion, however; it is, rather, the effect of the public character of religion, manifested as a social fact of the group and not as a spirituality belonging to the private intimacy of the individual. Religion becomes a political order to which one aspires, a political order whose coming is resisted by immoral beings lacking respect for the word of God.

This political order is not the coming of the kingdom of God on earth or the preparation of believing souls for eternal life. Islam does not permit

this fundamentalism. The Islamicists are not fundamentalists, and, although they proclaim the contrary, they do not confuse the spiritual and the temporal. Their objective is to construct not a divine order but a human order that obeys the prescriptions of the sacred test. This objective, if realized, will not ensure the individual's place in paradise but will permit better life on earth. Access to paradise is an individual and not a collective task.

This spiritual predisposition is shared by all believers in the land of Islam; in other words, Muslim societies are pregnant with a religious utopia from which they would like to draw political order. It is an Islamicist utopia, which stands as an obstacle not only to democracy but also to political modernism in general—at least in the latter's Western formulation. This utopia, latent in all Muslim societies, is politically active in those countries where great expectations have been disappointed, where the conditions of daily life are at the limit of the tolerable, and where repression can go no further. These three conditions applied in Algeria under the rule of Chadli Bendjedid.

But the Islamicist utopia is not an accident of circumstances; on the contrary, it belongs to the long term of history. The Islamic world held itself apart from the social debates that the Renaissance unleashed in Europe. Untouched by the dynamic of social criticism, it remained faithful to apologetic historiography. The Islamic renaissance, or Nahda, which took place in the second half of the nineteenth century beginning with Jamal al-Din al-Afghani, marks the beginning of the intellectual movement's attempt to integrate faith and reason. But, confronted with the expansion of colonialism, the Nahda fell back upon mythification of the past and apologetic discourse. Its last thinker, Rashid Reda, had Hasan al-Banna, founder of the Muslim Brotherhood movement in Egypt, as a disciple. Thus colonization did not help matters, since modernism was delegitimized by the very fact that it had brought with it colonial domination. This explains why, with the exception of a few isolated Arab intellectuals, whose positions were suspect, the paradigms of the Enlightenment had such feeble echoes in Muslim societies. In the rare cultivated milieu of the national liberation movements, the question was put off until after independence, which was supposed to ignite the dynamic of modernism automatically.

Nevertheless, a few decades after independence, national disenchantment appeared. Modernity had not been ignited at the desired speed or in the desired conditions. During the first years of independence—the 1950s and the 1960s—popular Marxism, at least in the universities, opposed the influence of Hobbes, Rousseau, Kant, de Tocqueville, natural law, and political freedom. It delegitimized them, labeling them "ideologies in service to the bourgeoisie, which produce alienation and exploitation." The Islamicist utopia became politically active, therefore, in a social and political context marked by a double disappointment: hopes invested in independence going unfulfilled and dissipation of the illusions of "developmentalism."

In this perspective, the system of education, in its legitimate task of teaching the past, reactivates the epic combat of Islam. In reaction against the West, the past is taught without any critical sense. Its specificity is emphasized to the detriment of universality. Historic events in the origins of modernity are minimized because they do not belong to the history of Islam. The discovery of America—why, in fact, did the Muslims not take part in it?—the Christian Reformation and the wars that followed it; the English, American, Russian, and French revolutions; the recomposition of national borders in Europe in the nineteenth century; the rise of Nazism in Germany—all these major events are considered foreign to the Muslim historical experience and therefore relegated to secondary importance. It is as if the Muslims did not consider themselves as taking part in the universalizing historical process and as if they sought to remake their history without drawing lessons from other people, especially people who set in march the process of modernity and the process of domination of which Muslims—along with other people—have been the victim. From the point of view of Islamic sensitivity, there is no modern reading of the American Revolution, the French Revolution, the Russian Revolution, and Hitlerism. Obviously, this is not a task for high school teachers. It belongs to the university, which should produce historical works from which the public school system can draw its lessons. In the absence of such research, the educational system spreads myths that deform the perception of the contemporary historical process, a deformation that results in a loss of the sense of reality. The system of mass education spreads the myths that feed the utopia, which is itself repressed when it expresses itself politically.

Muslim society is thus enclosed in a logic of ever-deepening repression. In this context, any opening to pluralism and democratization is condemned to failure, because the historical and ideological conditions for the privatization of public power have not been reached. Democratization threatens to change radically the verbal mode of legitimizing the neopatrimonial system. Historical legitimacy risks being replaced by religious legitimacy, but both put central authority above individuals and historical time; both refuse political citizenship and attack the dignity of individuals, making them administrative subjects who bow as the official vehicle passes by. Historical and religious legitimacy are the modality by which the dead exercise their dictatorship on the living. In the twentieth century there is only one legitimacy that conforms to the dignity of the free individual, electoral legitimacy. But electoral legitimacy is an inseparable part of democratic ideology, and the latter requires religion to lose the public character that predisposes it to be a basis of legitimacy and thus a political resource in the competition for power. Without democratic ideology, the political party presenting itself as most Muslim—or perceived as such—would be assured a crushing victory in democratic elections, and this would inaugurate the end of the democratic process.

POLITICAL MODERNITY AND PUBLIC RELIGION

It is necessary to show how political modernity is incompatible with the public character of religion and how modernity is built on the depoliticization of religion. But the notion of depoliticizing religion has a precise content, for the idea that religion must be separated from politics proceeds from a voluntarist, naive, and even religiously hostile vision. Clearly, every social act and collective or public manifestation contains a political dimension. Islam, like any other religion, contains a political dynamic that is impossible to deny. In Christianity, the church does not permit a believer outside the ecclesiastical hierarchy to speak to others in the name of religion. To the contrary, in Islam, the political aspect is limited to no institution, thus permitting any believer to claim religious authority and use it for temporal purposes over other individuals. For reasons deriving from the structure of its dogma, the political character of Islam is obvious. In addition, this character is emphasized by the recent history of Muslim societies struggling against colonial domination, during which Islam was mobilized as a political resource and a factor of identity—so much as to become a constructive element in national ideology and a constituent of nationality. Consequently, it is no longer possible to call for the separation of religion and politics.

But modernity does not require the separation of religion and politics or the marginalization of religion as a precondition. Nobody has the right to prevent the mosque from condemning corruption and arbitrariness or emphasizing the duty to assist widows and orphans. It is even desirable for the mosque to have moral authority in society, in order to appeal to the preservation of human values—fraternity, solidarity, and justice—that accompany the divine message and to denounce flagrant restrictions on human rights and social inequalities. But for the mosque to incarnate this moral authority, it must remain outside of the competition for power. That is, modernity and, more particularly, democratic ideology are incompatible with religion's having a partisan character.

Indeed, under modernity and democratic ideology, public debate about individual autonomy, political citizenship, juridical equality, and political liberty would be considered to be undermined were a party to claim divine authority in making its argument. Democracy means free elections and alternance in power, but it is also the public exercise of reason, as Habermas would say, on all issues concerning the individual and his or her relations with the community. Political parties that compete in elections try to convince their voters on the basis of supposedly rational argumentation. Of course, these parties defend the ideological interests of the group. But these interests, frequently not perceived as such, are theoretically rationalized in order to be presented as in the common interest of all members of society. Political debate, public in its essence, has the purpose of making group interests and political programs attractive

from the point of view of a broad rationality. The voter is supposed to choose, according to reason, the program most satisfactory to his or her own interests and vision of things. Without open public debate, without reference to the rationality of social choice, there can be no democracy.

If religion as such intervenes in the debate, that is to say, if the protagonists claim divine authority, there will no longer be debate or democracy. For citizens, most of whom are believers, cannot opt against the religious prescriptions for society. Once there is a religious party in the electoral competition or a party presenting itself as such, there can be no free national choice on the part of any voter who cannot imagine voting against the divine message. Human nature being what it is, there might even be voters who would vote for religious parties in order to assuage their conscience or to atone for bad behavior in the past (or in the future).

It is not the purpose of the electoral act to be transformed into a religious rite. It is not Islam as a text that transforms the electoral act into a rite; it is the culture of the believer, his or her capacity or incapacity to separate the sacred from the profane. In a society where the level of political culture is low, the theological content of the sacred text is altered. In such a case, the finality of the profane act is transformed: the profane becomes sacralized and the sacred profaned.

There is no contradiction, of course, between textual Islam—the Quran and the *sunna*—and modernism. The contradiction is with the way Islam is lived and practiced today. But a religion's public character is not inevitable or inherent; it is a product of history. Without succumbing to the illusion of hindsight, it can be said that the public character of Islam results from the medieval interpretation of the religion, an interpretation that remains active and formally rejects the notion of political sovereignty—only God is sovereign. It rejects, consequently, the logic of juridical positivism; it rejects political freedom, the abyss of the civil state founded on the Hobbesian-Rousseauistic notion of social contract; in short, as Charles Butterworth notes in his article in this volume, it rejects the modern construction of political life.

The Islamicist utopia is not, however, merely a relic from the past. On the contrary, it expresses, in a contradictory manner, a desire to join with modernism, while at the same time assuring the survival of community values. The Islamicist utopia seeks to construct a City where values of solidarity, equality, and justice will dominate, with respect for the word of God. That is, its goal is a City regulated not by politics—which showcase the ugliness of humankind—but by morality. Political parties are not the expression of preexisting divergences; in its view, they are the cause of these divergences. For the militant of the Islamic Salvation Front (FIS), for example, the so-called Berberist parties create the linguistic issues that serve as their stock in trade. Banning those parties, therefore, would be enough to make the issues go away. The same goes for all other parties that seek to divide the national community.

Economic battles and the ideological divergences that traverse Muslim societies would not exist except for the fact that humans have turned aside from the work of God. Let us come back to it, and we will once again become brothers, united by the love of God. The interest of the individual as well as the cupidity of the haves would stimulate the productivity of the workers, which would increase the riches to be shared. The Islamicist utopia is rooted in this ethical-religious anthropological optimism and therefore refuses to establish social relations on a juridical-political basis that implies the Kantian categories of civil law, rights and their subject, and individual will. To reorganize society on the basis of the anthropological pessimism of Hobbes, Spinoza, Kant, or Carl Schmitt would, for the Muslim consciousness, be a leap into the great unknown. The Islamicist utopia exists only because the categories of political modernism have not been reworked in the mold of Arab-Islamic culture. But such a creation of modernism by way of Arab-Islamic culture is theoretically possible, for there is no reason—everything else kept the same—why democracy should be inherently Western and absolutism inherently Muslim.

Thus the Muslim world is now in the throes of a debate it missed in the wake of its decadence. But now it is not the venerated thinkers who are forcing the debate. It is being forced by the streets, violently, murderously. As in the past, the thinkers of

al-Azhar continue to ponder the im-
mutable rules of grammar and the
placement of punctuation marks in
the sacred texts, bypassing the fundamental questions. In Algeria, it is
the FIS—the street—that poses, unwittingly, the essential questions
about the reconstruction of political
life in the context of local culture. The
Algerian democratic experience
would have shown that as long as the
Islamicist utopia remained popular,
as long as it remained anchored in
the collective imagination, it would
constitute an obstacle to the influx of
modern political categories without
which democracy is impossible. This
is why the democratic experience in
Algeria would have been decisive for
the whole Muslim world. Either it
would have succeeded, and the
Muslim world would have profited; or
it would have failed, and the Muslim
world would have returned either to
the wasting of the oil patrimony in
unproductive consumption or to international beggary.

FRATERNAL SOCIETY AS
A REFUSAL OF CHANGE

The interruption of the electoral
process—and probably of democracy
building—in Algeria at best restores
the situation before October 1988,
when the country went out into the
streets to protest government ineffi-
ciency. One may ask whether the defense of immediate interests and the
fear of eventual sanctions against the
ruling elite or the fear of political
anarchy by themselves explain this
interruption. There may well be
deeper reasons related to the very
perception of politics revealing fears

of radical breaks with the past and
historic changes. This does not mean
that the arrival of the FIS to power
would provoke a historic change in
the FIS's view of itself as the single
party of all Algerians; rather, it is
itself the refusal to change from the
single-party system of the National
Liberation Front (FLN). But from the
formal point of view, by coming to
power neither by riot nor by coup
d'état, the FIS would inaugurate a
new period of political history for the
country, a period that would have its
own dynamic in the recomposition of
political forces.

But the incumbent leaders did not
have the imagination and the courage to enter into the movement of
change. In this perspective, the banning of the FIS blocks change; for the
FIS, as an organized movement,
serves as a magnet for the ideology of
the fraternal society. This magnet allows the protagonists to define themselves in relation to each other. Banning the FIS means that the ideology
it bears will continue to dominate the
entire political space and to be present in all of the political groups. For
the FIS, far from being a party, is a
sentiment, a prepolitical culture.

From this point of view, all Algerians are members of the FIS to the
extent that we all swim in its prepolitical culture. The sense of historical perspective suggests that this
prepolitical culture will crystallize itself into a movement expressing a
utopian sentiment, even if this movement takes power by democratic
rules. Then, upon confronting the
contradictions of social life, it will be
repulsed to the point of losing any

political meaning. It is through political competition, public debate, freedom of expression, and the practice of political citizenship that a large part of the electorate will come to realize that the FIS is only a sentiment and not a management tool of modern political life and social contradictions.

Electoral competition forces the actors to situate themselves politically in the logic of alternance, in a political space defined by ideological rivalries. Political programs are not merely a trick to conquer and occupy central power. Any attempt to recover the adversary becomes futile, because political adversaries clash and publicly declare themselves to be irreconcilable. The bitterness of their struggle does not affect civil peace, however, because the struggle is regulated by democratic institutions and sanctioned by universal suffrage within the framework of an alternance accepted by all. This political game supposes above all that the society is permeated by irreducible political cleavages and that these cleavages are interiorized by the actors. Such a political game also presupposes that the historical subjects of political modernity are in place and that they have a more or less clear awareness of theoretical categories through which they perceive and practice politics. That leading figures of the FLN easily join the FIS or that leaders of the FIS easily participate in power only shows that the actors do not obey a rationality of political modernity that presupposes the insurmountable ideological and political contradictions compatible only in democratic institutions and in alternance in state power.

The refusal of political differentiation is founded on political fraternalism that the interruption of the electoral process destroys. Because it does not conceive of a national collectivity that is irreconcilably divided, fraternalism raises the possibility of recovering the adversary of the moment, allying with him if he is intransigent or sharing power if he is sufficiently strong. One must not believe that political fraternalism is justified by a fear of recourse to physical coercion. To the contrary, to the extent that fraternalism denies the political character of social contradictions, it offers no institutional means of resolution and therefore opens the possibility of bloody riots. In a fraternal society, central power is not the subject of political competition; it is the expression of a momentary relation of force. Maintaining oneself in power or conquering it supposes the use of physical force and violence. Violence is a banal means of political regulation in a fraternal society, as differentiated from a democratic society where parties declare themselves irreconcilable political adversaries without destroying civil peace and citizens' lives, whatever their political opinions.

On the day after the elections of 26 December 1991, Algeria was confronted with the choice of opting either for the fraternal society that had prevailed to this point, with its ideological handicaps and its political lethargy, or for a democratic society, with its competition and implacable logic. It chose fraternal society twice. The first time, it gave the majority to the FIS, which is an expression par excellence of fraternal society; the second time, it stopped the electoral process. Henceforth the great party of fraternal society will have to be reconstructed on the remains of the FLN and the debris of the FIS. The result, necessarily a single party, will have to reproduce the past and put central authority above political competition. Obviously, this does not prevent absolutism, corruption, or—even less—bloody repression of the riots that will arise within the logic of fraternal society.

What to do? There are two possible choices. The first one is to modernize the economy so that the Islamicist utopia cannot be joined to the social discontent that gives it its imprint. For Algeria, this choice will require a radical shuffling of the team in power and financial resources to the tune of $50 billion, earmarked for restructuring the economy. A different team in power—vested with a vision of the future, developing the economy, and releasing a dynamic of accumulation—would have enough authority to effect the necessary ruptures and to transform the education system. The social base of the Islamicist utopia would leave it a minority opinion expressed by a few firebrands whose startling actions would be human-interest stories without any impact on the democratic functioning of political society.

The second choice would be to permit the democratic process to bring about its own termination, by carrying the Islamicists to power. For a utopia, there is no antidote like reality. Utopia is an attempt to replace the real with the imaginary. As long as it is expressed by an opposition party, it can be pertinent and effica-cious. But once the party comes to power, it becomes reduced to reflecting reality—the harsh reality of concrete causality and human vice. History is the unhappy experiment. It has never followed the wise counsels of the Platonic sage. Westerners did not construct modernism and democracy with an ear to Hobbes, Rousseau, or Kant. Only after having suffered the tragic excesses of absolute power and tyranny, only after being instructed by Robespierre and Napoleon, did the consciousness of common interest prevail. The thinkers were not convoked until afterward, to provide the ideological justification for the new political order. That justification was traced back to Greek antiquity and primitive Christianity. Why could it not be found in the Islamic heritage as well?

It is clear that preference for the first or the second of these choices depends on the position of the chooser. If I, for example, were a Western politician, I would do anything to prevent the Islamicists from acceding to power, because that would provoke regional instability and threaten Western interests. For, after all, in the Islamicist discourse, the Evil Empire is the now-Christian, now-atheist materialist West. If I were an army officer or a high bureaucrat, implicated in the past mismanagement of the state, I would mount a coup d'état to prevent the Islamicists' accession. For, drunk with hatred for those whom they consider to be the enemies of God, would they not wish to throw some heads to the mob?

But I am neither a Western politician nor an officer of the Algerian army. I am an academic-Platonist, and the object of my reflection is the Islamicist utopia and its rootedness in society. As long as this utopia remains active, Algeria will twiddle its thumbs at the doorway of modernism. The Muslim consciousness will not awaken to modernism until after the clash between the Islamicist utopia and the political realities of human anthropology occurs. At what price? one might ask. To this I would be inclined to answer, "I am neither an officer of the Algerian army nor a Western politician."

ANNALS, *AAPSS*, **524**, November 1992

Islam in the States of the Former USSR

By VITALY NAUMKIN

ABSTRACT: Under the Soviet system, the rich intellectual life of Islam was eliminated, but a vigorous if unsophisticated popular tradition remained. After *perestroika*, an Islamic movement emerged as a form of political protest. But secular nationalism and ethnic conflict within and between the new republics also provided political dynamics. Throughout the time of change, Islam has served as a symbol of identity, a force for mobilization, and a pressure for democracy. But if successful politically, it faces economic challenges beyond its grasp.

Professor Vitaly Naumkin received his doctorate from Moscow University and has conducted research and taught in Russia and the Middle East. He is deputy director of the Institute of Oriental Studies of the Russian (formerly Soviet) Academy of Sciences, president of the Russian Center for Strategic Research and International Studies, and author of works in Russian, English, and Arabic on Soviet Central Asia and the Middle East.

THE former USSR held the fifth-largest population of Muslims in the world; according to various estimates, the population was 60-70 million. Since its formation, that state pursued a rigid policy of forcing out religion not only from public and political life but also from the life of the individual. The ideology of the ruling Communist Party was atheistic. Officially, religion was separated from the state, but even outside the framework of the state, the transmission of religious knowledge was extremely inhibited, primarily due to the strict limitation of the printing and distribution of religious literature and the absence of religious schools. The disintegration of the traditional way of life, industrialization, and urbanization also helped to lessen the weight of religion in the life of all peoples of the USSR, including the Muslims.

Muslims are found in Central Asia, Kazakhstan, Azerbaijan, North Caucasus, and the Volga region of Russia itself. The processes taking place before and under way after the disintegration of the USSR differed in each of these areas, though they have many traits in common. With that condition in mind, it is possible to focus on Central Asia and Kazakhstan.

During the years of Soviet power, Islam, though greatly restricted, did not completely lose its place in the life of Central Asian society. It was driven deep down and forced to hide under the surface of social structures. The greatest harm was done to intellectual Islam, represented, in the main, by the highly educated intelligentsia, many of whom in the early twentieth century were advocating reform and renovation of the religion. This intelligentsia was annihilated, and the intellectual Islamic tradition was fully suppressed.

A different fate fell to the so-called everyday or popular Islam based on the synthesis of classical Islamic values and notions with the elements of pre-Islamic beliefs. This Islam included a tremendous number of rites that were particularly vivid in the activities of the Sufi orders, with the Nakshbandiyya order having the greatest currency in Central Asia and the Volga area. For a number of reasons, this kind of Islam was able to survive within the borders of a very vast region comprising, inter alia, Central Asia. In other areas, this kind of Islam came to naught.

The place of the former stratum of theologians and shaykhs was occupied by official clergy institutionalized and integrated into the system of power and controlled with the help of Councils for Religious Affairs, which, in turn, were controlled by the Party bodies and the KGB. This new official clergy did not present a threat to the Communist regime, but to no small extent it facilitated the stabilization of the political situation in Muslim areas. Some researchers are also of the opinion that popular Islam, too, was organically interwoven into socialist life, also helping to consolidate the power of the party-state elite who did not violate the traditional norms of life and thus helping to strengthen the prestige of the authorities.

According to A. Malashenko, "after the completion of the struggle against the Basmach, the authorities practically stopped interfering with the internal affairs of Muslim communities, leaving them to the keepers of the old patriarchal traditions, i.e., the lowest stratum of the clergy who were ignorant of the canons of classical Islam but well versed in the aspirations and needs of the simple folk."[1] The imams of the underground mosques, unofficial village mullas, readers of the Quran, teachers of the secret *maktab*s ("schools"), and *mazar* shaykhs ("shrine officials") made up the stratum with the help of which religious tradition and knowledge were handed down. It was they who prepared the ground for the religious revival of today in that region.

The village community was one of the principal instruments for the preservation of popular Islam. Both prior to the Revolution and after it, irrigation facilities were in the hands of the state, but land was in the possession of peasants. Despite the large-scale establishment of state and cooperative farms, the state did not control the peasants' individual farms. The domination of that kind of economic life and the spread of private trade, which existed secretly despite formal bans, were instrumental in the preservation of traditional ways of life in the countryside. In the cities the role of the conserving element was played by the *mahalla*, the block community whose chairman acted in the same way as the *rais* ("leader") prior to the Revolution. He controlled the observance of Islamic norms and rites in everyday life.

There were very few mosques in Central Asia, and in most small towns and villages there was none at all. The local population used private or public facilities for prayers. Now village clubs, rest houses, and the like are used for this purpose. The setting up of so-called *hujras*, or agricultural settlements, on individual plots of local dwellers has become a common practice for the same purpose.

The cult of saints, always popular in the region, began developing on a large scale in the 1970s. In practically all Central Asian *kishlak*s there is a *mazar*—the tomb of the local saint—which is considered a holy place. Also considered sacred are almost all the graves of clergy, former members of the Emir and Khan administration, and leaders of the Basmach, the armed movement against Soviet power that was finally suppressed only in early 1941. According to S. Polyakov, there was no case in which a grave of a Soviet regime leader became a *mazar*. The *mazar*s were addressed with various requests, mainly about the curing of diseases, barrenness, the evil eye, and the like.[2] In Uzbekistan, Tadzhikistan, and Kazakhstan, especially revered were the graves of Khojas and Sayyids whose families descended from the Prophet Muhammad; in Turkmenia, the graves of the representatives of the "six sacred tribes" and the graves of the Turas, descendants of the Genghisides and also of the heads of the Dervish orders,

1. A. V. Malashenko, "Novy politichesky start Islama" [The 1980s: The new political beginning of Islam] *Oriens* (Moscow) no. 5, p. 54:80-e (1991).

2. S. P. Polyakov, "Tradicionaliam v sovremenom sredneaziatskom obscestve" [Traditionalism, the contemporary Central Asian society] (Moscow, 1989), p.75.

which are especially numerous in Samarkand, are held in special esteem. According to expedition data, the *mazar* shaykhs are usually children of mullas in North Tadzhikistan and members of the "sacred tribes" in Turkmenia; in Uzbekistan, Kazakhstan, and some areas of Tadzhikistan, they are representatives of the Khoja and Sayyid families.[3]

The 1970s and 1980s saw the rapid enhancement of the role of religion in the Islamic republics of the USSR as a result of greater access to information, the deepening of crisis in the society, and the influence of the Islamic revolution in Iran. The Islamic *jihad* of the Afghan opposition served as a strong impetus to that process in the southern part of the USSR, along with the increasing resistance to the Soviet presence in Afghanistan. As was stated at a symposium on Islam in Moscow, by the mid-1980s there were about 11,000 members of Sufi orders in the southern areas of the USSR.

PERESTROIKA AS CATALYST

With the beginning of *perestroika*, an Islamic movement emerged in the Soviet Muslim areas that started under the slogans of religious enlightenment, spreading religious culture among the Muslim peoples of the USSR, building and establishing Islamic traditions, and so forth. The ideas of Islamic enlightenment were quite rapidly adopted by various political forces, well aware that they were a reliable means of political mobilization. Believers expressed dissatisfaction with Party and state con-

3. Ibid., p. 76.

trol of religious communities and demanded the abolition of the system of councils and the renovation of the official clergy. The supreme Mufti of Central Asia and Kazakhstan, Shamsuddin Babakhan, was accused of godlessness and violation of Islamic laws and removed from his post. The process of splitting communities into smaller units began when they refused to be controlled by large regional religious boards. The democratic processes that started in the country as a whole opened the way to rapidly growing religious activity, which, under the conditions of greater openness and expansion of the Soviet Union's international links, won the support of the leading centers of the Muslim world, which began to help Soviet Muslims.

Alongside the trend of purely cultural enlightenment, the tendency of the politicization of Islam emerged in the USSR's Muslim areas in the mid-1980s. For instance, Tadzhikistan witnessed the call to set up an Islamic state. Some participants in the protest demonstrations in various republics voiced Islamic slogans.

Three main blocs of political forces gradually formed in the Muslim republics: former leaders of the Communist parties and the state apparatus, who changed their political face; new democratic parties and movements; and Islamic fundamentalists. Such movements as the Uzbek Birlik or Tadzhik Rastodhez were secular, but the advocates of the Islamic identity of the republics participated in them.

It is thought that the Islamicist movement emerged in Uzbekistan and Tadzhikistan as far back as the

1970s among the unofficial clergy. Its followers become known as Wahhabites; although they are not true followers of Muhammad ibn 'Abd al-Wahhab, they are akin to the Arabian Wahhabites because of their religious rigorism and ascetic attitude to life. In Tadzhikistan, the Islamicists found their main support in the less developed areas of the South; prominent positions in the Party and state apparatus were, as a rule, held by persons hailing from the North. In Uzbekistan, the main support was in the Ferghana Valley, known as the main agricultural area of the republic. The comparison of the data on the composition of the Islamic groups in the Ferghana Valley and a number of the Middle East countries yields a substantial difference. In Egypt, where we have concrete data on the composition of such groups, the urban youths—mainly children of migrants from rural areas—form their main social base. In the Ferghana Valley, where Islamic customs and values were preserved over the entire Soviet period, Islamicist groups consist mainly of rural people.

By the late 1980s, young leaders of the Islamicist movement became noticeably active. They accused the official clergy of conformism, collaboration, self-interest, violation of Islamic principles, and so on. In Tadzhikistan, several hundred inhabitants of Kulab, Kurgan-Tube, and Dushanbe attempted to enter the congress of Muslims of Central Asia and Kazakhstan, convened in March 1989.[4] At the same time, they tried repeatedly to depose the imams in the Dushanbe Karamirshiko mosque and the Kulab mosque.

Official Muslim clergy were against the politicization of Islam, rejecting the idea of establishing political parties on an Islamic basis. Evidently, this stand was prompted by the traditional loyalty of that clergy to the authorities and the apprehension that such a step might put unofficial mullas at the head of the Islamic movement. Naturally, the authorities, both in the republics and at the center, did not approve of this idea. Nevertheless, on 9 June 1990, a congress of the representatives of the Muslim communities of the country was convened in Astrakhan, Russia. It declared the establishment of the Islamic Revival Party (IRP) and adopted its platform and constitution. These documents of the party, as well as the speeches of its leaders, were of a moderate tenor, supporting the idea of equality of all religions and the readiness to collaborate with the state structures and other parties.

Among other things, the platform of the party stated that it

defends Islam from the attacks of its adversaries . . . advocates equality between believers and nonbelievers . . . demands an end to the propaganda of atheism . . . favors the enhancement of the role of women in families, believing that a woman is in the first place the mother of her children, and only afterward an industrial worker, public figure, etc. The society must provide them with the opportunity for education and all-round development, but the main thing is to give them real opportunity to be the keepers of the family hearth.[5]

4. *Grajdanskie politicheskie dvijeniya v Tadjikistane* [Civil political movements in Tadzhikistan, 1989-March 1990] (Dushanbe, 1990), p. 5.

5. *Komsomolec tadjikistana* (Dushanbe), 24 Nov. 1990.

The official clergy disapproved of the establishment of an Islamic party. The head of the Central Asia Muslims, Mufti Mohammed Sadik Mohammed Yusuf, declared: "We believe that Islam is a party in itself, having already existed for over 1400 years. We have a Constitution in the Quran and a platform in the Sunna of our Prophet. Moreover, Islam is above all parties."[6]

The authorities in Tadzhikistan, referring to the February 1990 riots in Dushanbe, prohibited the activity of the new party; the Tadzhik Kaziyat prohibited the leaders of the mosque from taking part in the activities of any political parties. But in the autumn of 1991, the IRP nevertheless held its constituent regional conference in the village of Chortut, near the capital of the republic. It formed the Tadzhik branch of the party, apparently with the aim of avoiding accusations of violating the ban. Only after the failure of the August 1991 putsch in Moscow did the republican parliament cancel the ban, and at the congress of the branch in the autumn of 1991 the decision for full independence of the Tadzhikistan party from the all-Union party was adopted.

The members of the branch party discussed the problem of the extent to which the Islamic movement should take into account the national interests of the Muslim peoples of the Soviet Union. The members of Turkic origin advocated the unity of interests of all Muslims. Thus one of the leaders of the party in Moscow, Gheidar Jamal, in his interview on Radio Liberty on 18 January 1991, stated, "Uzbekistan and Tadzhiki-

stan are the result of national partition and the undermining of integration principles in Central Asia. . . . Belonging to the Muslim world without boundaries is more essential than the national identity." Among Tadzhiks, a little apprehensive of the predominance of Turkic leaders, the tendency of the synthesis with national ideas prevails along with some pan-Iranian feelings. In that sense, the establishment of the Tadzhik IRP was in line with the aspirations of Tadzhik Islamicists.

In a short time, the IRP proved able to win some influence in a number of areas of Tadzhikistan, Uzbekistan, and other republics of the USSR. Its total membership was estimated to be 60,000 in early 1991, and after the disintegration of the USSR in December 1991, its membership increased. According to expert opinion, it enjoys the strongest positions in the south of Tadzhikistan. The election campaign showed that in Tadzhikistan, the IRP may be ahead of the democratic movement due to the weakness of the national intelligentsia, low political culture, and contradictions between different areas of the republic. In Uzbekistan, where democratic traditions are much stronger, Islamicists have as yet been unable to win such positions.

The Islamic Party of Turkestan, established in the Turkic republics, combines pan-Turkic nationalist and Islamicist ideas. As yet, that party has not won strong support in these republics, which have a mainly Turkish orientation, while Turkey is not interested in the encouragement of the Islamicist forces. At the same time, neither the Saudi Arabian nor

6. *Izvestiya* (Moscow), 14 Dec. 1990.

the Iranian Islamicists would like to encourage pan-Turkic aspirations. The former prefers mainly the support of purely Islamic forces. The latter, comprising Azerbaijani Shiites, resists the development of nationalist sentiments in Turkestan, for they may affect the population of Iranian Azerbaijan as well as the ethnically close Tadzhiks. The leaders of the Tadzhik IRP regard the activities of the Islamic Party of Turkestan with animosity.

The failure of the August 1991 putsch in the USSR opened up new opportunities for the democratic movement. In 1991, the democratic and Islamicist forces of the Islamic areas tried to make their election platforms more alike: the Islamicists strove to win over the democratically minded electorate and the democrats tried to make use of the religious sentiments of the population. Thus the Democratic Erk Party, of Uzbekistan, made an appeal to the ideas of Islamic revival. In Tadzhikistan, democrats and Islamicists acted jointly against the government and in August 1991 forced the Chairman of the Supreme Soviet, K. Mahkamov, to retire.

EXPLOSION IN TASHKENT

In January 1992, the establishment of the Islamic Democratic Party of Russia was announced in Moscow, but the number of its adherents is very small. In September 1991, before the presidential election in Tadzhikistan, the IRP of that republic decided to support the candidate of the democratic forces, D. Khudonazarov. Not only did their support not help the candidate, but, in the experts' view, it deprived him of the votes of those apprehensive of the prospect of an Islamic state of the Iranian kind. Assessing the situation, P. Mullojanov writes,

Democrats hoped that with the help of the IRP and the Kaziyat of the republic it would be possible to organize truly mass manifestations and meetings which would create a critical situation for the ruling structures. The Islamicists realized that if democrats were not with them in the square, the authorities would not hesitate to employ force. Using the democrats as their shield, they ensured the neutrality of the Center, the army, and the Ministry of the Interior. Thus, the alliance of democratic organizations and the IRP is rather a forced step prompted by special circumstances.[7]

In some places there was a tendency toward cooperation between the Islamicist leaders and the official clergy. But on the whole, the movement to discredit the official mullas continued. Thus, after returning from their pilgrimage to Mecca in 1991, some imams of Tashkent and the Tashkent region, in Uzbekistan, came out against Mufti Mohammed Yusuf, accusing him of violating Islamic norms and, among other things, of selling Qurans received as a gift of Saudi Arabia to the community. Soon afterward, the imams announced that they did not recognize the Mufti's power as the head of the Religious Board and declared their independence. The Mufti could no longer preach in mosques where the imams served, though his *fatwa*s were recognized. By the end of the

7. P. Mullojanov, "Islam i politika v Tadjikistane: Rukopis" [Islam and politics in Tadzhikistan: A manuscript], n.d., p. 29.

year, the relations between a part of the Muslim clergy of Uzbekistan and the Mufti and his adherents had become worse. In January 1992, the information agencies in Moscow announced the "removal of the Mufti by the Islamic leaders of the republic," but the Mufti himself denied the news.

The creation of independent states in the place of former republics, following the disintegration of the Soviet Union, and the beginning of radical economic reforms aggravated the internal situation in Muslim regions, as everywhere else. On 16 January 1992, the day of the announced liberalization of prices in Uzbekistan, there was a clash on the campus of the University of Tashkent between students who rebelled against the government and the internal forces. Finding themselves among the least provided-for of the population strata with the liberalization of prices, the Tashkent student community exploded. The students destroyed and put fire to several objects. As a result, one student died and dozens of people were wounded, including students and members of the internal forces. The youths' newspaper, *Turkestan*, produced two versions of the event. According to one, reported also by the official sources of information, "because of the price rise, students went out into the streets to take part in a meeting." The other version initially stated, "It can be the continuation of the previous, specially organized, bloody events."[8] After a few days, the President of Uzbekistan, I. Kerimov, actually repeated the second version, pointing out that students were

drawn into the political struggle. Both the democratic forces of Uzbekistan and Islamic forces were accused of participating in the riots. The students attending meetings handed their demands to the governmental commission headed by the Prime Minister, A. Mutalov, and vacations were announced early in many higher schools, but the students would not calm down.

The Presidium of the Uzbekistan Supreme Soviet mentioned in their statement that those who were behind the disturbances "are not content with our policy of national harmony. They would like very much to sow discord among people, to spread dissension, to occupy places in the power structures for the performance of their dirty deeds on an even greater scale."[9]

SECULAR NATIONALISM

Alongside the growth of an Islamic movement in the Muslim areas there is a developing secular nationalist movement. On the very eve of the Alma-Ata meeting of the leaders of 11 states of the former USSR, at which the declaration on the creation of the Commonwealth of Independent States was adopted, a special Turkic Assembly was brought to a close. It had been held on 18-20 December 1991, and delegations from the Turkic areas of the Russian Federation and a number of republics took part in it. The main issue discussed at the Assembly was the possibility of the establishment of Turkestan, a state uniting republics with Turkic populations.

8. *Turkestan* (Tashkent), 17 Jan. 1992.

9. *Komsomolskaya pravda*, 21 Jan. 1992.

The necessity of setting up a united Turkic state was the subject of speeches by the representatives of Kazakhstan, Azerbaijan, and Tatarstan. No delegation represented the will of its entire people, nor had any a mandate for adopting decisions on the main issue. Delegates were also unable to decide on the question of the borders of the Turkic state, but they formed branches of the Assembly in the Turkic regions of the former USSR—the Black Sea; Transcaucasus-Caucasus, with Baku as its center; Kazakh; and Central Asia. In addition, the formation of Turkic regions in the territory of the Russian Federation—the Urals, Yakut, and South Siberia—was announced.

It is significant that it was planned to unite regions based exclusively on ethnicity, irrespective of religion, in the proposed Turkic Commonwealth. The Yakuts and Turks of South Siberia, for example, do not practice Islam and are either Buddhist or Christian. In addition, rather than being drawn to their Turkic brothers in Central Asia and Transcaucasia, some gravitate toward Russia, others toward Mongolia. Despite those circumstances and the fact that there are many grave differences between the Turkic peoples, delegates were able to set up a Coordination Council of the Turkic Assembly. It was composed of representatives from all the regions and was to be in charge of relations between them so as to perform some of the functions of a common Turkic body.

The delegates agreed that all Turkic peoples should have one and the same alphabet. Since by then the Turkic peoples of the former Union had already used the same alphabet system for a long time, one based on the Cyrillic alphabet, it was clear that they were not content with it. The secular pan-Turkic orientation of the Assembly was particularly forceful in the decision adopted on that issue and proposed a transfer to the Latin alphabet, but one with 34 letters, following the model of Turkey. This means that political forces participating in the Assembly see Turkic unity not only as a union of all Turks of the former USSR but as a union with Turks living abroad. Moreover, it is evident that this union would be oriented toward Turkey as its leader. But there are no grounds to say that pan-Turkic organizations of Turkey itself took any part in these efforts. These organizations have not up to now enjoyed any support from Turkey's population. Delegates also agreed to set up a united Institute of Common Turkic Problems.

Secular or pro-Turkist concepts of the reform of the alphabet differ from the idea of going back to the Arabic written language. In the case of Muslim peoples, a return to written Arabic would mean a return to their former culture, but using written Arabic would be completely unacceptable to non-Muslim peoples. Though pan-Turkic aspirations do not reflect the views of the majority, they arouse the apprehensions of the non-Turkic peoples of Transcaucasia and also of Tadzhikistan.

Though official authorities in Kazakhstan and the Central Asian and Transcaucasian republics had no direct connection with the Assembly, some observers nevertheless noted their possible interest in the Assembly, held so soon after Russia, Ukraine, and Byelorussia announced in Minsk the creation of the Commonwealth of Independent States. In a way, it reflected the anxiety felt then by the leaders of the states of the southern belt of the former USSR. It was at that time that they decided to join the Commonwealth but expressed apprehensions about not being full-fledged founders of the Commonwealth but simply joining the states of Central Asia and Kazakhstan. The Alma-Ata meeting dispelled their doubts and reassured the political circles of these states, which were especially satisfied with the choice of Alma-Ata as the place to hold such an important meeting.

But other apprehensions were nevertheless expressed at the Turkic Assembly. A number of delegates said that the proposed alliance should defend the Turkic and Muslim world against possible expansion on the part of Russia. As the chairman of the Kazakh National Democratic Party, Hasan Hajiahmetov, stated, "The situation in Russia is very tense and unstable. It is not yet known what turn events in Moscow may take. At any moment the chauvinist Zhirinovsky or others like him may come to power. So here we must be prepared to resist possible intervention."

Shortly before the Assembly, another happening took place in Alma-Ata, affecting the tempestuous political history of the country in late 1991. On 13 December, the day of the Friday prayer, the opposition convened the Majlis of the Islamic community of the city in Alma-Ata. Leaders of the Alash Party of National Independence of Kazakhstan acted as the conveners. Declaring freedom of enterprise, individual rights, freedom of religious belief, and equality of nations since 1990, the party had been publishing its own newspaper under the slogan of "Turkism is our body, Islam is our spirit." The Majlis adopted the decision to depose the Mufti or head of the Muslim Religious Board of Kazakhstan, Ratbek Nysanbai-uly, for numerous violations of the *shari'a*. Members of the opposition called the Mufti a KGB agent, and the Majlis formed a working presidium to hold new democratic elections for the position of Mufti.

After that, seven men burst into the office of Nysanbai-uly and demanded that he resign because the people no longer trusted him. The Mufti, who was also a deputy in the Kazakh Parliament, refused to obey and was tied and severely beaten. Later it was discovered that his right arm and collarbone had been broken. While beating the Mufti, his assailants kept saying, "We have here in Kazakhstan two traitors: the President and Nysanbai-uly, a KGB agent." They also beat the bookkeeper of the mosque and took away his keys. The workrooms were searched.

Militia soon set the Mufti free, but the assailants captured the mosque and refused to leave it. The blockade of the mosque lasted from 13 to 15 December. Only on 15 December did a militia detachment for special purposes clear the mosque, detaining 41 persons, including several activists of the Alash Party. The chairman of the Alash Party, Aren Atabek, denied beating the Mufti, saying that the intervention by the militia detachment was similar to the suppression by the authorities of the Alma-Ata youth disturbances in 1986, which later was called unlawful by the new authorities of Kazakhstan. For his part, Mufti Nyusanbai-uly condemned the hooligans, saying that in his opinion they were incited by the mullas "who had been ousted from mosques for violations of the *shari'a* canons and embezzlement of money." Thus the Mufti clearly wanted to make the conflict look like a clash between the legitimate leadership of the community and the transgressors of law.

But representatives of the authorities gave the conflict a political interpretation. Kazakhstan's Attorney General Tukakbayev was confident that the reason for the attack against the Mufti was "the influence of Islamic fundamentalists." In his opinion, "many do not like the Mufti's attitude of being against the establishment of Islamic parties." Though there were no grounds for Tuyak-bayev to speak about the ban of the Alash Party, he hinted about such a possibility: it would be possible to speak about the ban, if actions of that kind were its programmatic tasks, said the Attorney General.[10]

Islamic factors also played a prominent part during the crisis in the Chechen republic, a part of the Russian Federation, which occurred in the autumn of 1991. President Dudayev made active use of Islamic slogans. Pathological anatomical postmortems were prohibited in the republic, and men were forbidden to work as gynecologists.

10. *Commersant* (Moscow), 16-23 Dec. 1991, no. 49, p. 18.

CONCLUSION

Assessing the situation as a whole, one should point out the following. First, Islam as the symbol of national identity, of the return to the original culture, became extremely popular among the peoples of the former USSR. Second, Islam is used as a means of political mobilization by various political forces, democratic, conservative, and nationalist. Third, the Islamicist movement as such still prefers to appeal to democratic or nationalist ideas. This last factor is due to an awareness of the sentiments of the masses of the population, who, in most Muslim areas today, are not ready to support the idea of an Islamic state in its direct form. But the Islamicist movement gains in impetus. Should present economic difficulties become more aggravated or the economic program of the authorities in the Muslim republics fail, the movement may have a good chance of success, particularly where the democratic alternative is weak.

It is not clear to what extent Islamic and nationalist trends will be combined in political life. In some situations they may unite, and this will make it possible for movements acting in concert with existing moods to become powerful; in other circumstances, they will be prone to act against each other. Nor is it clear what the result of the struggle within the Muslim clergy will be. If the struggle leads to a drastic renewal of the body of mullas and to the unification of the official and nonofficial leaders of the community, that also will enhance the political chances of the Islamicists. But it is hardly probable that, in the extremely complicated economic conditions existing in all the republics of the former USSR, Islamicist forces would be able to suggest an alternative capable of solving the crisis. Nevertheless, in the near future Islam and political groups guided by Islamic principles are, in all events, sure to remain one of the most influential forces in the region.

ANNALS, *AAPSS*, 524, November 1992

An African Case Study of Political Islam: Nigeria

By JOHN HUNWICK

ABSTRACT: Since the early nineteenth century, when Uthman b. Fudi established an Islamic state in northern Nigeria, there has been a close symbiosis between religion and political power. Since independence in 1960, the issue of regional or ethnic power sharing in Nigeria has shifted to a contest between Muslims and Christians, with the part-Muslim, part-Christian Yoruba of the southwest helping to hold the balance. Since the 1960s, Saudi Arabia has promoted its own austere interpretation of Islam, to the discomfort of the Sufi groups. More recently, Iran has been a model for younger militant Muslims. Calls by Nigerian Muslims for an Islamic state, and wider application of *shari'a* law, as well as the question of Nigeria's membership in the Organization of Islamic Conference have aroused the antagonism of Christians. Religious issues were behind several outbreaks of violence in the 1980s, some of which threatened the integrity of the Nigerian state.

John Hunwick has his B.A. and Ph.D. from the School of Oriental and African Studies, London. In 1981, after twenty years of teaching in Africa—in the Sudan, Nigeria, Ghana, and Egypt—he was appointed professor of African history and professor of religion (Islam) at Northwestern University. He is author of Shari'a in Songhay *(1985) and editor of* Religion and National Integration in Africa: Islam, Christianity and Politics in the Sudan and Nigeria *(1992).*

IN late 1991, a senior analyst of the Bush administration reviewing the current political situation in Africa was reported as saying that the most worrisome trend for policymakers was what he called " 'the march of Islamic fundamentalism.' "[1] This was shortly before elections in Algeria in which the Islamic Salvation Front, campaigning under the slogan "No laws. No constitution. Only the laws of God and the Quran" gained victory in the first round of national legislative elections. The analyst's remarks also came at the end of a decade in which various external forces have attempted to use sub-Saharan Africa as a theater for the implementation of political agendas inspired by or exploiting the emotive appeal of Islam. Using an eccentric blend of socialism, Islam, and Arabism, Libya's Muammar Qadhdhafi has wooed several African governments—notably Gabon, whose president, Omar Bongo, converted to Islam; the Central African Republic, whose former president Bokassa briefly adopted Islam; and Ghana—while at the same time supporting forces working for the overthrow of others, such as Senegal, Niger, and Chad. Saudi Arabia has poured untold sums of money into sub-Saharan Africa for the propagation of its own austere brand of Islam. Iraq before the gulf war used the appeal of both Islamic ideals and Arab nationalism in Mauritania and the Sudan to further its political ambitions. More recently, Iran, while rebuilding its bridges to the West, has begun to seek friends and influence in Africa and perhaps to use the Sudan for the training of Islamic militants.

The Sudan in the 1980s under various governments, but frequently ideologically guided by Dr. Hasan al-Turabi, leader of the National Islamic Front, has flirted with each of these external forces in turn. Despite an intractable civil war and virtual economic collapse, it presents itself as a role model for the establishment of Islamic states in Africa and is not without its admirers. Nigeria, launching its third attempt at democratic politics in 1992, is emerging from a decade of verbal and physical confrontation between Muslims and Christians, shrill debates over the place of *shari'a* (Islamic law) within the national legal framework, and several outbreaks of murderous violence sparked off by members of a Muslim underclass for whom the state had no meaning. As the most populous state in Africa and the one with the largest Muslim population, Nigeria has great diplomatic and cultural influence in Africa and is potentially the continent's economic giant. Both for these reasons and because of the way in which Nigeria illustrates so many of the problems associated with Muslim reassertion within a religiously diverse society, this article will focus on the relationship of Islam to politics, in the broad sense, within Nigeria since independence.

HISTORICAL BACKGROUND

Islam is no stranger to the political process in West Africa. Nearly a thou-

1. See Barbara Crossette, "U.S. Aide Calls Muslim Militants' Concern to World," *New York Times*, 1 Jan. 1992.

sand years ago, Islam was a factor in political change in the kingdom of Takrur on the banks of the river Senegal and a little later in Ancient Ghana and in the kingdom of Kanem near Lake Chad. Under the influence of North African Muslim merchants and itinerant teachers and preachers, many rulers and their courts adopted Islam between the eleventh and the sixteenth centuries, though they generally preserved much of their more ancient non-Islamic social and political praxis. However, rulers such as Mansa Musa of Mali (1312-37), Askiya al-Hajj Muhammad of Songhay (1493-1528), and Mai Idris Aloma of Borno (1564-96) made ceremonial pilgrimages to Mecca and engaged in diplomatic exchanges with various rulers of Morocco and, in the last case, also with the Ottoman sultan.

Trans-Saharan trade and the pilgrimage to Mecca provided continuing avenues of contact between the more or less Islamized kingdoms of West Africa and the heartlands of Islam in North Africa and the Middle East. Political as well as theological and mystical ideas passed along these conduits, and the eighteenth and nineteenth centuries saw a number of attempts—some more successful than others—to establish Islamic states in the area. One of the most successful of these was in the area of what is now northern Nigeria in the early nineteenth century. In 1804, a Fulani scholar and mystic, Shaykh Uthman b. Fudi, led a "withdrawal" (*hijra*) of his followers from the Hausa state of Gobir in northwestern Nigeria, established his own commu-

nity as the touchstone of true Islam, and declared a *jihad* first against Gobir and later against all the other Hausa states whose rulers he proclaimed "unbelievers" (*kuffar*). His efforts led to the unification of the Hausa states of northern Nigeria and the incorporation, more or less loosely, within the new Islamic state of other, non-Hausa lands and various polities to the north and west of Hausaland in what is now the republic of Niger.

Some areas of northern Nigeria, however, remained beyond the pale of this new Islamic state. Principal among these was the ancient Muslim kingdom of Borno in the northeast, which successfully defeated attempts by local Fulani to take control in the name of Shaykh Uthman. Other areas such as the uplands of the central plateau and much of what is loosely called the "Middle Belt," the bulk of whose inhabitants were not Muslims, also remained outside the grasp of the new Islamic state, whose capital was established at Sokoto. Little attempt was made to incorporate them during the nineteenth century; instead, they were exploited as reservoirs for slaves for internal use within the Sokoto state and for export to North Africa.

This new state, however, was not a unitary state. The former polities that were incorporated within it, such as Kano, Katsina, Zaria, Nupe, and Ilorin, retained their individual identities, though now they were governed by mainly Fulani dynasties descended from local warriors or scholars who were given flags and authority to rule by Shaykh Uthman.

These emirs, as they were now called, governed their territories with a large measure of autonomy, despite occasional Sokoto interference in succession, and demonstrated their loyalty to the caliphs of Sokoto by sending twice-yearly tribute.

This federal structure proved to be an ideal vehicle for the colonial policy of indirect rule introduced by Lord Lugard after the British conquest of northern Nigeria in 1902-3. Though controlled by British residents and though their power to enforce law was severely curtailed, the emirs still retained the respect, even the devotion, of their subjects down to Nigerian independence in 1960. Since then, their power and prestige have suffered considerable attrition at the hands of various federal governments, civil and military—a process aided by the creation and multiplication of states within the federation since 1967.

POSTINDEPENDENCE NIGERIA

When Nigeria became independent on 1 October 1960, it had an estimated population of some 50 million, of whom close to half were Muslims. It was a federal state with three regions—North, West, and East—and a political system at both the regional and federal levels modeled on the British parliamentary system. Of the three regions, the North was by far the largest in area, occupying some two-thirds of the land mass. Although its total population was only slightly greater than the combined total of the other two regions, it contained about two-thirds of the total Muslim population. Its Muslim pop-

ulation was distributed unevenly, however, seven provinces having Muslim majorities and five having a minority of Muslims.[2]

It would, of course, be convenient if one could give comparative figures for the present time. Unfortunately, none is available. Although a national census was taken in late 1991, it was decided that no data should be gathered on religious affiliation. The last figures we have that give such a breakdown are those of 1963, which show a total population of 55 million, of whom 49 percent were said to be Muslims, 34 percent Christians, and 17 percent animists.[3] While the percentage of animists has almost certainly decreased dramatically in the intervening period, due to conversion campaigns by both Muslims and Christians, it is not possible to say which faith has gained more converts, nor are figures available that might correlate birthrate with religion.[4]

This review of population statistics is a necessary prelude to what follows inasmuch as the fundamental political problem that has plagued Nigeria since independence has been how to share national wealth and

2. See John N. Paden, *Religion and Political Culture in Kano* (Berkeley: University of California Press, 1973), tab. 3, p. 44. Apart from a small number of converts to the Ahmadiyya sect, all Nigerian Muslims are Sunnites of the Maliki school.

3. Paden, *Religion and Political Culture.* The figures announced for the 1991 census show a total population of 88.5 million.

4. See further Jibrin Ibrahim, "The Politics of Religion in Nigeria: The Parameters of the 1987 Crisis in Kaduna State," *Review of African Political Economy*, 45-46:78 (1989), where attention is also drawn to the dramatic gains of Christianity vis-à-vis animism in the period 1931-63.

access to education, employment opportunities, and political office in a country of multiple ethnic identities and many and diverse regional and local loyalties overlaid by religious loyalties to Islam or Christianity. This has led to what have been termed "prebendal politics" in which individual and group access to education, employment opportunities, and the national wealth was closely linked to the political ascendancy of the political party or ethnic group of those who so benefited.[5] During periods of civilian rule—October 1960 to January 1966, and October 1979 to December 1983—dominance at the federal level, which was in the hands of essentially northern-based Muslim-led parties, was considered to be the key to economic development, jobs, and educational opportunity among the constituencies that voted the politicians into power. For example, at independence the Northern Region, by comparison with the Eastern and Western regions, was economically underdeveloped, virtually devoid of university-trained personnel, and grossly underrepresented in federal ministries and institutions. The regional prime minister, Alhaji Sir Ahmadu Bello, Sardauna of Sokoto, had already begun to take steps within his own region to "northernize" the regional civil service; in the early 1960s the federal government, dominated by the Northern People's Congress (NPC) and led by Sir Abubakar Tafawa Balewa, began to correct the regional imbalance in the federal civil service, often filling po-

sitions with northerners who were less qualified than their southern counterparts.[6] In the nature of things, a high proportion of these new appointees were Muslims.

During the First Republic (1960-66), the struggle for power at the center was essentially between the three regions (a fourth, the Midwest, was created out of the former Western Region in 1963), the politics of each of which was dominated by a single large ethnic group and a regional-based party: in the North by the Hausa and the NPC, in the East by the Igbo and the National Council of Nigerian Citizens and in the West by the Yoruba and the Action Group, though the National Council of Nigerian Citizens initially also had some strength there, too. Although the Eastern and Western—and Midwestern—regions in some sense viewed themselves as constituting the south as opposed to the north— the uproar over the 1963 census was about population balance between north and south—the controversy over power was never pitched in explicitly religious terms. On the one hand, the West was religiously divided with almost as many Muslims as Christians; on the other, the dominant party in the North, the NPC, had as its slogan "One North, One People," despite a 30 percent non-Muslim minority. There is little doubt, however, that the premier, Sir

5. See Richard Joseph, *Democracy and Prebendal Politics in Nigeria* (New York: Cambridge University Press, 1987).

6. Taylor Cole, "Bureaucracy in Transition," in *The Nigerian Political Scene*, ed. Robert O. Tilman and Taylor Cole (Durham, NC: Duke University Press, 1962), p. 109. A regional quota system for recruitment of army officers was also established in which 50 percent of the places were reserved for candidates of northern origin.

Ahmadu Bello, at least latterly, looked forward to an eventual coincidence of northernness with Islam. Hence in 1963-64 he undertook conversion campaigns among the animists of the Middle Belt area and among the Maguzawa, who are non-Muslim Hausa, and hoped to extend these campaigns to other areas of Nigeria.[7]

The power struggle in the civilian realm was superseded in 1966 by a similar one in the military realm. First, a coup brought an Igbo-led military regime to power, and seven months later a second coup thrust a northern—but Christian—officer, Lieutenant Colonel (later General) Yakubu Gowon, into the headship of the Nigerian state. In May 1967, in an attempt to forestall the secession of the Eastern Region, Gowon replaced the four regions composing the federation with 12 states, thus defusing power and allowing ethnic groups other than the "big three" a greater share in their own governance. Since then subsequent decrees by military governments have increased the number of states to a current total of 30 plus a federal territory around the new capital, Abuja. The old North thus disappeared, though its shadow lingered for a decade longer, and with it disappeared what many southerners had perceived as a threat of northern—Muslim—domination.

Civil war, however, was not averted, and between July 1967 and January 1970 a federal army of very mixed ethnic and religious complex-

7. See John N. Paden, *Ahmadu Bello, Sardauna of Sokoto* (London: Hodder & Stoughton, 1986), pp. 566-78; Ibrahim, "Politics of Religion."

ion fought its way into the secessionist Republic of Biafra; this republic was originally the entire old Eastern Region, but finally only the Igbo heartlands. Biafran war propaganda liked to paint the federal attack on it as an Islamic *jihad* against embattled Christians, but the absurdity of this claim was patent. In fact, the war was about retaining a Nigerian federation—very much in the interest of the landlocked Muslim majority states and ethnic minorities in all areas—and federal control over the prime economic asset, oil, of which the former Eastern Region had an abundance.

These events—military rule, civil war, and the abolition of hugely powerful regions in favor of more and weaker states—had a number of consequences. The crushing of secession made it clear that hiving off was not an option no matter how great the grievance. The creation of states, while it diffused some political energies, in the end only underlined the importance of the federal center. The armed forces—and we should remember that the much smaller navy and air force have also shared in government along with the army—who phased themselves out of power in 1979 demonstrated that they were no worse at governing than civilians and were ready to step in again, as they did in 1984. The diffusion of political energy and the absence of normal political life under military rule, however, were contributory factors in the politicization of religion, or, rather, the use of religion as a tool for creating a political constituency. The emergence of a small very wealthy class and the general impoverishment of the urban masses, resultant upon the oil boom of the mid-1970s followed by a sudden slump in the 1980s, created discontent and frustration, and Nigerians—both Muslims and Christians—turned to religion both as a refuge and as a political weapon.

THE *SHARI'A* LAW ISSUE

The first indications that religion might begin to play a major role in national political life came during the 1977 debates in the newly created Constituent Assembly on the draft constitution for the Second Republic. The issue was the creation of a Federal Shari'a Court of Appeal which could hear appeals from state Shari'a Courts of Appeal rather than sending them directly to the Supreme Court of Nigeria. Before the creation of states in 1967, *shari'a* cases, which were confined essentially to matters of personal status, could be sent on appeal to a Northern Region Shari'a Court of Appeal. In other areas of the country, there were neither *shari'a* courts nor Shari'a Courts of Appeal.

The proposal to create a Federal Shari'a Court of Appeal unleashed a storm of protest from Christian members of the assembly who claimed that this privileged Islamic law, created a dual system of law in the country, and opened the door for the creeping Islamization of the Nigerian state. Muslim members countered that the application of *shari'a* lay at the core of their lives as Muslims and to deny them the exercise of the *shari'a* rights to the highest level was discrimination against them and an attack on Islam. In the end, a compro-

mise was fashioned with the support of Yoruba Muslim members—reflecting traditional Yoruba tolerance in religious matters—under which there would be within the Federal Court of Appeal a panel of three judges "versed in Islamic law" who would decide cases sent up by a state Shari'a Court of Appeal.[8]

Despite the dissatisfaction at such a compromise expressed by many Muslim members from northern states, the then head of state, General Olusegun Obasanjo, accepted the amendment and had it written into the constitution. The issue did not, however, die there. It surfaced again with equal or greater passion in similar debates over a constitution for the Third Republic in 1989. This time the then—and current—head of state, General Ibrahim Babangida, simply foreclosed debate on the issue, and the constitution for the Third Republic, published on 3 May 1989, shows no change on this matter from its predecessor. There is little doubt that this issue will continue to surface. Indeed, it would be no surprise if some states with Muslim majorities eventually seek to arrogate to themselves the right to impose *shari'a* as the only form of law within their territories. The imposition of *shari'a* has been at the cutting edge of all recent debates about the Islamic state, whether in Pakistan, Iran, the Sudan, or, now, in Algeria, where the Islamic Salvation Front has made implementation of *shari'a* the cornerstone of its program.

8. On this issue, see David D. Laitin, "The Sharia Debate and the Origins of Nigeria's Second Republic," *Journal of Modern African Studies*, 20(3):411-30 (1982).

While the *shari'a* debate of 1977 first brought Muslim-Christian antagonism into sharp focus, it was the issue of Nigeria's membership in the Organization of Islamic Conference (OIC) in 1986 that caused Nigerian Christians to suggest there was a conspiracy to turn Nigeria into an Islamic state—an issue on which many have since become virtually paranoid. Nigeria had long been an observer at OIC meetings, but suddenly it was rumored that Nigeria had become a full member. Christians argued that the OIC was more than a club of friendly states that mutually aided one another in the economic sphere; rather, it was an organization for the promotion of Islam that required member countries to be headed by Muslims and encouraged movement toward the implementation of Islamic legal and social norms. The brouhaha created was very considerable. The government set up a committee to inquire into the matter, but the affair only quieted down when the government announced that the question of Nigeria's membership in the OIC had been shelved. Christians remained suspicious that the full truth had not been disclosed, and they continue nervously to monitor the actions of Muslim organizations for any hint, real or imagined, that Nigeria may be moving toward an Islamic state.

REGISTERS OF
ISLAMIC DISCOURSE

The 1980s witnessed an increasing polarization between Muslims and Christians as symbolic power blocks within Nigeria. In both Muslim and Christian milieus, there were attempts to galvanize and radicalize the faithful and persuade them to give primacy to an identification based on religion. At the same time, there has been considerable infighting among various Muslim groups and an extraordinary multiplication of sects, churches, and charismatic movements among Nigerian Christians.[9] There has also been a sustained attack in some Muslim quarters on the idea of the secular state, which one writer described as " 'a child, albeit a bastard, of Christianity . . . [which] has become a sinister but convenient mechanism to blackmail Muslims and impede the progress of Islam.' "[10]

The principal cleavage between the Muslims of the northern states has been between the proponents of an Islamic discourse dominated by strict adherence to the Quran and the *sunna* largely reflecting the reformist teachings of Uthman b. Fudi and the political legacy of the Sokoto Caliphate, on the one hand, and, on the other, those who belong to Sufi *tariqas*—often, misleadingly, called brotherhoods—in particular the Tijaniyya, which has had its strongholds in Kano and Zaria, with important links to the West African Tijani

9. See Rosalind Hackett, ed., *New Religious Movements in Nigeria* (Lewiston, NY: Edwin Mellen Press, 1987). See also Don Ohadike, "Muslim-Christian Conflict and Political Instability in Nigeria," in *Religion and National Integration in Africa: Islam, Christianity and Politics in the Sudan and Nigeria*, ed. John O. Hunwick (Evanston, IL: Northwestern University Press, 1992), pp. 101-24.

10. Ibrahim, "Politics of Religion in Nigeria," p. 77, quoting remarks of Ibrahim Suleiman published in the Nigerian *Sunday Triumph*, 24 Apr. 1986.

headquarters in Kaolack, Senegal.[11] The leader of the first tendency is Alhaji Abubakar Gummi, a close associate of the late Sardauna Sir Ahmadu Bello and for many years Grand Kadi of Northern Nigeria. He accompanied the Sardauna on his twice-annual pilgrimages to Saudi Arabia between 1955 and 1965, formed close relations with members of the Saudi ruling family, and imbibed the austere and anti-Sufi interpretation of Islam preached there. These links have ensured him financial support for his cause and in 1988 earned him the King Faisal Prize—a fitting Islamic riposte, so it was seen, to the award of the Nobel Prize for Literature to the non-Muslim Wole Soyinka.

It was Abubakar Gummi who advised the Sardauna in 1962 to establish the Jama'atu Nasril Islam (Group for the Victory of Islam), conceived of as an umbrella organization to promote Muslim interests. After the Sardauna's assassination in 1966, Gummi, though still a functionary of the Jama'atu Nasril Islam, began to attack the *tariqa*s more vociferously. His attacks in fact helped to bring together the Qadiriyya and the Tijaniyya, which had hitherto often been hostile to one another. In 1977, for example, the Kungiyar Jama'ati Ahlis-Sunna was formed as a sort of union of Sufi *tariqas*.[12] Gummi soon began to feel the need for an independent

platform of his own and in particular one upon which he could promote more effectively his Wahhabi views. The result was the emergence of a group that finally became formalized in 1978 as the Jama'at Izalat al-Bid'a wa-Iqamat al-Sunna (Group for the Eradication of Innovation and the Upholding of the Sunna), commonly known as the Izala. In the 1980s, it recruited a large membership, opened branches in many Nigerian towns, and established its own separatist mosques. Using both traditional methods such as open-air preaching, when such was not banned by government, and modern methods of communication such as radio, television—including Quranic exegesis during Ramadan—and recorded audiocassettes, it harangued the Sufis—often in immoderate language—and called on Muslims to follow only the Quran and *sunna*. Gummi himself became notorious for provocative statements including an assertion that no Muslim would join a political party led by a non-Muslim and hence the two-party system announced as the model for democratic politics by General Babangida would become a contest between Islam and Christianity.[13]

Another important Muslim group in Nigeria—more influential than its name would suggest—is the Muslim Students Society. Founded as far back as 1954 in Lagos, its originally Yoruba leadership passed into the hands of northern Nigerian students

11. See Ousmane Kane,"La confrérie 'Tijâniyya Ibrahîmiyya' de Kano et ses liens avec la zâwiya mère de Kaolack," *Islam et sociétés au sud du Sahara*, 3:27-40 (1989).

12. See Muhammad Sani Umar, "Changing Islamic Identity in Nigeria, 1960s-1980s: From Sufism to Anti-Sufism," in *Muslim Identities in Sub-Saharan Africa: Contemporary Transformations in Muslim Societies*, ed.

L. Brenner (London: Christopher Hurst, forthcoming).

13. See Peter Clarke, "Islamic Reform in Contemporary Nigeria: Methods and Aims," *Third World Quarterly*, 10(2):530 (Apr. 1988).

in the 1970s as it entrenched itself and expanded its membership at universities such as Ahmadu Bello University, in Zaria, and Bayero University, in Kano. Its now radical leadership began to call for "total application of the Sharia and its full entrenchment in the constitution."[14]

The overthrow of the Shah and the installation of an Islamic republic in Iran in 1979 had repercussions in Nigeria and in particular among the members of the Muslim Students Society, now led by Aminudeen Abubakar, a student of Gummi. A split occurred, with one wing, the Da'wa, under Abubakar, supported by Saudi and Kuwaiti funds and stressing the fight against "innovations" (bid'a) and with the other, the Umma, taking a stronger line on the implementation of shari'a and the establishment of an Islamic state. The Umma wing itself split again into two groups: one, called Hodaybiya, recalling the Prophet Muhammad's truce with the Meccans, favored an accommodation, at least temporarily, with the secular state, and the other, often referred to as the Yan Shi'a, taking its inspiration directly from events in Iran and from the mujahidin struggle in Afghanistan and preaching a more radical message that brooked no compromise with the ungodly state.[15] Iran has, indeed, been active

in seeking sympathizers to its cause in Nigeria, largely, it would appear, to attempt to neutralize the well-entrenched influence of its archrival Saudi Arabia. Much Iranian Shiite literature in English and Arabic has been distributed, and an Iranian magazine in Hausa, Sakon Islam [The message of Islam] is being published. Given the anti-Sufi stance of the Saudis, it was natural for the Iranians to woo the tariqa leaders as well, and in 1987 a prominent Tijani leader, Dahiru Bauchi, was invited to Iran for the eighth anniversary of the revolution.[16]

RELIGION AND VIOLENCE

None of the foregoing movements is, in and of itself, a real threat to political stability in Nigeria, though each is a breeding ground for the ideologization of various forms of political and social discontent and each represents an attempt to dominate the discourse about what is normative Islam and hence what kind of society Muslims should create for themselves—and perhaps others—in Nigeria. The greatest threat to the state lies in the growing general antagonism between Muslims and Christians, most vividly seen in the frontier areas of northern Nigeria—Kaduna, Plateau, and Bauchi states—where militant Christians—many, especially among university students, "born again"—conduct their own crusades. A Christian preacher,

14. See the press release of the Muslim Students Society of Nigeria, Ahmadu Bello University, Zaria, n.d., in Peter Clarke and Ian Linden, Islam in Modern Nigeria (Mainz-Munchen: Kaiser-Grunewald, 1984), pp. 167-68.

15. On these developments, see the excellent summary in Ousmane Kane, "Mouvements religieux et champ politique au Nigeria septentrional: Le cas de réformisme musulman au Kano," Islam et sociétés au sud du

Sahara, 4:7-24 (1990). The term "Shia" seems to be used loosely in Nigeria, without doctrinal connotations, to stigmatize radical, militant Muslim groups.

16. See Umar, "Changing Islamic Identity."

a convert from Islam,[17] was the focus of rioting in Kaduna State in March 1987 that claimed many lives and caused destruction of millions of dollars' worth of property—in particular, churches and hotels—over a three-day period.[18] While a religious issue was the ostensible cause of this outbreak, the head of state, General Babangida, characterized the riots as "carefully planned and masterminded by evil men who saw the incident in Kafanchan as an opportunity to subvert the Federal Military Government and the Nigerian nation." It was, he said, "the civilian equivalent of an attempted coup d'état organized against the Military Government and the Nigerian nation."[19] He did not elaborate on these sibylline utterances and no "masterminds" were ever indicted.

In 1991, there were other riots that pitted Muslims against Christians with ensuing loss of life. One began near Bauchi over the use of a slaughtering place by adherents of the two religions and spread quickly to Bauchi Town. The other erupted in Kano when foreign evangelists arrived to lead a revival campaign among Christians in the Sabon Gari ("New Town," that is, the strangers' quarter outside the old city), leading to a number of deaths and the burning and looting of property—mainly

that of Igbos—bringing back memories of the 1966 pogroms.[20]

Undoubtedly, the most serious manifestation of Christian resentment of perceived domination by Muslims in Nigeria came with the attempted intra-army coup in April 1990. Fighting, including the use of tanks, raged for some 12 hours in the capital, Lagos, after an army major from the Middle Belt, supported by others from what is now Edo State, set in motion a move to topple the Babangida government and kill its leader—his aide-de-camp was in fact killed in the fighting. In his single broadcast, Major Gideon Orka attacked "those who think it is their birthright to dominate till eternity the political and economic privileges of this great country to the exclusion of the Middle Belt and the South" and threatened to excise the five majority Muslim states of the north from the federation until, as he put it, a delegation would come "to vouch that the feudalistic and aristocratic quest for domination and oppression will never again be practiced in any part of the Nigerian state."[21] General Babangida's loyal troops won the day; had they lost, the country would inevitably have been plunged into a second civil war. It was a close call.

Space precludes full discussion of the most violent religious episodes of the 1980s—the so-called Maitatsine disturbances—which, though they were intra-Islamic rather than interfaith, nevertheless had the potential

17. It may be noted that, had *shari'a* been applicable, the man would have suffered the death penalty for his apostasy from Islam.

18. According to an official inquiry, 19 people and eight animals were killed, and 169 hotels or beer parlors, 152 churches, five mosques, and 95 vehicles were destroyed or damaged. See Ibrahim, "Politics of Religion," p. 67.

19. Ibid., p. 68.

20. A Muslim preacher from South Africa had earlier been denied a permit to hold meetings in Kano.

21. As reported in *Punch* (Lagos), 24 Apr. 1990, p. 8.

for creating considerable political destabilization. The original disturbances took place in Kano in 1980, and subsequent outbreaks occurred over the next five years in Maiduguri, Kaduna, Yola, and Gombe. In these upheavals, groups of poor and mainly illiterate men who had set up a type of commune existence got into—possibly provoked—clashes with the police, effectively using bows and arrows and knives and in return were slaughtered in large numbers by the police. In two instances, the police were backed by army units.

The original leader, Muhammad Marwa, whose nickname Mai Tatsine ("the one who says, 'cursed be!' ") gave the name to these disturbances (although it is unclear to what extent they were all organically linked), was a preacher from Marwa, in Cameroon, but long a resident in Kano. He preached deviant interpretations of Muslim belief and ritual; according to some, they included human sacrifice and magical use of body organs. He was fiercely antagonistic to all Muslims outside his community, extremely anti-elitist, and probably a chiliast. He was killed in the first disturbances in Kano, and his followers refused to talk about him or about his message.

Many varying interpretations of his movement and the copycat disturbances that followed the 1980 Kano riot have been given. What is clear is that those involved were economically and socially marginal men with a strong sense of grievance against the state and its agents and those who had grown rich from association with it or through entrepreneurial activity. In and of themselves, Mai Tatsine and his followers and emulators were irrelevant to the greater politicoreligious discourse. The question has remained, however, as to whether they were, or could potentially be, manipulated by larger political forces, whether external, as some alleged at the time, or internal, as some have since suggested.[22] The existence of any such thing as a Maitatsine sect or movement seems very doubtful, but it is clear that rapid urbanization in northern Nigeria, the oil boom, and subsequent economic decline have created extraordinary social and economic problems and an atmosphere of uncertainty and anger in which violent movements of protest can flourish. In the Hausa political idiom, it is not surprising that such movements should express themselves within the framework of religious discourse.[23]

PROSPECTS FOR THE 1990s

The prospects for an end to violence between Muslims of different persuasions or between Muslims and Christians do not seem very encouraging. The overall economic situation of Nigeria in a world currently plagued by severe economic troubles is unlikely to improve dramatically in the near future. The planned return to civilian rule in January 1993, provided nothing happens to defer it,

22. Kane, "Mouvements religieux," p. 21.
23. The Maitatsine phenomenon has provoked a literature of explanations. A convenient bibliography of this literature is to be found in Niels Kastfelt, "Rumours of Maitatsine: A Note on Political Culture in Northern Nigeria," *African Affairs*, 88:83-90 (1989), an article that analyzes the power of rumor in political myth-making in the Nigerian context.

ought to provide more multifaceted outlets for political energies, but in fact the religion question in one form or another has been an integral part of Nigerian political discourse since the beginning of party politics. Most constitutional and political thinking has refused to face this stark fact, mainly for fear of the animosity that might be stirred up. Much will depend on how the elections for federal and state assemblies go, since the ban on the participation of former political personalities has been lifted; the crucial test will be the election for an executive president who, in the nature of things, will belong, or be perceived to belong, to either the Muslim or the Christian constituency.

In any future moves to gain greater recognition for *shari'a* at the federal level or to dilute in any way the secular nature of the Nigerian state, the role of the Yoruba will be critical. Historically, there has been a lack of consonance between Yoruba Muslims and northern Muslims, not least because Yoruba religious thinking tends to favor a plurality of views, even allowing different members of the same family to belong to different religions without divisiveness. It should not be assumed that this situation is incapable of change. Indeed, there are signs that change is occurring. Shifting political alliances, too, might bring Yorubas closer to Hausas, as they did during the latter days of the First Republic.

External influences will also play a role in determining the fortunes of differing political and social interpretations of Islam in Nigeria. There are many and diverse historical links between Nigeria and the Sudan, and one may expect that the experiences of the Sudan in Islamization will be closely studied by activist Muslim groups in Nigeria. Iran and Saudi Arabia will continue, covertly or overtly, to attempt to influence the course of Muslim debates in Nigeria, and, if the Islamic Salvation Front dominates Algerian politics, Algeria, too, can be expected to play a more active role in promoting its own interpretations of Islam in sub-Saharan Africa and not least in Nigeria.

ANNALS, *AAPSS*, 524, November 1992

Political Islam in Asia: A Case Study

By ALAIN-GÉRARD MARSOT

ABSTRACT: The phenomenon of Islamic resurgence, the so-called fundamentalism, has had important political effects, but it is often viewed as a Middle Eastern issue, just as Islam is essentially perceived as a Middle Eastern religion. In point of fact, the major Muslim nations are found in Asia, where most of the world's Muslims live. Islamic resurgence is also found, in various degrees, in all the countries of Asia where there are Muslims. The intensity and character of this phenomenon, however, depends on several factors, such as geography, historical background, and the relative size of the Muslim communities. While it is both a religious and a political phenomenon, as Islam itself, this Islamic resurgence should also be considered a response to the global issue of modernization and development, in all its complex and unsettling dimensions.

Born in Vietnam of French origin, Alain-G. Marsot received a law degree, took the bar exam, and received a Ph.D. in political science from the University of Paris. He also received an advanced degree from the University of Oxford. Dr. Marsot has taught at different universities in England, France, Egypt, Thailand, and the United States and has lived and traveled in many countries of the Middle East and South and Southeast Asia, which have also been the subject of his publications.

WESTERN stereotypes associate Islam with the Middle East and North Africa, as geographic areas, and with the Arabs as people. Most of the Muslims, however, are found in Asia, where the largest Muslim nations are located: Indonesia, Pakistan, and Bangladesh. Furthermore, there are other nations in Asia where either Islam is the religion of the majority—or of the largest group, as in Malaysia—or there are sizable Muslim minorities, as in India, the Philippines, and Thailand. In point of fact, there are more Muslims in the Indian subcontinent than in all of the Middle East and North Africa. Were it not for Eurocentric notions, the Middle East, more appropriately, would be referred to as West Asia and North Africa. But this article is concerned with regions traditionally considered Asian, such as South and Southeast Asia, keeping in mind that there are also sizable Muslim communities in Central Asia and China.[1]

Just as in the Middle East and North Africa, most Asian countries with Muslim communities were colonized and then again became independent in the aftermath of World War II. Therefore, those communities have been faced with the issue of nationalism and the struggle for independence leading ultimately to decolonization. Following the end of colonization, new problems appeared in the shape of attempts at modernization and development. More recently, a major phenomenon has spread through the Muslim world, giving religion—Islam—a major role in political, economic, and social matters. This phenomenon has been characterized, by outsiders, as a resurgence of Islam or, more commonly, as "fundamentalism." This so-called fundamentalism, or, more accurately, Islamic activism, has affected Asian Muslim countries as well as the countries of the Middle East and North Africa. It has become a major political issue, especially in the wake of the establishment of an Islamic regime in Iran, which has had an impact far beyond the borders of that country.

PRELIMINARY OBSERVATIONS

Before discussing the role of Islam in the politics of Asia, a preliminary observation has to be made, as well as some considerations regarding the character of Islam in that part of the world.

First of all, in Islam there is no separation between the realm of the religious and that of the political, or, as commonly stated in the West, between church and state. While all religions affect and are affected by the political, to a greater or lesser degree, Christianity early on claimed such a separation, expressed in the New Testament as "Render unto Caesar the things that are Caesar's, and unto God the things that are God's." The whole history of Christianity contradicts this statement, from the quarrel of the Two Swords in medieval times to the war of religions in the age of the Renaissance and Reformation, to the temporal powers of

---

1. Some of the information and observations in this article are the result of research and interviews conducted between 1988 and 1991 in Southeast Asia—Malaysia, Thailand, Indonesia—and India on the subject of Muslim attitudes toward modernization.

the Papacy and many other instances down to the present time. But in Islam, there has never been such a disclaimer. Islam was political from the very first day, concerned with the governing of the religious community and with any and all political questions, as well as with dogma and religious problems. Over time, and in different historical and geographic contexts, the connection may have loosened, but it is always in the background and ready to reassert itself.

The second question that arises, keeping in mind that Islam originated in the Middle East, is whether the form of Islam practiced in Asia is any different from that practiced in the Middle East and North Africa. While one can expect that distance from the beginning and source of Islam as well as different geographic and cultural contexts in the areas affected by the spread of Islam might somewhat modify the character of the religion, the essential factors of differentiation between Middle Eastern/ North African Islam and Asian Islam are related to the historical circumstances in which Islam reached various Asian countries.

FACTORS AFFECTING
THE IMPACT OF ISLAM
ON ASIA: CONVERSION

Before discussing the role of Islam in the contemporary politics of Asia, one has to recognize that it is determined, or at least affected, by three sets of factors, which are sometimes intertwined.

The first factor is the way Islam came to Asia. From its birth in the Arabian peninsula in the seventh century, Islam spread its political control through military conquest over the Middle East, Persia, North Africa, and Spain with extreme rapidity. The Islamization of the conquered territories, however, took place progressively, given the tolerance displayed by the Arab conquerors toward the religious beliefs of the conquered peoples, essentially various brands of Christianity, considered worthy of protection (dhimma). This first phase in the spread of Islam is marked by a close relationship between the religion, the Arabic language of the conquerors and of the Quran, the fusion of the spiritual and temporal powers of the caliph, and consequently the intertwining of political and religious questions.

South Asia

In the second phase of the spread of Islam, the leadership of the Muslim community had passed from the hands of the Arabs into those of Turks from Central Asia, the Ottomans, following the destruction of the Abbassi Caliphate in Baghdad. It is during this phase that Islam really reached the South Asian subcontinent. The impact of Islam on South Asia was marked by somewhat contradictory factors. The first wave of Arab conquests in the Middle East and North Africa, along with subsequent Islamization, was accompanied, overall, by a fair amount of toleration due to the fundamental closeness of Islam to Christianity. Moreover, the conquered Christians in the Middle East found their Muslim masters more lenient in terms of both taxation and religious dogma than their previous Byzantine overlords, who practiced a different form of Christianity and persecuted them for that reason.

In South Asia, on the other hand, apart from a brief Arab incursion in the Sind province (now Pakistan), conquest was carried out by Turkic bands from Central Asia, who were recent converts to Islam and overzealous, as new converts usually are. Those Turkic elements justified their looting and massacring of the local populations by the fact that Hindus and Buddhists were idolaters, not entitled to the protection afforded the People of the Book—Christians, Jews, and Zoroastrians—and therefore were to be offered only the choice between death and conversion to Islam. Successive Central Asian and Mongol leaders conquered and lost various parts of the northern Indian subcontinent between A.D. 1000 and 1500, but with the passage of time the Muslim conquerors came to some sort of accommodation with the peoples of the Indian peninsula who had remained Hindus.

This modus vivendi was the result of several factors. While quite a few Indians converted to Islam, especially people from the lower castes escaping the oppressive Hindu socioreligious structure, the Muslim ruling class was still very small in number compared to the Hindu masses. Therefore, it had to call upon uppercaste Hindus to serve as officials at its court and in the administration of the country.[2] Because the Muslim

rulers were no longer Arabs and Arabic speaking, they were less knowledgeable of the sacred law and texts and consequently less intransigent regarding Islamic norms. This increasing tolerance reached a high point under the early Mogul emperors, marked by intermarriage with high-caste Hindu princesses, notably Rajput, and most of all by the Mogul Emperor Akbar's attempt to create a syncretic religion combining Islam with local contributions. This attempt, by the greatest of the Moguls, ultimately failed and there were resurgences of intransigence and persecution of non-Muslims, notably by Emperor Aurangzeb.

From the thirteenth century onward, armies of Muslims no longer expanded south and east; instead, the Muslim religion was peacefully introduced by traders and preachers who carried it all the way to the limits of Southeast Asia and to China. In this process, Islamization was helped in no small measure by the appearance of mystics, or Sufis. Sufis attempted to reach the transcendent through inner or intuitive knowledge, rather than book learning, presenting a popular understanding rather than an intellectual one. That approach found a fertile terrain among many mystically inclined people in India and in the Malay world.[3]

Southeast Asia

The progressive Islamization of most of the Malay world thus took place in a peaceful fashion. In many ways, this process was similar to the Indianization of the area in either its

2. Marshall G. S. Hodgson, *The Venture of Islam* (Chicago: University of Chicago Press, 1974), 2:557.

3. Ibid., p. 542.

Hindu or its Buddhist form several centuries earlier. Many of the local potentates were merchant-rulers. Muslim traders would marry into those princely families and spread Islam to the ruling elite, to those who soon found it expedient to adopt the new creed for trading purposes, as well as to others who believed its tenets. The Arab traders, present in the area and in south China since pre-Islamic times, had refrained from proselytizing after the birth of the new religion. Islamization was therefore carried out by Indian Muslim traders from Gujarat and, to a lesser extent, by Tamils from the Coromandel coast in southeast India. Those Gujaratis benefited from the prestige attached to India, in terms of advanced culture and technology, and, like their Hinduizing predecessors, superimposed their creed and culture over the existing beliefs and traditions they found, be they Hindu, Buddhist, or animist, without erasing them.[4]

Thus traditional laws and customs (adat) survived in the Indonesian archipelago. One finds there the attitude, so prevalent in most of Asia, of blending new beliefs and cultures with preexisting ones without exercising exclusion, intolerance, or fanaticism (there were always a few exceptions). The result has been a widespread propensity toward syncretism, either formally or simply in practice. It should be added that when Islam arrived in the Malay world, the local Hinduized empires and kingdoms had become exhausted, thereby weakening the Hindu-Bud-

dhist traditions.[5] In other Southeast Asian regions, Islam did not make any inroads, save in Champa (southern Vietnam). Finally, in the Malay world, Islam essentially reached the elites, the coasts, and the port cities. Inland populations were little touched by the new faith, or only progressively so at later periods.[6] Small Islamized communities also appeared in China as a consequence of trade, either on the southern coast or in the far west on the Silk Road.

EUROPEAN COLONIZATION

The arrival of European traders in the sixteenth century and later European colonization constitute the second factor that has had direct and profound effects on the place and role of Islam in Asia. It is ironic that initially the first Europeans, the Portuguese, unwittingly helped the spread of Islam in the Indonesian archipelago.[7] Their missionary zeal was so brutal and heavy-handed, marked by a mix of crusading, Iberian peninsula reconquista spirit, visceral anti-Muslim feelings, not to mention the spirit of lucre and plunder, that they often succeeded in unifying the local populations under the banner of Islam, perceived as a barrier against such abuses.

The Western presence, through traders and missionaries, even when it used military means, did not at first lead to outright colonization except in the Philippines. There, the

4. Ibid., p. 548.

5. D.G.E. Hall, A History of Southeast Asia, 4th ed. (New York: St. Martin's Press, 1981), p. 221.

6. Ibid., p. 231.

7. Ibid.

Spanish emphasis on proselytizing and the absence of strong religious traditions on the islands led to successful Christianization and to arresting the progress of Islam. Only the large island of Mindanao became Muslim. The Spanish government's commitment and use of violence accounts for this lone victory of the cross over the crescent in Asia. Elsewhere, European interest in the Malay world was of a commercial nature, even if it did occasionally use the argument of Christianization as a pretext for their endeavors; the Portuguese were a case in point. When European governments became involved in South and Southeast Asian affairs in the eighteenth and, most of all, the nineteenth centuries, progressively supplanting private commercial companies instead of simply giving them assistance, the stage was set for outright colonization. This was to have a much greater impact upon the local peoples and their traditional cultures.

South Asia

On the Indian subcontinent, the eighteenth century saw a struggle for power and influence between British and French companies, each supported by its respective government, especially the British, which resulted in the victory of British concerns. In the first part of the nineteenth century, there was a steady increase of British governmental control and interference in Indian affairs, accompanied by high-handed and superior attitudes that increasingly antagonized the locals and were partly responsible for the Sepoy mutiny of 1857. Following the mutiny, which the British tended to blame on the Muslims, the Muslims were ostracized by the colonizers; but the birth of a Hindu nationalist movement led the British to practice a divide-and-rule policy on the subcontinent. Threatened by this Hindu resurgence, the Indian Muslim minority looked to the British for protection against the Hindu majority.

When the British had to grant some measure of self-government to the Indians, they instituted separate electorates for the Muslims and the Hindus. Some of the Indian nationalist leaders, Hindus and Muslims alike, were westernized and secular in attitude, but the utterly fragmented nature of the socioethnic scene in India made it imperative to emphasize religion as a factor of unity. This was true most of all for the Hindus, and, in consequence, the Muslims were forced to adopt the same approach, making impossible a durable alliance between the communities in the struggle for independence.

The outcome, in 1947, was the partition of British India into two states—India and Pakistan—based on communal lines. Partition was accompanied by massive transfers of population and much bloodshed between the communities. Thereafter, while India has attempted with some success to follow a secular and democratic policy, the genesis of the birth of Pakistan, the nature of its political elite, and irredentist claims based on religion, as in Kashmir, have placed Islam squarely at the center of politics in Pakistan. In any case, from the beginning of British rule in India, the Hindus had been more willing to adopt Western ways, while the Muslims, displaced as the ruling elite, had remained somewhat on the sidelines, sulking, so to say. In the first years of independence, Islam had been the common bond between the two wings of Pakistan, until insurmountable differences brought about the breakup of the country and the birth of Bangladesh in the east wing, following the Indo-Pakistani war of 1971.

Southeast Asia

In the Malay world, on the other hand, where the large majority of the population was Muslim and where the colonizers were more interested in profits than conversion to Christianity, the British and the Dutch essentially practiced indirect rule. They maintained at least the facade of the preeminence of the local aristocracies and traditional rulers, taking care not to upset the peoples' beliefs and customs. An Islamic-based political movement, however, appeared in Java in 1825-30 with the Dipo Negoro war, which was based as much on Dutch meddling in dynastic affairs as on the increasing role of the Chinese in the economy. Throughout the nineteenth century, there were numerous instances of 'ulama'-led peasant resistance against Dutch rule, including the long Acheh wars between 1871 and 1908.[8] The founding in 1912 of the Sarekat Islam (Islam Association) in Java was motivated by identical economic rea-

8. Ira M. Lapidus, *A History of Islamic Societies* (New York: Cambridge University Press, 1988), p. 758.

sons. Sarekat Islam had a socialist orientation, but it soon split into several tendencies, and the leadership of the budding nationalist, anticolonial movement in the Dutch East Indies came to be in the hands of more secular leaders, either nationalists or Communists. The Japanese occupation during World War II accelerated the drive toward decolonization and independence throughout Southeast Asia, but Islam per se did not play a major role in this process either in Indonesia or in Malaya. Once independence had been achieved, however, Islam reemerged as a political force, increasingly so in the wake of the so-called Islamic resurgence.

THE MUSLIM POPULATION

The third factor that has affected the place and role of Islam in Asia is the size of the Muslim population in various Asian countries at the present time. With respect to population, there are three categories of countries. Some countries have an overwhelmingly Muslim majority. These include, first, Indonesia, the largest Muslim country in the world and the fifth most populous country, with a total population of 186.9 million people, of which 168.2 million, or 90 percent, are Muslims; second, Pakistan, with a total population of 120.8 million, of which 117.2 million, or 97 percent, are Muslims; and third, Bangladesh, with a total population of 117.8 million, of which 97.8 million, or 83 percent, are Muslims.

The second category comprises one country, Malaysia, which has a bare majority of Muslims: 9.3 million out of 18.6 million.

The third category comprises several countries with a Muslim minority. In India, the minority is nevertheless large in numbers, with 96.3 million geographically dispersed Muslims composing a mere 11 percent of the population. In the Philippines, the Muslims number 3.16 million, constituting 5 percent of the total population of 63.3 million; in Thailand, they are 2.3 million, 4 percent of the total population of 57.6 million; in China, they are 11.4 million, or about 1 percent of the total population of 1,147.6 million.[9] In the case of both the Philippines and Thailand, however, the Muslims are concentrated in specific geographic areas and, in the case of the Thai, Muslims belong to a different ethnic group from that of the Buddhist majority of the population.

All three factors discussed earlier—the spread of Islam, European colonization, and population patterns—have had a direct correlation with the behavior of Muslims and the role of Islam in the various countries of Asia. Looking at the record since independence, one can determine two periods regarding the role of Islam in the politics of Asia. Following independence, with the exception of Pakistan, the leadership in most countries was essentially secular, concerned with problems of foreign policy, nation building, modernization, and development. Then, from the late 1960s, and in some places even earlier, one witnesses the alleged resurgence of Islam, the rise of

9. *World Development Report 1991* (New York: Oxford University Press, 1991). Figures are population projections for 1992, based on statistics in ibid., p. 254.

Islamic fundamentalism. In point of fact, this was not the resurgence of a religion, which had always been there, but an attempt to interpret Islam holistically by using principles derived from Islamic teachings to guide politics and economics, as well as society in general. What attracted the attention of the West was the political dimension, which used Muslim idiom instead of Western terminology and which distanced itself from westernization while preaching reform.

Revivalism or fundamentalism—whatever term one uses—is not a new phenomenon in Islam. It has occurred many times in the past centuries. The present conditions in the world, in terms of rapid change and modern means of communication and transportation, have given this resurgence a global character that it could not have had in the past.

ISLAM IN ASIA: CASE STUDIES

The reappearance of Islamic idiom as a political factor in Asia has taken different forms in different countries, both before and after the watershed constituted by the Iranian revolution.

Pakistan

Religion played an essential role in the birth of Pakistan. After independence, it continued to play a major role in the politics of the country and not just because the official name of the country is "The Islamic Republic of Pakistan." Less westernized than India, or at least less receptive to Western ideas of political and economic organization, Pakistan did not succeed in establishing a durable semidemocratic system within the framework of a secular ideology. The first years of the new state were marked by political instability, aggravated by the successive deaths of its most able leaders, Mohammed Ali Jinnah and Liaqat Ali Khan. The only anchor that could be used to keep the country together was religion, and it was not sufficient to prevent the breakup that produced the new nation of Bangladesh in 1971. Since 1958, Pakistan has been under military rule, except for brief civilian interludes with Zulfikar Ali Bhutto and, more recently, his daughter, Benazir. But whatever type of regime operated, Islam has been used as a guideline in both domestic and international affairs. From the very beginning of the new state, there has been a struggle for influence between the modernists, often coming from the Muslim League and trained at Aligahr Muslim University, a modern institution, and the traditionalists led by the *'ulama'*.[10] At least in theory, the traditionalists have been successful in imposing their agenda on the political system, both under civilian and military regimes.

Both types of leaders were under pressure to establish or maintain their Muslim credentials. Military rulers, such as Zia ul-Haq, were eager to preempt the most extreme demands of Muslim traditionalists in order to justify and maintain their hold on power. While Pakistan's three constitutions (1956, 1962, and 1973) contained Islamic provisions governing, for instance, individual moral or social behavior, General Zia after 1977 attempted to enforce the more extremist interpretations of *shari'a* law in judicial and criminal matters, such as in punishments for theft or adultery, to enforce a strict observance of the Five Pillars of Islam, even forcing a dress code on government employees and women in general.[11] There was also to be the establishment of "Islamic economics and banking," which would prohibit interest and usury. The attempt was to bring about a society fairly similar to that of Khomeini's Iran.

An additional factor on the path of Islamization had been the breakup of Pakistan in 1971 and its reorientation in international affairs toward the traditional Muslim heartland, the Middle East, which was initiated by the secular and socialist Bhutto.[12] This was further reinforced by the 1973 Arab-Israeli war and the subsequent rise in oil prices, which have exacerbated anti-Western feelings and given added leverage and influence to traditional and conservative regimes such as Saudi Arabia. The anti-Soviet, anti-Communist struggle in Afghanistan waged in the name of Islam, the influx of Afghans into Pakistan, and Saudi financial support of the resistance have played in

10. Kemal A. Faruki, "Pakistan: Islamic Government and Society," in *Islam in Asia: Religion, Politics and Society*, ed. John L. Esposito (New York: Oxford University Press, 1987), p. 54. See also Barbara D. Metcalf, "Islamic Arguments in Contemporary Pakistan," in *Islam and the Political Economy of Meaning*, ed. William R. Roff (Berkeley: University of California Press, 1987).

11. Metcalf, "Islamic Arguments in Contemporary Pakistan," p. 74.

12. John L. Esposito, "Pakistan: Quest for Islamic Identity," in *Islam and Development*, ed. John L. Esposito (Syracuse, NY: Syracuse University Press, 1980), pp. 150-51.

the same direction. It remains that ethnic, linguistic, economic, and social differences, and dissensions within Pakistan remain profound and are unlikely to diminish.

Bangladesh

The new state of Bangladesh, born in 1971 as a result of the breakup of Pakistan, initially emphasized national, secular goals.[13] This was understandable, since the secession had broken the bond between the two wings of a union that was based only on the common religion, Islam. Later, especially in the wake of military coups and takeovers, an Islamic fundamentalist orientation somewhat similar to that of Pakistan, but so far not carried to the same length, has appeared. In spite of the phenomenon of Islamic resurgence, which has also reached Bangladesh, the Islamic idiom in the politics of that country has remained moderate because of the circumstances of the country's birth, its connections with India, present rule by a democratic regime, and the existence of a substantial non-Muslim minority.[14] What might give the Islamic political idiom a renewed influence would be a demand for greater social justice, given the extreme poverty of the country, one of the world's poorest, and its vulnerability to recurrent natural disasters such as floods.

13. Lapidus, *History of Islamic Societies*, p. 747.

14. Peter J. Bertocci, "Bangladesh: Composite Cultural Identity and Modernization in a Muslim-Majority State," in *Change and the Muslim World*, ed. Philip H. Stoddard et al. (Syracuse, NY: Syracuse University Press, 1981), pp. 77, 78.

India

Of the three countries of the subcontinent, India is the only one where Muslims constitute a minority. But it is a very large minority in absolute numbers, nearly as large as the Muslim majority in neighboring Bangladesh and twice as large as the Muslim majority in any Middle Eastern country. Nonetheless, the situation of the Muslims in India is a difficult one. First, they suffer from the circumstances of the partition, which has left durable rancors and antagonisms, especially in northern India, where most Muslims are to be found. On the other hand, over most of the postindependence years, the official government ideology has been secular, committed to nondiscrimination on the basis of race, caste, or religion.[15] Some Muslims have reached very high positions in the government structure, up to and including head of state. But the Muslims are also subject to special provisions governing their personal status, such as family matters.

The attempt to combine nondiscriminatory provisions at the public level and a special status at the private level has generated tensions between the communities. In practice, discrimination against the Muslims is widespread, both at the public level—with respect to government jobs, for instance—and at the private, such as with jobs in the private sector, bank loans, and so on.[16] Some, but by no means all, such practices may be justified by the overall lower

15. Syed Shahabuddin and Theodore P. Wright, Jr., "India: Muslim Minority Politics and Society," in *Islam in Asia*, ed. Esposito, p. 155.

16. Ibid., p. 164.

educational achievements of the Indian Muslims. Intercommunal riots and violence have been widespread, exacerbated by a renewed Islamic consciousness on the part of some elements of the Muslim community and accompanied by a renewed Hindu consciousness, communal disputes over the location of a mosque or Hindu temple on the same site, and, lastly, the situation of quasi civil war in the Muslim majority province of Kashmir.

In the recent past, for the Indian Muslims, Islam played a major role at the devotional level, not perforce at the public one, and in fact the more affluent Muslims have reached a fair level of accommodation with the Hindu majority.[17] But the conjunction of the continuing religio-ethnic strife in India—affecting communities other than the Muslim one—and the Islamic resurgence can only increase, albeit in a limited way, the political role of Islam within the Indian Muslim community.

Indonesia

In Southeast Asia, one finds a wide array of situations with respect to the political role of Islam. In Indonesia, governments since independence have managed to maintain a secular approach within the state ideology of Pancasila, whose principles include a belief in God and are acceptable to other communities as well as the Muslims. This secular approach was followed both under Sukarno, in the first years of the Republic, and the military under Suharto and the New

Order, since 1965.[18] It seems paradoxical that the largest Muslim country in the world appears to be one of the least influenced by Islamic political activities. But several reasons account for this situation.

While Muslim parties or movements were active under Dutch colonization, during the Japanese occupation, and in the struggle for independence, the leadership of the independence movement and then of the independent Republic remained in the hands of committed secularists. Under Sukarno, some Muslim parties led secessionist movements;[19] others spent their energy fighting Communist influence. Under the New Order of General Suharto, some fringe Muslim groups have been involved in terrorist acts, giving the military government a pretext for keeping a tight control over all Muslim movements and activities.

The historical and geographic contexts have made the emergence of a strong, unified Islamic political movement difficult. There is the geographic, ethnic, and linguistic diversity of the Indonesian islands and their inhabitants. There is the survival of pre-Islamic, animist, Hindo-Buddhist traditions in a tolerant and syncretic environment. Religious and cultural pluralism is a fact of public life and a matter of pride for many Indonesians.[20] An added factor of fragmentation is resentment in the outer

17. Lapidus, *History of Islamic Societies*, p. 748.

18. Nasir Tamara, "Islam under the New Order," *Prisma* (Jakarta), June 1990, no. 49. pp. 6-31.

19. Anthony H. Johns, "Indonesia: Islam and Cultural Pluralism," in *Islam in Asia*, ed. Esposito, pp. 211-12.

20. Ibid., p. 204.

islands caused by the domination of heavily populated Java. It remains that reformist Muslim movements continue to exist and to advocate a polity more in tune with the precepts of Islam but equally in tune with the demands of a technological world. Devotional Islam is on the increase, as is Islamic education, encouraged but controlled by the authorities. As in many other places in the Muslim world, the tensions created by modernization contribute to a reinforced sense of Islamic identity at the national and global level.

Malaysia

The picture is very different in Malaysia, providing an interesting contrast with Indonesia in terms of the Islamic dimension of politics. In Malaysia, the Muslims constitute a bare majority but control the political system, while the Chinese and Indian communities have long controlled the economic life of the country. As opposed to the autocratic civilian or military regimes that have governed Indonesia since independence, Malaysia has, so far, enjoyed a fairly democratic form of government. That government, based on an alliance of representatives of the various communities, but under the leadership of Malays—which in Malaysia means Muslims—attempted at first to follow a secular policy balancing the interests of the different communities. In more recent years, however, the phenomenon of Islamic resurgence, more obvious in Malaysia than anywhere else in Southeast Asia, has pressured the political system into moving in the direction of a greater

Islamic presence in public life, accompanied by a policy of affirmative action for the Malays.[21] Such a trend might ultimately upset the precarious balance that has kept the communities together.

But the Islamic resurgence, apart from some regional influence, including financial support from the oil-rich countries of the Middle East, is essentially for domestic and global reasons. Under colonization, the Malays were content to remain peasants, and the British had to bring Chinese and Indians to work in the tin mines and on the rubber plantations. In time, those overseas immigrants drifted into cities, which they pretty much populated and whose economy they dominated. When the Malays started to move to the cities, they became exposed to modernization and urbanization in an environment dominated by those communities of foreign origin with different cultures and religions, which generated confrontations. This has led to a reassertion of the Malays' self-identity, naturally centered on Islam.[22]

Increased possibilities for education in this dynamic, partly alien economic environment have exposed young educated Malays to the materialistic, westernized cultural aspects of modernization, which, more often than not, they find offensive to their deep-rooted ethical values. While they realize that modernization is probably a one-way street, they want it to take place within an

21. Margaret Scott, "Where the Quota is King," *New York Times*, 17 Nov. 1991.
22. Fred von der Mehden, "Malaysia: Islam and Multiethnic Politics," in *Islam in Asia*, ed. Esposito, p. 192.

Islamic framework respectful of their values.[23] More in evidence in Malaysia than possibly anywhere else in the Asian Muslim world is the difference between modernization, which is desired, and westernization in its conspicuous-consumption aspects, which is rejected, together with its capitalist, neo-imperialist dimension. Some signs of the Islamic resurgence have been the growth of *dakwah* ("missionary") movements, the increasing place given by the politicians and the media to Islamic issues, and the popularity of the Islamic type of dress.[24] The government's answer has been to co-opt some of the movement's leaders and to try and raise the economic level of the Malays through policies aimed at increasing their share in the economy.

In two other Southeast Asian countries, the Philippines and Thailand, Muslims constitute small minorities, concentrated in specific areas. Policies of either benign neglect or semi-forced cultural assimilation have radicalized the Muslims' resistance, leading to insurgency, often supported from outside. Examples of this resistance are that of the Moros of Mindanao in the Philippines and the Muslims of southern Thailand, who feel greater affinities with their Malay cousins of Malaysia and have been further politicized by the phenomenon of Islamic resurgence.

23. Fred von der Mehden, *Religion and Modernization in Southeast Asia* (Syracuse, NY: Syracuse University Press, 1986), p. 108.

24. Ibid., p. 107. See also Muhammad Kamal Hassan, "The Response of Muslim Youth Organizations to Political Change: HMI in Indonesia and ABIM in Malaysia," in *Islam and the Political Economy of Meaning*, ed. Roff.

CONCLUSION

After this all too brief overview of the most significant countries of Asia with a Muslim population, one can attempt to draw some tentative conclusions as to the role played by Islamic activism in the politics of these countries. First, the phenomenon of Islamic "resurgence," with its holistic approach to politics as inseparable from religion, is not a new one. It has occurred many times before, in different places, at different moments. What is new is its global character, how it is widespread throughout the Muslim world from North Africa to Southeast Asia, from Central Asia to sub-Saharan Africa, and in fact everywhere where there are Muslims. Part of the reason for its ubiquity is the modern means of transportation and communication, which have facilitated contacts and transfers of ideas.

A more profound reason is also rooted in the advent of modernization, due first to the advent of a global society, then to the change from an agricultural society to an industrial one and subsequently to an information society, progressive in the Western world, often partial or telescoped in the developing world, to which most of the Muslim countries belong. This rapid change is profoundly disruptive and even traumatic. While old securities inherent in the stability of traditional societies are vanishing or under considerable challenge, the modern world offers alternatives, which both in their Western and Communist versions—before the latter's collapse—appear exploitative, mindless, and dehumanizing.

On the one hand, modernization seems inevitable to most Muslims.

The only way to "tame the beast" is to have an anchor, a sense of purpose, an ethical foundation, which Islam seems to offer because it is a Weltanschauung with a promise of a just and integrated society. This is why the phenomenon of Islamic resurgence has had, and continues to have, such an impact. In Asia, the extent of that impact has varied depending, as we have seen, on such factors as historical and cultural backgrounds, geography, size of the Muslim community, and government policy. But whatever its degree of intensity, it has affected, affects, or will affect the politics of those countries. In many ways, the rapid political decolonization following World War II did not fulfill widespread expectations for a better life in the former Western colonies. What we may well witness in the making is a political phenomenon of the first magnitude, a second decolonization, a cultural dewesternization spearheaded by resurgent Islam.

ANNALS, *AAPSS*, 524, November 1992

Maghrebi Immigration to Europe:
Double Insertion or Double Exclusion?

By RÉMY LEVEAU

ABSTRACT: In Europe, Islam became a significant form of collective behavior among migrants from the Maghreb, Turkey, Western Africa, and India during the 1970s, when that group of people decided to settle abroad and raise their children in what they considered, at the beginning, to be a lasting exile. In that way, Islam appeared as an instrument for building new identities and transnational solidarities for the purpose of negotiating with the states and societies of settlement. But that peaceful approach has been taken as an unacceptable challenge by secular societies, which are no longer used to dealing with religious values as a way of collective self-assertion. In a future open Europe that will include 5 to 6 million Muslims, it will be necessary to establish a new doctrinal framework of cultural pluralism that includes Islam.

Rémy Leveau is professor at the Institut d'Études Politiques de Paris. He has taught at the Universities of Rabat, Michigan, and Beirut (St. Joseph) and New York University. He has spent many years as a civil servant with the Ministry of Foreign Affairs (cultural affairs). He has published Le fellah marocain: défenseur du Trône *(1985);* Les musulmans dans la société française *(with Gilles Kepel) (1987); and many articles on subjects related to the Middle East, the Maghreb, Islam in France, and migration.*

IN today's Europe, everyone's attention is focused on political changes in the East and the potentially important modifications of migratory flows that may go along with these changes. Interest in the Maghreb awakens only when events like the Persian Gulf crisis, martial law in Algeria, or the Islamic Salvation Front's success in legislative elections provoke passionate reactions. But a new social and human alignment has been building up between the Maghreb and Europe as a result of an immigration that was unplanned and largely unrecognized in either place. Since 1970, a slow, sometimes painful awareness of the scale and implications of this migration have developed, along with reactions of rejection in European, particularly French, society.[1]

At the same time, a sense of identity among Maghrebi immigrants

1. Particularly useful works on the topic of the present article are *Être français aujourd'hui et demain* (Paris: La Documentation française, 1988); Gilles Kepel, *Les banlieues de l'islam* (Paris: Le Seuil, 1987); Rémy Leveau and Gilles Kepel, *Les musulmans dans la société française* (Paris: Presses de la Fondation nationale des sciences politiques, 1987); Dominique Schnapper, *La France de l'intégration* (Paris: Gallimard, 1991); Patrick Weil, *La France et ses étrangers: L'aventure d'une politique de l'immigration 1938-1991* (Paris: Calmann-Lévy, 1991); Michel Wieviorka, *La France raciste* (Paris: Le Seuil, 1992); Catherine Wihtol de Wenden, *Les immigrés et la politique* (Paris: Presses de la Fondation nationale des sciences politiques, 1988); Rémy Leveau, "Les partis et l'intégration des 'beurs'" in *Idéologies, partis politiques et groupes sociaux,* ed. Y. Mény (Paris: Presses de la Fondation nationale des sciences politiques, 1989), pp. 247-62; Fathia Dazi and Rémy Leveau, "L'intégration par le politique: Le vote des 'beurs,'" *Études* pp. 179-88 (Sept. 1988).

and their descendants has been developing that focuses on Islam. By choosing Islam, this sense of identity, which has allowed these insecure new immigrants to legitimize their presence within European society, blurs the traditional European boundaries between public and private affairs. On the other hand, the language of the French extreme right, the National Front, represents a typical example of the reaction of a majority group that adopts minority group behavior and redefines its own identity on the basis of cultural and religious values.

The process of collective negotiation that uses Islam as the focal point, however, is in turn affected by the changes that occurred in Europe, particularly the opening to the East and the unification planned for 1993. Competitive, conflictual, and interactive situations are taking shape, presaging a new type of North-South relationship, which could be compared with some of the factors at work in the plans for a common market between the United States, Canada, and Mexico. It may also create conflicts of a new type and magnitude.

To start with, the ambiguity of the situation is amplified by the world's perception of a coincidence between Maghrebi immigration, its assertion of an Islamic cultural identity, and the Iranian revolution of 1979. It is true that the French political system has long been familiar with Islam because of the French colonial history and since the 1930s has known a significant Maghrebi influx. That immigration has continued long after decolonization, although since then talk about going back to the countries of origin has accompanied the move away from them.

Change has been taking place since the 1970s, when, officially, immigration to all the European countries was stopped and Islam became a tool for collective negotiation. First of all, Islam has occupied that private space to which religious behaviors have been confined since the separation between church and state that occurred in France in 1905. However, it has voiced a demand for recognition in the public space, constituting a community capable of becoming a legitimate collective actor to face the various French authorities. The religious factor has become a substitute for political participation, which is lacking, and for economic and cultural integration that is insufficient. Religion is a provocative way to ask for integration, and the French system cannot answer the questions it raises without having to modify itself. On the part of the migrants, the religious demands have been peaceful ones, most often made on the basis of human rights revendications.

Since the 1970s, the phenomenon has taken a pan-European dimension. First of all, the Maghrebi diaspora has not limited itself to France. It has existed in Belgium, in Germany, and in Holland since the 1970s, going through the same changes, especially in becoming a family immigration. A more recent immigration, but nevertheless similar to the previous ones as far as behavior is concerned, is nowadays occurring in Spain and Italy.

The problems linked with the nationality of either the countries of origin or the host countries are creating what will probably become a new type of citizenship in the community. The Maghrebi case is similar to that of the Turks, settled essentially in Germany, and the Indo-Pakistanis in Great Britain.

As a consequence of the groups' immigration, the old nation-states can no longer define the rules of citizenship as they once did.

Communities of a new type are coming into being in the transnational space. Their presence modifies the rules of the game and tends, in the long run, to add to the pressures for a European federal system on the verge of being elaborated, evoking some aspects of the American system and more clearly giving the preference to the *jus solis* (place of birth) over the *jus sanguini* (descendance) as the determinant of citizenship. In the meantime, the developing system is unable to adopt immediately a precise attitude without conflicting with various national heritages.

Moreover, the groups that assert their collective identity by valorizing their cultural and religious heritage nevertheless adopt a cautious behavior in their relationships and display an adhesion to collective rules, especially in French society. Two recent events, the crisis over wearing the so-called Islamic scarf at school in October 1989 and the Persian Gulf crisis, may have, paradoxically, helped to demonstrate that there exists a largely predominant allegiance attitude among Muslims. On the one hand, Muslims are looking for a collective visibility by respecting food taboos, by having identifiable places of worship available, and by searching for a group representation capable of negotiating on their behalf. On the other hand, they see to it that they do not become too provocative in the eyes of the majority of the population. Polls show that more than half of them are against the wearing of the scarf and nearly as many do not want a call for prayer from the mosque. Nearly all favor private practice of Islam, accept intermarriage with a non-Muslim person, and support ongoing relations with a relative who has abandoned Islam. But collective reactions that some perceive as related to the management of a private space appear to the outside world as being characteristic behaviors of a community group and as a kind of intrusion into the public space.

In the same way, during the Persian Gulf crisis, at a time when French society feared particularly the impact of solidarity conflicts, Muslims in France recognized the legitimacy of the right of the President of the Republic to involve France in a war against an Arab and Muslim country, although they preferred negotiations as an alternative. In February 1991, François Mitterrand received favorable opinions from 67 percent of Muslims, while Saddam Hussein found favor with only 26 percent. The discourse of Muslims in France was above all anti-American and anti-Israeli, and Muslims tried, on the contrary, to find excuses for the behavior of French leaders.

Confronting the new situation of a minority trying to negotiate its space without disappearing, in the 1980s the French political system created interlocutors from among the migrants, by converting Maghrebi intellectuals into social workers. Of-

ficially committed to the earlier policy of individual integration, the French political system gradually came to accept dealing with intermediaries acting on behalf of the community. But, in the process, the state got the impression that it no longer had complete control over the norms of society. Other actors, especially local powers, have, since 1982, had greater autonomy and, since 1985-86, with the construction of the new European political space, have been competing with the central state for the definition of values and collective practices.

THE PRESSURES ON EUROPEAN STATES

At a time when the state is doubting its capability and is losing part of its efficacy because of the economic crisis that affects particularly the youth, are there any signs of a policy for the integration of Maghrebi immigrants within the European Community? Officially, there is no policy or institutional answer to this question. For the time being, immigration does not belong to the areas of supranational authority. The only collective actions on the subject concern groups of experts from the Interior Ministries of the 12 countries, who, at first, had been directed to study terrorism and drug problems and then the circulation of nationals from outside the European Community.

More than the others, the northern European states, where outmoded industries—steel, mining, public works, automobile—were in crisis at the end of the 1970s, are directly concerned with the immigration problem. Thus they are the ones that have gone the furthest in coordinating the control of population moves. As with the Turks in Germany, and the Indo-Pakistanis in Great Britain, an economic and social phenomenon—the integration of a population of Mediterranean and Asian origin—is linked with a cultural and political phenomenon comprising the assertion of an Islamic identity. This raises a collective anxiety over an imported and extremist Islamism, and these fears lead to the rise of an extreme-right electorate.

Nevertheless, the simple assertion of an Islam, most of the time peaceful, challenges the principles that are at the basis of centralized states. The Rushdie affair has been an illustration of those tensions at the European level. The opening up of Eastern Europe has led to the confused notion that migratory movements from the East would compete with those of nearby Third World countries. They would discourage questioning the principles defining the relationships between centralized states and the non-European culture's migrant groups. It is very tempting to create a community barrier at the southern and eastern Mediterranean shores, while applying flexible controls on the eastern border. This comes into conflict with the policy of the free movement of capital and goods that accompanies the triumph of the free-market economy and presides over the evolution of today's Europe.

The main obstacle to the free movement of people across borders stems from the fact that immigration has become a major political issue within the northern European countries of France, Germany, and Great Britain. The coincidence between the North African and West Asian settlement of Europe at the end of the 1970s and the assertion of an Islamic identity has meant, above all, for the migrants, a desire not to be diluted in the mass of the populations of the host countries and, at the same time, a desire to pass on to their children some of their own values and memories. But, because of the 1979 Iranian revolution, that strategy has been perceived as an external threat linked with Middle East terrorism and the taking of European hostages.

For that reason, starting with the communal elections in France in 1983, the immigration problem has become a major political issue, causing the rise of a populist movement under the leadership of Jean-Marie Le Pen. The National Front does not limit itself to the recruiting of a classical, marginal, extreme-right electorate, which may represent about 5 percent of the votes. In 1986, and again in 1988-89, it more than doubled that figure, indicating, according to 25 percent of opinions expressed in opinion polls taken in a time of crisis, that even Socialist and Communist voters were inclined to adopt positions close to the National Front program when it came to immigration problems.

The settlement of Turks in Germany and the de facto disappearance of the myths about the guest workers have given rise, under similar conditions, to the success of the Republican Party in that country. For a long time, Great Britain has been able to manage the tensions created by the integration of an Indo-Pakistani minority, thanks to Britain's acceptance of multiculturalism and to the minority's participation in political life, facilitated by Commonwealth citizenship. For the whole of the European Community, the immigrants of Islamic culture certainly do not represent more than about 6 million people: 2.5 to 3 million in France, 2 million in Great Britain, 1 million in Germany, and a few hundred thousand in Belgium and Holland. In France as well as in Great Britain, the majority of these migrants, or at least their children, are on their way to becoming citizens of the host country. In Germany, that practice is more difficult, but their right to stay is nevertheless recognized.

Taken as a whole, the immigrant group, if one imagines it as a coherent unit, represents only a small segment—2 percent—of the European population. But, in some countries, that share may rise to 5 percent locally, and in other places to 20 percent, due to high concentrations in housing. These concentrations favor the identity reactions translated into communitywide strategies, but also the rejection reactions or a low threshold of tolerance. In France, in the 1970s, these reactions led Communist city councils to enact quotas for dwellings, for entering nurseries, or for access to social services. In this way, the councils dealt with very high concentrations of immigrant populations that often adopt a type of blockbusting strategy and compete with the oldest strata of the working class, which, due to the economic crisis of the late 1970s, can no longer improve their living conditions and find their social mobility blocked. That confrontation has engendered, since the be-

ginning of the 1980s, a slide toward the extreme right, particularly among the middle class.

Thus local tensions coupled with the general decline in the influence of the Communist Party might, during the next municipal elections—in 1994—lead to the crumbling of those traditional Communist Party strongholds that the city councils in the suburbs of big cities—Paris, Lyons, Marseilles, Lille—have represented and where the major part of the immigrant populations undergoing integration are living. If, at that time, the Communists' decline among the working-class electorate has not been compensated for by the involvement in political life of the new generations of Maghrebi immigrants through the Socialist Party, then these city councils risk coming under the control of the National Front. That development will make even more difficult the realization of integration policies on which a reasoned management of local affairs greatly depends.

Decentralization measures taken since 1982 make it extremely difficult for the state to interfere directly in these policies especially when mayors who exclude the immigrants either from entering schools or from getting a home are supported by their electorate. Today, these mayors are able to control either directly or indirectly the housing market, including private housing, through the use of their right to preempt sales. A great number of (illegal) actions to prevent immigrant children from entering nurseries or primary schools lead the immigrants into conflict with state authorities. In the end, their decisions are abrogated by the administrative jurisdiction after the education authorities have initiated a request. But by then, local elected representatives have gained a real popularity and probably discourage immigrants from settling down in their area. In the same way, by broadly interpreting their rights, they now use their control over housing certificates to hinder access to three-month visas.

Their statements about illicit immigration use examples of tourists who settle down, saturate the labor market, and add to the demands for social assistance. They justify in the eyes of their electorate the excessive practices of most of the town councils, whether dominated by the right or the left. Interventions of the same sort tend to develop, aiming at limitations on possible family regrouping.

The state gradually finds itself confronted with a tricky situation in the sense that, if the immigrants continue to be excluded at the local level of government, any rational policy of integration will become impossible. The state might even have to face, here and there, violence engendered by these exclusions. Today, it cannot consider recovering direct control of the areas that, since the 1982 decentralization law, have been delegated to local authorities without provoking a major political crisis. But the evolution toward local management of the problems linked with immigration has given birth, within some decentralized political systems such as Great Britain and Germany, to high concentrations of population that claim, even more than in the French system, a strong and separate identity, leading in the end to a ghetto phenomenon.

One can witness blockage at the local level in France, but the state is still responsible for integration policies. Integration is advanced when leaders belonging to the immigration association movement become involved in social and political life. In the classical ways of the French political system, that involvement runs through the parties and, primarily, the Socialist Party. It is incarnated essentially in the personality of the President of the Republic, who is viewed positively by migrants as a supreme recourse in the face of misunderstanding and hostility on the part of the local and administrative services. But this integration by political channels, which might be characteristic of the French system and is derived from its history, comes today to a dead end, as much as a consequence of local authorities' reactions as of some of the claims presented by the immigrant populations. The immigrants' felt need to mobilize the community and to accentuate their pressure on the central government increases their tendency to resort to the expression of cultural and religious identities. That strategy comes in conflict with the traditions of hostility toward intermediate groups and of confining religious matters to the private sphere, which are part of the basic principles of the modern French state. Therefore, it becomes difficult to find a satisfactory solution to the crisis on a purely national level. To abandon the principles of state secularism and to recognize that legitimate community actors exist would mean giving birth to a major internal crisis. To assume control of the managing power now exercised by local authorities would equally engender opposition beyond the single issue of immigration.

THE NEED FOR A
COMMUNITY RESPONSE

A broad compromise is needed, establishing a level of decision making that combines local management, state policies, and some forms of pan-European coordination. As for the management of immigration, the absence of a European policy will be an embarrassment, both for the member states and for the Community, on the eve of 1993. The states wish very strongly to keep their authority over any question related to population movements that, in the long run, could affect their own society. They might, though, find it practical for a community authority to be established to present externally a restrictive immigration policy, in order to minimize contradictions between state policies, local authorities, and community groups, the inner logics of which lead to conflict.

There is a real need to define a common policy toward an Islamicist movement based in the Maghreb. Too strong a solitary reaction on the part of the French authorities would provoke opposition on the part of the Islamicist movement's new leaders along the theme of colonialist interference. The expression of a policy on the Community level would be more difficult to condemn. A European policy on immigration could help as much to establish common rules for the management of visas and residence conditions as to define arbitra-

tion terms concerning the methods used by local authorities. A common policy could prevent them from engaging in an opposition game with national authorities. In addition, if the European power gives itself the judiciary and political means necessary to enforce its general lines, then the local authorities would be led more easily to abandon their discriminatory practices. The collective structure may not immediately be as efficient as one wishes, but the blockages of state mechanisms, the fear of external pressures, and the rise of community dangers may force the establishment of new procedures.

The previous analysis of tensions refers essentially to the French case, in which visibility strategies chosen by the immigrants have thrust religion into the public space, thus spurring conflict with the secular tradition at the heart of the political system. While Islam is part of the immigrants' assertions of identity in Germany, its religious presence in the German public space does not appear to conflict with common rules. Rather, the conflict relates to the principle of dual citizenship as requested by Turkish associations, which is as much in opposition to the constitutional rules of the German nation as the contesting of secularism is in France.

Is the implication in both cases that conflict is, in essence, linked to an integration process and aims above all at redefining the terms of a new social contract? If so, it would be even more urgent to contemplate redefining the contract at a global and European level rather than through a series of national adjustment processes that might be contradictory.

A study of group perceptions, collective memory, and values, and not only of security, is the only way to establish a new contract. It can constitute a guideline for the judges who will have to regulate immigration in a legal common space, before the state-level powers take charge of it. Such a study will also give material to political leaders for defining their strategy and will help the negotiation with minority elites who tend increasingly to locate their identity in the European space. Reflection on collective memory and on the way groups are perceived ought to avoid the sort of incoherences and hasty opinions that accompanied both official and popular reactions at the time of the Rushdie affair or the Islamic scarf crisis. Great Britain as well as France appears as a precursor when it comes to those identity crises, inasmuch as they symbolize opposite ways of managing the minority phenomenon.

Germany is probably in a more favorable position because of the federal and decentralized character of its political system and the solidity of its economic system, making it possible to grant economic compensation to those who have no hope of entering the political field. Given a tradition of religious pluralism that is evidently more integrated into Germany than into France, the fact that Islam constitutes the third religion in Germany seems to engender less rejection of immigration than either in France or in Great Britain. The challenge that the Muslims present is related more to the idea of a homoge-neous nation seeking incarnation in a state. Turkish and Maghrebi immigrants have settled in industrial cities where their percentages have risen to levels similar to those in France. The fact that the term "foreigner" has been substituted for "guest worker" clearly indicates the idea of a lengthy residence, but it also indicates that the application of *jus solis*, which, in the long run, would grant citizenship to immigrants' children born in Germany, is not even contemplated. That country remains unwilling to accept dual citizenship, a measure capable of facilitating integration.

Meanwhile, one ought to note that, in spite of legal uncertainty, Germany does not expel more foreigners than does France. But German reunification and East German hostility toward Turkish immigration will probably accentuate pressure for them to leave the country; the result will be a move westward rather than a return to Anatolia. Because French citizenship is easier to obtain, it may be used to allow Turks from Germany to move freely in the European space.

The signing, on 19 June 1990, of the Schengen agreement by the five countries of northern Europe—Belgium, France, Germany, Luxembourg, and the Netherlands—might create difficulties. That agreement, which Italy joined in November 1990 and Spain in May 1991, provides for the generalization of visa procedures that are applied by each country. A computer network established for control at the external borders will ensure that the traveler is in possession of all the necessary papers. Such strict measures will permit foreigners to move freely within the whole of the Community space from the Polish border to Algeciras or Bari. The establishment of that Schengen space will create a new type of relationship with the non-Community foreigners.

The consular procedures of the signing countries will be harmonized and made quite dissuasive for those who may be suspected of intending permanent settlement. Administrative controls will be reinforced through the airlines and maritime companies in charge of repatriation, which will have to pay heavy fines in cases where travelers are turned back. Interconnected computerized management ought also to permit identification of those who have extended their legal stay. It is highly probable that overextending one's legal length of time will be punished not only by expulsion but by inclusion on the list of undesirable foreigners who will thereafter not be granted another visa. Indeed, these procedures will affect the relationship between the immigrants settled in Europe and their external bases.

To avoid abuses by overexuberant leaders and their police services, a centralized service in charge of controlling the various national authorities should be established. That would mean moving toward a European authority similar to the American federal Immigration and Naturalization Service, which calls for a strong executive and appropriate legal control. Beyond those technical procedures, the major political issue at stake in the relationships between the European ensemble and its southern Mediterranean environment is taking shape. It would be illusory to think that the tight barrier that is the aim of the Schengen agreement's procedures may be kept very long, especially because the minorities settled in those countries will wish to keep contact, through family networks, with their countries of origin. Their insertion in Europe would be made easier through a flexible management of interests rather than breaking off with those countries.

On the other hand, it would be contradictory, at a time when Europe is developing a philosophy of the free movement of capital, goods, and persons, to establish a lasting barrier vis-à-vis the South. But, since the free circulation would engender tensions that the European society would not be capable of managing, it appears more appropriate to filter and regulate flows. In the meantime, this could be compensated for through economic assistance so as not to accentuate tensions within southern Mediterranean societies.

The welfare state, along with European television images, which today can be received directly by millions of people in the Maghreb or in Turkey, provokes both a fascination and a frustration inherent in the desire to go elsewhere. But those images reflect, at the same time, an inaccessible society that rejects them and therefore justifies a withdrawal into their own identity—a self-ghettoization—favorable to Islamicist movements. In the short run, that evolution is also translated into a new exodus of middle-class people who, having been educated in a modern system, no longer find a place in Maghrebi societies. It would be futile to believe that one is going to put an end to these cultural, economic, and social flows by using visas, computerized controls, and other repressive measures. Such a policy may, indeed, slow down and delay pressure from southern Mediterranean countries, which tends to become an exodus of middle-class persons. But the gains will be meaningful only if a true policy of economic transfers to those countries is coupled with a policy aimed at the integration of minorities with respect for their double culture and interests. If the only objective is to gain time in order to quiet European fears, then it is very risky, for that might engender situations of tension and violence both in Europe and in those countries.

ANNALS, *AAPSS*, 524, November 1992

Democracy and Islam: The Cultural Dialectic

By I. WILLIAM ZARTMAN

ABSTRACT: Current history is marked by the meeting of two powerful currents, democracy and political Islam. Islam itself is the subject of a cultural dialectic between a modern and an authentistic form, out of which a synthesis tends to arise, only to be attacked again by a new authentistic antithesis. Political Islam is the current antithesis, attacking the unpopular states for impiety and materialism. Democracy is also rising in popularity as a criterion of good government, with special meaning as the consummation of nationalism for new states recently free from colonial rule. The two currents are not necessarily incompatible, but they have different sources and will have a profound effect on each other whenever they meet.

I. William Zartman is Jacob Blaustein Professor of International Organization and Conflict Resolution and director of African studies at the Nitze School of Advanced International Studies of the Johns Hopkins University in Washington, D.C. His doctorate in international relations is from Yale. He is past president of the Middle East Studies Association and founding president of the American Institute for Maghrib Studies. He is coeditor and coauthor of Beyond Coercion: The Durability of the Arab State *(1988) and* Polity and Society in the Contemporary North Africa *(1992).*

MUCH of the world finds itself today at the crossroads of two historical political currents. They deal with the highest question of political life: How will individuals and societies decide their own future? Will it be by repeated and updated acts of choice in a rapidly evolving world or by a single referendum on faith in millennial verities? One of these currents is democracy; the other, political Islam. It is unlikely that either current will win totally; more probably, the result will be a turbulent mixture of the two in varying proportions. The outcome, however, will have momentous consequences for the people involved and also for the rest of the world.

The confrontation concerns two rising tides of attention, surging from their own sources, spreading through their own dynamics, and flowing together in many places throughout the world. They meet wherever governance is debated in the land of Islam (*dar al-Islam*), but they also meet in the streets of Paris, in the hidden house of Salman Rushdie, author of *The Satanic Verses*,[1] and in the District Building in Washington, D.C., when it was taken over by the Hanafi sect in 1977. From one side, democracy, flowing from the West since classical Athens, has suddenly resurged as a popular demand and a political criterion in response to the failures of authoritarian rule in both the Second and Third worlds. On the other side, Islamic revival and its extension as a political formula have also arisen, in reaction to the failures of modernization and secular socialism in developing countries.

This is not to say that Islam is the successor to communism as a threat to the West, as some U.S. government spokespersons have suggested.[2] Islam as a personal religious belief has no necessary consequences for either domestic governance or foreign relations, despite the inherent unity of social and religious life in Islamic teaching; it is only when the religious beliefs about piety and correct behavior are promoted as the basis of the political system that they shape the practices of domestic governance and international relations.[3] Even then, as previous articles in this volume have shown, regimes that call themselves Islamic may pursue their interests in cooperation with Western states, as governments in Saudi Arabia, Pakistan, and Mauritania have done, whereas others also calling themselves Islamic may see themselves necessarily and primarily in conflict with the West, as governments in Iran and the Sudan have done. Moreover, in all of these states, opposition parties calling themselves Islamic have contested their own governments.

Nonetheless, as currents of political philosophy, and so of practice, both Western democracy and politi-

---

1. Salman Rushdie, *The Satanic Verses* (New York: Viking, 1988).

2. Barbara Crossette, "US Aide Calls Muslim Militants Big Concern in World," *New York Times*, 1 Jan. 1992; David Ignatius, "Islam in the West's Sights: The Wrong Crusade?" *Washington Post*, 9 Mar. 1992.

3. See James Piscatori, ed., *Islam in the Political Process* (New York: Cambridge University Press, 1983); Adeed Dawisha, ed., *Islam in Foreign Policy* (New York: Cambridge University Press, 1983).

cal Islam are systems of thought and action with their own integrity, neither containing the precepts of the other. In reality, in the earthbound workings of politics and governance, the two sets of ideas and practices challenge and contaminate each other wherever they meet. How to be a democrat in an Islamic state? How to be an Islamicist in a democratic state? How democratic can an Islamic state be? How Islamicist can a democratic state be? All are real and important questions for sincere citizens not only in Saudi Arabia, Pakistan, Iran, the Sudan, and Mauritania but also in France, Nigeria, England, India, the Russian Confederation, and the United States.

ISLAM: THE CULTURAL DIALECTIC

Arab writers and Western analysts have long debated two poles of attraction for Muslim society in its search for a model for the kingdom of believers on earth. One is an Arabo-Islamic model of revealed values, calling for a return to religious inspiration to bring the kingdom of God to his followers. The other is a worldly model of materialist values, designed to bring modern success to the community of believers. To some, the first is seen as authentistic but traditional, and hence outmoded; to others, the second is considered as modern but secularist and often foreign, and thus alien. This dichotomy represents not merely a clash of conceptions and of criteria for desirable conduct but the basis of a dynamic process of conflict and creation that acts as a dialectic.

Out of this clash between thesis and antithesis came not simply a clear-cut victory but rather, in time, a synthesis of the two cultures into a political system that combined the material values of the state with religious values for the individual, as Lapidus records in his article in this volume. In time, however, the synthesis itself has come under attack, usually from a new antithesis in the form of a religious revival that castigates the incumbent political culture for its materialism and worldliness. The confrontation reopens, and is resolved in turn not by a clear defeat of one side but by a new synthesis combining elements of both models. The dynamic goes on.

This dialectic was the basis of the famous analysis of the fourteenth-century Arab philosopher Abdurrahman ibn Khaldun,[4] who saw the dynamic of history as a conflict between desert zealots and urban materialists. The rulers of Arab society became caught up in the corrupting material culture of their capitals, arousing the corrective zealotry of the hardy communities living on the desert fringes of the countries. They emerged from the wilds to conquer the cities and install austere government based on religious principles. But in time the urban life got to them and their rule became a synthesis of the two cultures. In a cyclical fashion, new zealot groups, bound together in their coarse life by a strong spirit of

4. Abdurrahman ibn Khaldun, *An Arab Philosophy of History*, ed. Charles Issawi (New York: Grove Press, 1950); idem, *The Muqaddimah: An Introduction to History*, ed. Franz Rosenthal and N. J. Dawood (Princeton, NJ: Princeton University Press, 1967).

solidarity, again came over the mountains to clean out the urban fleshpots and, in turn, fall into them.

In the coming of Western colonialism, the dialectic took on a new meaning. The materialistic thesis became the colonial society, which drew in imitators fascinated by Western material success but which offended the colonized society because of its foreign and secular worldliness. This time the antithesis came from abroad, through contact with Europe, producing reform governments in the Ottoman core—Tanzimat—and in Tunisia at the end of the nineteenth century. In the Arab world, the clash of values produced a notable synthesis of faith and reason in the works of Jamal al-Din al-Afghani at the same time. However, the corruption of this synthesis through association with reinforced colonial rule in World War I produced a new antithesis in the ideas of Hasan al-Banna and the organization he founded in 1928, the Muslim Brotherhood.

Throughout the depression and World War II, Arab nationalism and Islam combined to form a powerful message to be used against colonial rule. The most successful nationalist leaders, however, were those who could wield that message but could also speak the language of the colonizer and negotiate an agreement for independence to create a modern society based on both national and modern values. North African nationalist leaders such as Allal al-Fassi, the 'alim ("doctor of theology") from Qarawiyin University in Fez who led the Moroccan Independence Party, or Habib Bourguiba, the French-trained lawyer from Monastir who founded the New Constitution Party and for thirty years was Tunisia's first president, embodied the new synthesis of modern Western and Arabo-Muslim national values.

In time, however, this synthesis, too, has come under attack from a new wave of corrective zealotry from the margins of modern society. Bourguiba, President Anwar al-Sadat of Egypt, King Hassan II of Morocco, and, outside the Arab world, Shah Reza Pahlevi of Iran have drawn heavy attack for being too modern, materialistic, secular, tied to the West.[5] Their governments have been charged with corruption, impiety, and neglect of the national culture and heritage but also with disrupting traditional national society in the name of modernization without providing the promised benefits in compensation. Basic values have been destroyed, the city has corrupted the soul, but poverty is more pervasive than it ever was in traditional times, the wealth of the few is more ostentatiously flaunted, and yet the developed world surges ahead, mocking the house of Islam. This is the language of the new antithesis, turned against the former national synthesis of modernity and authenticity and carrying the banner of resurgent political Islam.

These moments of confrontation and challenge to a former synthesis

5. Mohammed Tozy, "Islam and the State in North Africa," in Polity and Society in Contemporary North Africa, ed. I. William Zartman and W. Mark Habeeb (Boulder, CO: Westview Press, 1992); Douglas Magnuson, "Islamic Reform in Contemporary Tunisia," in Tunisia: The Political Economy of Reform, ed. I. William Zartman (Boulder, CO: Lynn Rienner, 1991).

do not arrive by chance, and it is no accident that Islamicism is on the rise at the end of the twentieth century. Such times occur when the current order is in difficulty and no longer a source of stability and satisfaction. When order, identity, and resources collapse, believers flock back to their religion and seek in it not just a means of salvation in the afterlife, in its normal personal role, but also an answer to unsatisfactory conditions in the earthly life. Previous instances in the collapse of regional orders were associated with the coming of colonialism at the turn of the century and then with its destruction in the aftermath of the world wars, both of them strong markers in the disruption of the twentieth-century world order. Steps in the colonization and decolonization of the Muslim world were disruptions in the sense of identity in the region; people literally no longer knew who they were in the clash between authentism and modernity.[6]

But these moments of confrontation are not merely philosophical matters; they concern material conditions as well, and perhaps above all. When the economy is no longer able to fill the needs of its inhabitants, when the disruptions of modernization dismantle the peasant and traditional urban commercial economies, and when the state falls short in assuming the colonial promise of social services as well as general responsibility for welfare, believ-

ers tend to see the cause in divine retribution for the adoption of alien models and for the corrupt deviance of the rulers, and the corrective in a return to the straight path revealed in God's word.

The antithesis, in the words of Addi's article, comes in the form of a religious utopia, which promises jobs and good government here and now, because its economic program "is in the Quran," in the words of Islamicist campaigners from Algeria and Tunisia to the Sudan and Iran. Because the response bears the stamp of religious legitimacy, it must succeed, again not in terms of bringing salvation in the hereafter—where it cannot be verified—but in terms of bringing successful governance in the temporal immediacy. If it does not succeed immediately, it is not because it is wrong but because it is thwarted by the incompletely eradicated forces of impiety. In the best dialectical terms, the antithesis does not seek a compromising synthesis; it seeks to win.

What is required for a new synthesis, therefore, is a vigorous confrontation between the two forces, modernist and Islamicist, and, eventually, a new figure with a following who can combine the best of the two into a nationalist-modernist program for society. That synthesis cannot come too early, or it weakens the force of the debate that is needed to reveal and purge the depths of corruption and irresponsibility in the modernist thesis and the shallowness of utopia and atavism that is in the religious antithesis. Only then can the scientific understanding of modernism and the mobilizing inspiration of nation-

6. See Albert Memmi, *The Colonizer and the Colonized* (Boston: Beacon Press, 1967); Frantz Fanon, *Black Skin, White Masks* (New York: Grove Press, 1967).

alism be combined to produce a program of commitment and productivity that will meet the need for order, identity, and resources in society.

DEMOCRACY:
THE CONSUMMATION
OF NATIONALISM

There have been many stirring and insightful treatises on democracy, from which it is necessary to draw two apparently contradictory but defining elements into this discussion. On the one hand, democracy is a procedure. It is the provision of a choice of rulers, at regular intervals, from among contending candidates. It does not guarantee results at any particular time; it is not synonymous with good government in the short run. It is the way in which both good results and mistakes are produced, and the procedure cannot be annulled merely because of a momentary mistake. In the longer run, however, it is the only guarantee of accountability and responsibility by the governors, the only way of correcting mistakes, the only way both of getting the rascals out and reducing rascality while they are in. Democracy is the ability to choose *and* the ability to repent.

On the other hand, democracy is not just procedure. It is government conducted by democrats, by people who live within the rules that provide for repeated choice and who believe that losing does not threaten their security, nor winning guarantee their privilege. While it does not guarantee good results at any one election, it is based on the deeper belief that only by open debate will the best alterna-

tive be brought to light and that open debate will—perhaps with a little lag time—produce the best alternatives. Perhaps the most difficult part of democracy lies in the surrounding attributes that allow for its success, attributes that comprise social preconditions such as literacy and urbanization[7] but also include an adherence to such democratic ideals and values as those indicated previously. Literacy and urbanization have independent sources of development, but adherence to democratic values is hard to come by without experience in democracy, posing a chicken-and-egg dilemma.

Colonialism tried to resolve this dilemma by giving a threefold training in democracy to its subjects. It taught colonial peoples about its own ideals of governance, in terms of parliamentary democracy, for example, or liberty, equality, and fraternity. It gave them something to emulate by showing how colonial governments were responsible to settler populations, a process from which the colonized peoples were excluded. Finally, it forced them to create democratic nationalist movements as the means to achieve national self-determination, since masses and then legitimacy were the only instruments of power that the colonial ruler did not monopolize, unlike arms, money, organization, and international support, for example.

As a result, democracy, too, has come in waves across the world. Early waves came with the great rev-

7. Seymour Martin Lipset, *Political Man* (New York: Doubleday, 1960).

olutions—American and French—of the later eighteenth century, and again with the lesser revolutions—Paris Commune, Hungarian rebellion, Italian revolt, Frankfort assembly—of the mid-nineteenth century. More recent waves were brought by Woodrow Wilson's Fourteen Points and the emphasis on national self-determination as the outcome of World War I and then, as the result of colonial training, through the Atlantic Charter and the collapse of the colonial order after World War II. But colonial training in democratization was necessarily skewed and truncated.

Nationalist movements were the embodiment of the mass democracy of Rousseau's General Will, targeted against the colonial order. They were an exercise in national self-determination, taking government into their own hands and restoring it to the people, often using institutions that the colonizer had brought and left them. But the nationalist governments were so heavy with legitimacy and unity that they were unable to carry the democratic argument to the conclusion it required. They were unable to condone division, debate, parties, and repeated elections between competing candidates, and they were therefore unable to provide for successors to the father of the new emancipated countries. The democracy of the colonial succession remained a dead letter, a truncated exercise.

Thus, at the end of the millennium, half a century or so after independence, there is a new wave of democracy sweeping the world, a renewed pressure for popular sovereignty that has a special meaning for developing polities and for the Muslim countries among them. It is the fulfillment of the logic and promise of the nationalist movement and the culmination of self-determination, in which government itself is determined on regular intervals by the people, and not merely the independence of the state determined in a one-time vote. The current wave of democracy, which began in the late 1980s, draws its major impetus from the collapse of the Communist system of social or totalitarian democracy[8] in the Soviet Union and Eastern Europe and from the culmination of the colonial liberation movement in the exhaustion of the apartheid system of hijacked democracy in South Africa. But it is in the Muslim world where it has a special impact, since it meets the historical current of Islamicism, which is rising at the same time.

In addition to its importance as the culmination of the nationalist movement, the current wave of democracy gains significance from two other aspects in the operation of the post-colonial state. One is the enormous expansion of the functions of the state, into areas of socioeconomic services and regulations that far exceed the scope of state activities in the precolonial or even colonial times. Typically, in the Third and especially the Muslim worlds, the state is the largest employer and the largest investor; nearly all university faculties are civil servants and all students live on state subsidies, expecting—

8. J. L. Talmon, *The Origins of Totalitarian Democracy* (Boulder, CO: Westview Press, 1985).

and sometimes guaranteed—state jobs upon graduation. Basic food staples are subsidized to a low consumer price, and medical treatment, like education, is free or low-cost. But it is also a source of intrusive regulations, as a legislator of labor laws, currency controls, exit visas, curriculum reforms, and social norms. As a result, the state is an important prize for democratic—or any other—control and not just a source of privilege for a ruling few.

Yet the other element in the struggle for the state is that in fact it has been viewed in the Arab world—and elsewhere in the Third World—as the hunting preserve of the few, alienated from the people, ruling not so much by coercion as by manipulation, and without the charismatic leaders who dominated Arab politics in the 1950s and 1960s. The decade of the 1980s saw significant outbursts of popular disapproval in most Arab countries, protesting not only shortfalls in goods and services provided by the government but a lack of trust and faith in the leaders themselves. Riots in 1981 and 1984 in Casablanca and 1990-91 in northern Morocco, in 1986 in Constantine and then 1988 throughout Algeria, in 1984 in Tunis, in 1986 in Cairo and other cities of Egypt, in 1989 in Amman, and in 1986 in the Great Mosque in Mecca and, of course, the revolution of 1979 in Iran are all strident and bloody instances of popular protest against the governors of the Muslim Middle East.

Alienated rulers controlling a powerful state and confronting a sudden rise in the pressures for democracy as the consummation of nationalist self-determination have made for a most explosive combination. Unfortunately for a lasting commitment to democratic values, the situation has meant that democracy is not viewed merely as a healthy procedure but as a guarantee of the results that the previous system failed to produce. That is a tough challenge to throw in the face of a new system of government in which its practitioners have had little experience, at a time of falling foreign aid, unfavorable terms of trade, and shrinking and redirected investment. Democracy in the Middle East, and elsewhere in the Third World, is threatened with becoming yet another system of government that did not produce the expected results, because so much is expected of it. If the democratic resurgence threatens incumbent authoritarians in the Muslim world, the charismatic demagogue in turn threatens to deform democracy into xenophobic populism. But the most powerful form of this challenge is political Islam, which promises the restoration of morality, authenticity, and earthly success and the exclusion of corruption and error, backed by God's word as a guide and as a guarantee.

DEMOCRACY AND ISLAM

There is no inherent incompatibility between democracy and Islam. Like all scripture, the Quran can be interpreted to support many different types of political behavior and systems of government. It contains no direct support for democracy, the closest statement being an indication that "what is with God is better and more lasting for those . . . who [conduct] their affairs by mutual consultation [shura]."[9] As would be expected, its emphasis lies much more on the pious qualities expected of a ruler than on the way in which rulers should be chosen. As indicated at the outset, each of the two currents comes from different sources and addresses different issues.

The conflict arises when the particular form of political Islam precludes the procedural essence of democracy, the repeated provision of debate and choice between a free range of options. When political Islam, in the name of cleaning out the stables of corruption and alienation, promises to install a system where only those who subscribe to the true path are allowed into the contest for power, then the incompatibility arises. When parties led by devoted leaders inspired by religious beliefs vie among others for a role in government, there is no incompatibility. But when the party arrogates for itself the mantle of the national religion, monopolizing its symbols and delegitimizing its opponents, open democratic debate and the guarantee of future free elections are hard to insure.

Islamic parties and regimes are usually rather straightforward about their intentions, although not always to the Western press. Although the leaders of the Algerian Islamic Salvation Front (FIS) profess their devotion to democracy before Western journalists, they also tell local audi-

9. Quran 42:36, 38; this *sura* ("chapter") is named *"al-shura"* because of the reference to discussion that it contains.

ences that "democracy is heresy" and "all parties who subscribe to the Way can compete freely," clear statements of incompatibility with democracy. It should be remembered that the position of democracy and that of political Islam on the matter of open debate are similar but different in an important way. Both maintain that truth will prevail in open debate, but democrats are proponents of the debate whereas Islamicists are proponents of the Truth.

More complex is the usual division of Islamic parties into a moderate, usually visible leadership and a radical militant wing, often underground, creating a situation where, as in any revolutionary movement, the moderate leadership is controlled and can eventually be replaced by the militants once its usefulness in achieving power is spent. Thus the compatibility of political Islam and democracy must be judged not only by public statements but also by an analysis of probable political dynamics.

While the confrontation is going on, what can be done to create conditions for a functioning synthesis, so that democracy can be preserved in the presence of political Islam rather than being destroyed by it? One way, adopted by most Muslim countries, is through constitutional provisions declaring Islam to be the national religion but prohibiting Islamic parties, often along with ethnic and other religious parties. Many Muslim states' constitutions have both provisions— including Algeria, where the FIS was authorized in 1989 despite its unconstitutionality! A similar method involves the use of a national charter of agreed principles to register a national consensus of values on which participation and competition can be based. This device has been used both in Egypt and in Tunisia, and in the latter case included an Islamicist representative as a signatory but did not permit the legalization of the Islamicist party.

A second measure is the development of a credible opposition. The crisis in the current confrontations between a decrepit authoritarian regime and a new Islamicist opposition arises from the absence of alternatives. In Algeria, in the elections of 1990 and 1991—and the canceled elections of 1992—it was not that the FIS won but that the discredit of the old single party, the National Liberation Front, left no party known and attractive enough to draw the votes. As a result, the FIS, mobilizing all the voters it could, won 47 percent of the votes cast but only 25 percent of the eligible voters. The crisis came from the fact that there was no party that could win majority support from the nation and, more specifically, that could even draw out the majority of the population to vote. In Tunisia and Egypt, strong government parties, even if tied to the old regime, handily overcame Islamicist opposition, running as independents in Tunisia in 1989 and among several parties in Egypt in 1990 and 1991. But in both countries, third parties, try as they did, were too new, inexperienced, and unknown to present a serious challenge to the incumbents, and the old parties were hampered by ties to previous regimes. Yet, as the experience of Iran under the Shah shows, incumbents are in a poor position to help develop credible oppositions to their own regimes.

A third measure is to use the technicalities of elections to encourage pluralism and limit the hold that an Islamicist party could gain on the government apparatus. An electoral system of proportional representation gives seats to smaller parties and prevents an overemphasis of the majority. It often leads to coalition governments and less coherent policies, however. Majoritarian systems, either for single-member districts or for large-constituency lists, tend to focus on prominent alternatives, to the underrepresentation of small and regional parties. Establishment of a minimum percentage for inclusion, usually set between 5 and 8 percent, keeps tiny parties from producing many splinters and overvalued coalition partners. Parties may be required to show clientele or candidates in all regions or all voting districts, in order to establish their national character. These and other aspects of election laws can be used to limit extremist parties, encourage coalitions, eliminate splinters, and strengthen credible options.

A fourth measure would be to delay political democracy until its preconditions are established or at least begun. Literacy levels and urban concentrations have been mentioned as social requisites, but other political correlates of democracy include a free and pluralistic press, an independent judiciary, autonomous associations including labor unions and public affairs discussion groups, and respect for civil liberties and human rights. The problem is that these conditions are as difficult to establish as free elections themselves and more difficult to maintain. Their existence does not guarantee their continuity, and their imperfection can be too easily used as a pretext to postpone the exercise of democracy that would help perpetuate them. Yet without these conditions, it is hard to maintain the democratic values that undergird free elections. The bundle of measures should go together, and it is important to begin wherever one can.

A fifth measure would be to practice the forms of democracy whenever scheduled, let the most popular—including the Islamicists—win, and let them learn democracy on the job. The lesson of many experiments with radical groups is that responsibility moderates, but that lesson is not absolute. Another lesson is that experiments in moderating revolutionary groups tend to take up to a generation, as the Iranian experience shows. Such experiments make for exciting stuff for social science analysts, but they are hard on the subject populations and disruptive for the world around them. The dialectical conflict within Islam and the confrontation of the two waves of political Islam and democracy also have their costs. Ultimately, it is the populations themselves, acting as masses or as political leaders, who will have to make the choice of which costs to bear.

Book Department

PAGE

INTERNATIONAL RELATIONS AND POLITICS 192
AFRICA, ASIA, AND LATIN AMERICA 194
EUROPE 203
UNITED STATES 209
SOCIOLOGY 215
ECONOMICS 223

INTERNATIONAL RELATIONS AND POLITICS

OBERDORFER, DON. *The Turn: From the Cold War to a New Era: The United States and the Soviet Union, 1983-1990.* Pp. 514. New York: Poseidon Press, 1991. $25.00.

FEINBERG, RICHARD F. et al. *From Confrontation to Cooperation: U.S. and Soviet Aid to Developing Countries.* Pp. 229. New Brunswick, NJ: Transaction Books, 1991. $24.95. Paperbound, $15.95.

These two very different books share the commonality of looking at the end of the Cold War and its consequences for the operation of the international system. In terms of style, audience, scope, and intent, however, they are quite different.

Don Oberdorfer's *Turn* is the larger of the two, in just about every sense. Oberdorfer is a *Washington Post* correspondent by trade, and in his professional endeavors, he attended and covered many of the events that cumulated to produce the dramatic change—the "turn" —in Soviet-American relations. His methodology, in addition to direct observation, was to read extensively in the secondary literature but, primarily, to interview an astounding array of current and former governmental officials—both American and Soviet—to whom his position gave him access.

The result is a panoramic chronology of the period beginning basically with the rise of Gorbachev and carrying through 1990. Oberdorfer's purpose is "instant," if provisional, history of the kind found in Robert Woodward's *Commanders,* and the book is very similar in style and impact to Woodward's. Undoubtedly, it will receive the same mixture of reaction.

As a first attempt at the history of this epoch—and given that there is more to be added in the future—it is an insightful chronology that adds some richness and detail to what we knew or suspected. His depiction of the Reagan-Gorbachev summit at Reykjavik and how close the two men actually came to agreeing to essential nuclear disarmament reveals how

192

two people at the top can nearly change the world essentially without consulting anyone else. The evolution of the personal relationships between Gorbachev and both Presidents Reagan and Bush adds texture to our understanding of how the world has changed.

This is a very rich, even heavy book, but it is a fascinating read. Small insights abound; I was particularly fascinated to learn that one of the people most responsible for convincing Gorbachev of the need to invest in high technology was no less than Secretary of State George Shultz.

This book will be widely read both for its content and for its highly readable style. Oberdorfer has gone out of his way to avoid interpreting and editorializing on events. Although he recognizes this to be an interim history of the era, it is still a highly valuable source.

The Feinberg et al. volume is a good bit narrower and more specialized. As its subtitle suggests, it is an investigation of how the Americans and Soviets can cooperate in providing developmental assistance to the Third World in the future. Its unique perspective is that it is the product of a conference under the joint auspices of the Overseas Development Council and the Institute of World Economy and International Relations of the USSR Academy of Sciences.

The book is both an analysis and an advocacy of future joint ventures. In the early chapters, Soviet and American scholars look at how they operated competitively in the past and move on to how they may be able to cooperate in the post-Cold War world. When the analysis moves to advocacy, it loses some of its rigor; for instance, the participants argue that funds spent on military competition during the Cold War might now be used for funding developmental assistance.

This book clearly has a much more limited audience. Moreover, the timing of its appearance could hardly have been worse, since its suggestions for collaboration are almost certainly going to evaporate as rapidly as has the former Soviet Union itself. Still, it is an interesting example of just how far the Cold War relationship has moved away from confrontation toward cooperation.

DONALD M. SNOW

University of Alabama
Birmingham

TRACHTENBERG, MARC. *History and Strategy*. Pp. xii, 292. Princeton, NJ: Princeton University Press, 1991. $44.50. Paperbound, $14.92.

In recent years it has been frequently argued that the most interesting scholarship is appearing along the interstices between traditionally defined disciplines. Marc Trachtenberg's brilliant and richly detailed book provides a superb example of this phenomenon. Trachtenberg was trained as a historian, and his first, highly regarded, book dealt with a classic topic in diplomatic history, the issue of reparations after the First World War.

History and Strategy, a series of discrete essays, is in large measure a sophisticated dialogue between diplomatic history and political science, focusing on American nuclear policy and strategy between 1945 and the late 1960s. Included are three important studies of how that strategy was implemented in moments of crisis. Trachtenberg pays close attention to the tremendously important literature on strategic theory, produced by a hybrid breed of intellectuals associated with governmental and private think tanks and various university institutes of advanced study, who are closest to political scientists in method and approach.

The first essay deals with strategic thought in America between 1952 and 1966. It is a powerful and original analysis of the influential writings of such theorists as Bernard Brodie, Thomas Schelling, and Albert Wohlstetter, mostly affiliated with the RAND Corporation. All the other essays, except the second, build upon the premises developed in this more theoretical chapter. The studies of the Berlin Crisis and the Cuban Missile Crisis offer convincing reconstructions of terrifying moments in our recent history. Trachtenberg uses recently declassified material most effectively, and he ingeniously works around key documents that are still classified, making plausible hypotheses about what actually transpired. His inferences—based, of course, upon very different and much less reliable evidence—about Soviet attitudes and responses during various crises are remarkably persuasive.

My one regret is that Trachtenberg— or his editors—felt obliged to include his 52-page essay on the coming of World War I, which in itself is an excellent overview of one of what remains probably the greatest historical controversy of this century, if not of all time. But it does not fit with the rest of the book and should have been published separately. A slimmer but more satisfyingly structured volume would have resulted.

Trachtenberg's book was completed before the dramatic reductions in nuclear weapons put into effect by Presidents Bush and Gorbachev in the fall of 1991. As of this writing, in late November 1991, the Doomsday Clock has just been reset at 17 minutes before midnight, the best setting since this unnerving, if effective, graphic image began to appear in the *Bulletin of the Atomic Scientists* more than forty years ago. Trachtenberg warns us that in the more relaxed climate of the late 1980s Americans were suffering from "what can only be called an extraordinary case of collective nuclear amnesia." This careful, judicious reconstruction of a time when the hands on that clock were much closer to midnight and global catastrophe goes a long way toward helping us recover

from that amnesia. Trachtenberg's book should be widely read and debated by academics and political and military leaders alike.

DAVID L. SCHALK

Vassar College
Poughkeepsie
New York

AFRICA, ASIA, AND
LATIN AMERICA

FORESTA, RONALD A. *Amazon Conservation in the Age of Development: The Limits of Providence*. Pp. x, 366. Gainesville: University of Florida Press, 1991. $49.95.

Here is a specialized study that richly deserves a readership far wider than those persons customarily interested in a book by a geographer about conservation in one foreign river valley, albeit the world's largest one. On a topic where advocacy writings often bordering on the polemical have enjoyed much greater attention than those founded on serious and objective scholarship, Ronald Foresta has combined rigorous research with eminently sensible analysis in a readable work that goes far to frame the increasingly salient issue of tropical rain forest preservation in truly meaningful terms. With the 1992 world ecology conference having taken place in June in Rio de Janeiro, this well-grounded study could hardly be more timely. Although it carries the detailed story of Brazilian Amazon programs only through the mid-1980s, Foresta's impressively documented book provides all the elements necessary to place the present policy debate in proper focus and set the broader philosophical issues in perspective.

Foresta is highly concerned with putting biological conservation into a broader sociopolitical context. To this end, he closely examines the programs and activities of Brazil's Forest Development Institute and environment secretary within the immense area of the Amazon basin, always with an eye for lessons from this experience that can be applied to successful strategies for conservation in the future. Following an overview through the 1970s in his first three chapters, Foresta focuses upon the difficult and only partially successful task of developing a continuing political constituency for conservation and consolidating the gains made to 1980. He perceptively portrays the heavy impact of economic and political interests whenever conservation and development clashed frontally. In large part owing to the economic recession of the late part of the 1980s, the long-awaited return to civilian democratic politics after 1985 resulted in loss of headway by the Brazilian conservation movement rather than the gains that environmentalists had expected. Although Foresta does not foresee a major upsurge in domestic political support for conservation in the years immediately ahead, he does believe that external pressures will have a significant positive impact.

Important as this book is to the comparative study of conservation, it is equally valuable as a case study of public policymaking in Brazil over a time span of two decades, for Dr. Foresta has developed a competence with respect to Brazilian government and politics extremely rare among scholars outside the closely related disciplines of political science, sociology, and economics. Indeed, his grasp of political factors involved in policy toward the Amazon—closer to masterful than merely competent—surpasses that of all but the best of the latter and the cream of historians working on Brazil.

RONALD M. SCHNEIDER

Queens College
Flushing
New York

HAERI, SHAHLA. *Law of Desire: Temporary Marriage in Shi'a Islam*. Pp. xiii, 256. Syracuse, NY: Syracuse University Press, 1989. No price.

Shahla Haeri's study of the unique Shi'a Muslim practice of temporary marriage has, in the short time since its publication, already become a classic work. This should ideally be the fate of every well-researched, well-written book. But Haeri's study has the added attraction of being virtually the only study of this social institution—exotic even within the world of Islam, since it is prohibited by Sunni Muslim law.

Haeri's study is masterful because she is able to use the investigation of temporary marriage to explore so many aspects of Iranian society: male-female relationships, Shi'a-Sunni religious divisions, and the nature of contract in Islamic legal codes. She is also able to shed light on processes of social adaptation and modernization through exploration of the ways in which Iranians have adapted this institution to contemporary use.

In Shi'a Islam, men and women may enter into temporary contract marriages (*mut'a*, or, more popularly, *sigheh* marriage) at any time. These marriages differ from "permanent" marriages (*nikah*, or, more popularly, *'aqd*). Here English fails in simple translation, since both *sigheh* and *'aqd* literally mean "contract." It is the nature of the contract that differentiates temporary from permanent marriages.

Sigheh marriages differ from *'aqd* marriages first in that they are contracted for a predetermined length ranging from a few minutes to a hundred years or more. Second, a man may have an unlimited number of these marriages simultaneously, whereas he may contract only four permanent marriages at one time. Third, since the temporary marriages are contracted, the Quranic restrictions and limitations on permanent marriage regarding paternal and spousal permission, inheritance, divorce, and equal treatment of multiple wives are effectively not operative or are constructed differently. The most intriguing aspect of the two forms of contracts, as Haeri demonstrates, is that permanent marriage is constructed as a contract of sale whereas temporary marriage is constructed as a contract of lease. In both cases, specific payment must be made as part of the contract. *Mut'a* marriage, if sexual in nature, carries the additional restriction that the woman must wait nine months before contracting a new relationship, presumably to determine paternity. In terms of control of personal choice, perhaps the crucial difference is that permanent marriage is a contract between the father of the bride and the groom (and his family), publicly written and recorded, whereas temporary marriage is a direct contract between a man and a woman that may be written but that can be only a private verbal agreement.

Sigheh marriage is most often sexual in nature, and it has been institutionalized in a number of ways. Often the marriages are contracted in shrines, one location where the sexes can mix freely. Here men and women approach each other and agree to a relationship. This kind of liaison is often associated with prostitution and is the source of much public ambiguity about *mut'a* marriage.

Not all temporary marriage is suspect, though. One of the most frequent uses of the institution is for the family to hire a maid and make her a *sigheh* wife to the husband of the house or, occasionally, to a teenage son. Haeri reports that for the maid, being a *sigheh* wife confers additional status and solves a social problem concerning the presence of an unrelated female in the house. A *sigheh* marriage can also become a kind of surrogate motherhood in the case where a permanent wife is barren.

The temporary marriage can also be nonsexual in nature. This is a fascinating twist both in human relations and in legal scholarship, for, as Haeri states: "nonsexual *sigheh* is truly a product of popular 'imagination.' It is continually improvised by people who come face to face with moral barriers imposed by the paradigm of sex segregation." In one case cited by Haeri, a family traveling with the wife's widowed aunt contracted a *sigheh* marriage between the elderly woman and the couple's two-year-old son so that they could travel together in a train compartment without the need for the aunt to veil herself before the husband, since the marriage made her his daughter-in-law. In revolutionary Iran, women and men working in rural areas on development projects contracted nonsexual *sigheh* marriages for the duration of their projects so that they could work together with no threat of impropriety. Clearly, the use of this institution is limited only by the imagination. Indeed, in post-Khomeini Iran, *sigheh* marriage is seen by religious officials as a direct benefit of the Iranian revolution. It is also used as a defense against overzealous officials anxious to arrest people for moral impropriety. Haeri reports one Islamic notary who issues *sigheh* documents to his friends to present to the police whenever questioned about their association with a female.

Haeri's book would be excellent if it dealt only with these institutional and legal matters, but she also appends a set of wonderful biographical sketches of women and men who have entered into *sigheh* relationships. This gives the entire institution a human face. The women in Haeri's sketches universally show vulnerability and a need for protection both as a way of attracting men and as a justification for *sigheh* relationships when permanent marriage has not been possible. For both men and women, however, eroticism is an explicit component in the decision to contract these kinds of marriages. Both men and women seem to initiate the suggestion to enter into the relationship.

This book raises some penetrating questions about women in Iran. *Sigheh* marriage uncovers a range of contradiction about women and their status. They are revealed as both active and passive socially and sexually, both helpless and cunning, independent and dependent, controlled and free. There is no easy resolution to the contradictions inherent in these gender issues, but Haeri has used this investigation to provide a unique and provocative view of their complexity.

WILLIAM O. BEEMAN

Brown University
Providence
Rhode Island

HOURANI, ALBERT. *A History of the Arab Peoples*. Pp. xx, 551. Cambridge, MA: Harvard University Press, Belknap Press, 1991. $24.95.

Albert Hourani, a doyen of Middle East scholarship whose previous works have become required for students of the region, has contributed still another volume that should be required reading for those with more than a passing interest in the subject. Unlike his previous studies, this is not a piece of original research but a summary of his own broad perspectives covering not only conventional history but the economic, cultural, and intellectual history of the Arab peoples from the seventh to the late twentieth centuries.

The book distills from the rich history of the Arab world the essence of most major trends and developments since the rise of Islam to the upheavals throughout the region during the 1980s. What emerges is a luxuriant tapestry blending with unique coherence a variety of historical trends. These include descriptions of changes in regimes, governments, leaders, and intellectual currents; scientific progress, literature, and the arts; and the progress of economic development or the lack of it. Few other single-volume surveys of the region have so skillfully integrated these diverse aspects of Arab and Middle Eastern history.

The 26 chapters are divided into five parts covering Islam from the seventh to tenth centuries, medieval Islam from the eleventh to the fifteenth, the Ottoman era from the sixteenth to the eighteenth, European empire building in the region from 1800 to the eve of World War II, and the emergence of independent Arab states since 1939. Within each of these five principal divisions, chapters are devoted to the evolution of Islam, everyday life as lived by the common person, Middle Eastern perspectives of the outer world, and Western perspectives of the Middle East. The role of non-Arabs and non-Muslims is described as is the status of women, themes not generally treated in survey histories of the Middle East.

Subjects such as the Arab-Israeli conflict are covered objectively but not without critical insight. The recent popularization of emphasis on Islamic revival/fundamentalism is avoided. Indeed, a unifying thread in the total history of Arab peoples since the seventh century has been Islam in one form or another, as Hourani and most other scholars make plain.

The book includes over thirty pages of photo illustrations, twenty pages of maps, genealogies of principal dynasties, a general index and index of terms, and a thirty-page, chapter-by-chapter bibliography. Since the book is not intended as a work of original scholarship, notes are sparse, some chapters having none at all.

DON PERETZ

State University of New York
Binghamton

HUNTER, F. ROBERT. *The Palestinian Uprising: A War by Other Means.* Pp. xx, 312. Berkeley: University of California Press, 1991. $24.95.

F. Robert Hunter's analysis of the Palestinian *intifada* from December 1987 through August 1989 focuses on five related topics: the events of the *intifada* itself; the mobilization of the Palestinian community in the occupied territories; the response of the Palestine Liberation Organization and its constituent organizations; Israeli government attempts to combat the *intifada*; and the diplomatic activity aimed at starting negotiations between Israel, Palestinians, and other Arab countries. The work is based primarily on newspaper accounts and on interviews with Palestinian and Israeli informants that Hunter conducted during 1988 and 1989. The broad scope of Hunter's concerns, the limited duration of his investigation, his reliance on available published sources, and questions about his use of informants combine to make his book valuable more for the many questions it raises than for the answers it provides.

Hunter's most interesting discussion focuses on the mobilization of Palestinian society to develop a national and local *intifada* leadership. Hunter argues that one important result of the *intifada* was some restructuring of Palestinian society due to the weakening of many economic links between Israel and the territories, primarily those based on the employment of Palestinians in Israel. But he never presents systematic data that would indicate the extent of this disengagement or the degree to which local initiatives actually compensated Palestinians for losses resulting from the breakdown of cross-Green Line employment and commercial ties.

Hunter recognizes the difficulties of studying history in the making, and his use of Palestinian informants reflects them. It is hard to evaluate the words of anonymous sources, though Hunter makes some attempt to do so. His subtitle, "A War by Other Means," can also apply to what outsiders are told.

Hunter's analysis of Israel often lacks the sensitivity he displays to the intricacies of Palestinian society. His view of "oriental" Jews in Israeli politics, for example, is simplistic. He treats Israel and Palestinians almost exclusively as opposing communities, emphasizing how their long joint history has kept them apart but not appreciating sufficiently how it has also joined them.

A book such as this cannot help being overtaken by events. In an epilogue, Hunter speculates that the *intifada* "has already delivered what it can. Political change can now come only from the brokers outside, the United States, the Soviet Union, and other powers." But the Soviet Union is no more, and its collapse sent more than 350,000 Jews to Israel in the past two years. It remains to be seen whether the peace talks that began in Madrid will reflect these changes.

CHARLES S. KAMEN

University of Connecticut
Storrs

KOHLI, ATUL. *Democracy and Discontent: India's Growing Crisis of Governability.* Pp. xi, 420. New York: Cambridge University Press, 1990. $59.50. Paperbound, $17.95.

Democracy and Discontent is an important book, not only for the study of India but also for comparison with other Third World countries and the operation of democratic systems in the developing world. Atul Kohli states that his study is analytical, but "two policy prescriptions emerge from the discussion: the need to strengthen the organizations of the major parties, and the need to narrow the gap between the state's commitments and capabilities."

In reaching these policy recommendations, Kohli follows a path begun by Myron Weiner in his *Party Building in a New Nation: The Indian National Congress* (Chicago: University of Chicago Press, 1967). Weiner chose five districts for study: Kheda, Gujarat; Belgaun, Karnataka; Guntur, Andhra Pradesh; Madurai, Tamil Nadu; and Calcutta, West Bengal. There was an obvious flaw in this selection in that none of the districts were from the "Hindi heartland." Kohli, deliberately following Weiner, restudied the same districts. He mentions in a footnote (p. 184) that he also investigated Deoria in Uttar Pradesh but little of the results of the investigation are contained in the note. He does, however, add state-level studies on Bihar, which is often selected as a disaster area for governance; Gujarat; and West Bengal, concluding, as have others, that Communist-led West Bengal now may well be the best-governed state in India. He also looks at two national issues: economic liberalization and the Punjab crisis. His analyses are excellent, as were Weiner's almost 25 years earlier.

Kohli's fieldwork was done in the mid and late 1980s. His conclusions might be even more dismal had he seen the two consecutive failures of the Congress Party to gain parliamentary majorities. Indira Gandhi's populism—displaying the gap between commitments and capabilities—and her failure to maintain the party organization, Sanjay Gandhi's "goons," and Rajiv Gandhi's "incompetence" figure prominently in the analysis, although he adds in reference to Indira: "Would a different leader have done things very differently?"

Kohli cites—correctly in my view— four factors that have been key to the "crisis of governability": poorly organized and deteriorating political parties, undisciplined mobilization of various groups, conflict between classes, and the weakness of leaders.

Kohli's work should lead the way to further country-specific studies on the ability of state systems to govern and to do so in a democratic framework. South Asia might be a good place to begin, with the laboratories of Bangladesh, Pakistan, and Sri Lanka close at hand and each with some type of democratic system; however, these may be perverted by their leaders.

CRAIG BAXTER

Juniata College
Huntingdon
Pennsylvania

NESTER, WILLIAM R. *The Foundation of Japanese Power: Continuities, Changes, Challenges.* Pp. 418. Armonk, NY: M. E. Sharpe, 1991. $49.95.

William Nester provides an in-depth description and analysis of the Japanese political economy since World War II. He describes in detail the neomercantilist policies designed and implemented by the conservative political, bureaucratic, and corporate elites since 1945. These policies, many of them initiated or made possible by the U.S. occupation, focus almost single-mindedly on spurring Japanese economic growth with little regard to their consequences for other nations, the global environment, or even for the Japanese people.

Nester rejects the currently popular "Japan is unique," "Japan, Inc.," and "Japan as number one" theories as well as neoclassical theories of the Japanese political and economic development "miracles." The neomercantilist policies forged by Japan's elites have drawn upon existing institutions, culture, and values, but they are not in any sense a natural or inevitable outgrowth or carryover of a "samurai ethic," Japanese Confucianism, or the "Japanese spirit." Japanese workers, for example, work the longest hours in the industrialized world not because the workers, imbued with a Japanese spirit, are exceptionally loyal and committed but because the system of labor discipline leaves them little opportunity to resist employers' demands that they work these hours. Similarly, the impressive household savings rate is shown to be the product of government and industrial policies, not culture.

Charges of Japan bashing leveled against any critics of Japanese policies and practices are revealed as a carefully orchestrated lobbying effort that has served well to minimize American and other foreign retaliation against Japan's protectionist trade practices. Myriad complex nontariff barriers, erected expressly to protect the Japanese domestic market from foreign penetration, keep profits high for Japanese businesses, keep foreign countries from obtaining more than a minuscule market share in Japan, and encourage foreign countries to sell their technology to Japanese companies as a substitute for direct access to the Japanese market.

Japanese consumers pay much higher prices than do residents of other industrialized countries. The per capita income of Japanese people is the second highest in the world at $19,500, but the price parity purchasing value of that income reduces them to a more moderate $13,000. Japanese people are convinced to accept these high prices through government- and business-sponsored campaigns portraying foreign goods as inferior, tainted, and dangerous.

The analysis in this book is thorough, accurate, and detailed. Nester draws upon the best of current scholarship in his area and synthesizes and organizes it into a valuable introduction of the Japa-

nese political economy. There is little in the book that would be new to another specialist in the area, but it is an excellent choice for the nonspecialist who really wants to understand how Japan got to where it is today, what lies behind its seeming miracles, and what implications this has for the future for all of us.

CHARLOTTE G. O'KELLY

Providence College
Rhode Island

TAPPER, NANCY. *Bartered Brides: Politics, Gender and Marriage in an Afghan Tribal Society*. Pp. xx, 309. New York: Cambridge University Press, 1991. $54.50.

Nancy Tapper's book describes marriage in detail among the Maduzai, a subtribe of the Durrani Pashtuns of northwestern Afghanistan. The book's aim is to show marriage as a means of managing political conflict. The economic and political ideal of a household, argues Tapper, is independence, self-sufficiency, and noninterference from outsiders. Households compete vehemently for the control of resources and prestige, which are obtained by maintaining male unity and cooperation in a household. Hence marriages, inextricable from politics, are an attempt to maintain this unity, particularly among closest agnates, who constitute the greatest potential threat to each other. Strict endogamy is thus the rule.

Tapper divides the book into four parts. The first is introductory, providing background information on her own fieldwork, on marriage in the Middle East, and on the Durrani of the Saripul region. Part 2 describes the indigenous classification of social groups and how it is reinforced by marriage practices.

Part 3 includes the most detailed description of marriage. First, marriage types are discussed in terms of bride-price and exchange. The direct exchange of women for women, claims Tapper, is done to regulate the increasing competition between households, particularly close agnatic households. Ceremonies, gift exchange, and marriage choice are all discussed as political moves between households.

The last part of the book concerns a household's ability to control its resources, especially in terms of marriage and the behavior of women. The lack of political and economic control in weak household heads is reflected in their corresponding lack of control over their wives and daughters. Powerful men, on the contrary, exercise tight control over their women, who have the fewest means of alternative personal expression or of improving their situation.

Tapper provides a fifty-year marital history between several leading Maduzai families, including bride-prices, feuds, deaths, and consequent marriages. This narrative clearly shows the variety of marriages and how most marriages are contingent on those that have preceded them.

Several issues remain ill defined throughout this work. First, the precise total length of fieldwork, conducted between 1970 and 1977, is not stated. The book reads like a grammar of rules, a myriad of general cultural facts charted onto tables and figures, which are at times difficult and time-consuming to follow. More disturbing is the lack of mention as to informants. It seems that a work dealing with gender would at least specify whether the voice behind quoted statements and opinions is male or female.

This last criticism leads to what is perhaps the book's greatest shortcoming: the lack of any feminine voice. Tapper claims that she worked among women, gained their trust, and even taped much material. Yet, the cases, the marital history, the general voice of the book are all given from male leaders' accounts, with the assumption that women have no real say. This is surprising and disappointing from a woman researcher who could have had access to, and might have at least mentioned, women's perceptions of marriage. Despite her in-depth discussion of exchange, Tapper speaks of women as objects of exchange, with no mention of exchanges between women. This solely male perspective raises doubts as to how much fieldwork was actually done with women.

Nonetheless, this long-awaited and long-needed book is a great contribution to the literature on marriage practices in the Middle East and certainly increases our awareness of the major differences between Arab and Mediterranean Islamic models, on the one hand, and Eastern Muslim models, on the other.

BENEDICTE GRIMA

University of Pennsylvania
Philadelphia

VAILLANT, JANET G. *Black, French, and African: A Life of Leopold Sedar Senghor*. Pp. 388. Cambridge, MA: Harvard University Press, 1990. $29.95.

Janet G. Vaillant, associate director of the Soviet and East European Language and Area Center at Harvard University, seems well qualified to give the reader a fascinating account of one of Africa's foremost leaders, Léopold Sédar Senghor. Although Africa is not an area of her expertise, Vaillant presents a vivid composite portrait of Senghor, not only as an individual African but also as a national and continental leader in search of solutions to the problems of a continent desperately in need of new directions. The environment that exists at Harvard University to promote international studies has combined with her experiences at Queens College, Barbados, Radcliffe, and

Boston University to give Vaillant an unquestionably high level of knowledge about world leaders, which she has adequately utilized to give the reader a credible narrative of Léopold Senghor.

To understand and appreciate Vaillant's credibility as Senghor's biographer, one needs to follow closely the sequence of events in his life that she discusses so well. His birth in October 1906, his early education in Senegal, the recognition by his teachers of his ability and their assisting him in his endeavors to secure more education in France beginning in 1925, his determination to acquire basic elements of French culture in order to function in the colonial setting, his serving as president of Senegal from 1960 to 1980, and his election to the prestigious Académie française for his literary contribution to the advancement of the French culture are among the major events that Vaillant captures to portray Senghor as a national leader who has demonstrated commitment to the emergence of a democratic society.

In Vaillant's depiction of this aspect of Senghor as his major contribution to the development of postcolonial Africa lies the sad contradiction so characteristic of "successful" Africans who were products of both colonial conditions and their own cultural background. Although Vaillant discusses the relationships that existed between Senghor's personality, his family background, his literary efforts, and his political philosophy and behavior to suggest the organized mind of an individual who sees his place in society as being determined by a combination of what he is and what he does, one is still struck by the extent of the contradiction that is tragically part of the character of most African leaders. This contradiction has taken a heavy toll on Senghor.

On the one hand, Senghor systematically sought to accommodate himself to the French culture in order not only to survive and function under oppressive colonial conditions but also to assert himself in a fashion that compelled him to question the values of his own African cultural identity. From his arrival in France in 1920, Senghor decided that his future was inseparably intertwined with anything French. Any relationships that he might have with his native Senegal were intended to reinforce his perception of himself as a French national whose origins were African. Slowly Senghor began to drift into the dark shadows of the colonial corridors, where his acceptance by the French was by no means certain and his relationships with his own people were strained beyond repair. This is the dilemma that many educated Africans face.

On the other hand, realizing that he had lost contact with himself and his own people, Senghor groped for rescue where there was none. Claiming in 1948 that "Western technology and culture might set in motion change that would shake African society to its foundations," Senghor used his French cultural discomfort to launch a movement he called Negritude to redirect the thought process to stress what he called positive attributes of African culture, including socialist ideological precepts and claims of rejection of the capitalist and material greed of the West. But when he was seeking his own place within the French cultural setting and the African sense of collective destiny, Senghor "castigated as deserters of Negritude those Africans who espoused Marxism." This contradiction alienated Senghor and badly tarnished his image as a continental leader seeking to assert his leadership role in a tragic vacuum created by Nkrumah's demise.

That Senghor would never fully recover from this crushing dilemma suggests the confused mind of an individual whose perception of self had been lost in the inevitable cultural conflict cast in a limiting environment. Senghor was losing both himself and the course he had charted for his nation. Was he French, black, or African? Senghor did not seem to know. This is the reason why Vaillant entitles the book the way she does. In 1984, four years after Senghor had retired as president of Senegal and sensing the predicament in which he found himself, the French did what they thought they had to do to restore the tarnished image of their favorite African cultural agent and give him back some of his lost sense of self: they voted him into the prestigious Académie française, the only African to have this honor. That this further alienated Senghor from the mainstream of African thought process simply compounded the identity crisis he was facing. When Abdou Diouf succeeded Senghor in 1980, he was highly sensitive to the need to bring Senegal back into the circle of the continental family that Africans have been yearning for since the founding of the Organization of African Unity in May 1963.

The power and relevance of this book lie not so much in its biographical insights into one of Africa's foremost leaders but in its perception of what Africa has been in relationship to what it could be in the context of the life of an individual. The limitation of the book is its limited effort to see issues beyond a biographical portrait; however, this is overshadowed by its candid discussion of the controversial African leader. Everyone who has the interest of Africa at heart will read this book with great interest.

DICKSON A. MUNGAZI

Northern Arizona University
Flagstaff

EUROPE

CHRISTIAN, DAVID. *Living Water: Vodka and Russian Society on the Eve of Emancipation.* Pp. x, 447. New York: Oxford University Press, Clarendon Press, 1990. $74.00.

Throughout the nineteenth century, Russia raised about a third of its public revenue from the sale of vodka. With a largely subsistence agriculture and less dependence on foreign trade than most other countries in Europe, Russia had to depend quite heavily on the taxation of commodities traded in the domestic market. Vodka was the obvious choice.

Public revenue from the sale of vodka was acquired by tax farming until 1864, by excise taxation from 1864 to 1894, and by public monopoly of production and sale from 1894 to the present day. *Living Water* is about the organization of the tax farm and the reasons for its eventual replacement by excise taxation.

The choice between these methods of taxation depended for the most part on the impediments to tax collection in nineteenth-century Russia. Excise taxation, such as imposed in most countries on cigarettes today, would presumably have been feasible in Russia during the early years of the nineteenth century, but it was generally considered to be a poor source of revenue in a society where accounting was rudimentary, officials corrupt, and black markets difficult to detect.

The problem with the pure excise system was to find some guarantee that the money would actually reach the government . . . "where the very life of the inspector may be endangered by smugglers determined to make their way with arms if necessary . . . [and where] . . . honest officials will refuse to serve, and those that do agree to serve will aim merely at enriching themselves at the expense of the treasury" (p. 356).

The tax farm was an exclusive right to sell vodka within a certain territory, for a fixed period of time, and subject to restrictions on price and quality. Public revenue was raised from tax farming by putting the farm to auction. Every four years the exclusive right to sell vodka in each district of Russia was granted to the merchant who offered the largest annual revenue to the government. Clearly, public revenue would have been maximized and there would have been a considerable discouragement of drunkenness—one of the professed objects of public policy—if tax farms had been awarded to the highest bidder, with no restrictions on the price or quality of the vodka sold to the public. Restrictions were nonetheless imposed, in part because the czarist government refused to allow the price of vodka to rise as high as it would go in an unconstrained monopoly and perhaps because it was in the nature of that government to regulate wherever possible.

Regulation of the price and quality of vodka gave rise to cheating by tax farmers and to an almost inevitable complicity on the part of public officials. Tax farmers and their agents, the tavern keepers, had every incentive to charge customers more than the maximum allowable price for any grade of vodka, to adulterate vodka, or to sell low-grade vodka as high-grade vodka. Customers surely understood what was going on but were powerless to stop it as long as actual prices were less than the market would bear and officials were unwilling or unable to enforce the regulations. But the profit from cheating, from not adhering to the regulations on price and quality, would be automatically passed back to the government as merchants capitalized these profits in their bids for the right to become the tax farmer. It was inherent in the institution of tax farming that the government became the beneficiary at the expense of the peasants of the violation of its own regulations.

The most effective evader of the rules could afford to offer the highest bid for the tax farm, and the government became increasingly unwilling to prosecute the malfeasant tax farmer once it had accepted from him a sum that he could afford to pay only by breaking the rules. Contemporary observers were under no illusions about how the system worked.

In the words of one commentator, " 'under the existing system the government is obliged to accept revenues from tax farmers which it knows are higher than can be recouped by honest means. . . . Such a demand is bound, in reality, to appear as farming out the right to commit abuses.' "

The choice between tax farming and excise taxation was a balancing of considerations. Though the case for tax farming seemed the stronger in the earlier part of the nineteenth century, it appeared less persuasive later on when "the government itself had finally acquired the bureaucratic reach necessary to undertake on its own account the functions it had previously entrusted to tax farmers." A special corps of young, well-trained, well-paid, and well-disciplined officials was established to administer the excise tax.

Christian tells the story of the rise and fall of the tax farm, including accounts of the culture of drinking in czarist Russia, the organization of the taverns, the "sobriety movement" to stop drunkenness, and the "tipling theory," put forward as justification for public sponsorship of drinking. According to this theory, steady drinking, day by day, is salutary as long as one does not allow oneself to go on a binge. The tipling theory can be recognized from its modern counterpart in which, for instance, the government of Ontario, with the same deep respect for its people that the czarist government showed for the peasantry, advertises on billboards and television to encourage people to gamble in the state lottery every single week.

The story is well told. The book is a pleasure to read. The research is, insofar as an amateur like me can tell, thorough and sound. Christian is judicious and fair in his presentation of contemporary opinion. Sometimes, however, material that might usefully have been collected in one place is scattered throughout the book. In particular, I would have liked to have seen an early chapter on the regulation of tax farming and the detail of the auctioning procedure so that when corruption was discussed, the reader would know precisely what rules were being violated. It would have been helpful to include a summary of the Russian public accounts and to express time-series of monetary values in real terms so that the reader could tell when an increase in a monetary value was something more than the normal consequence of inflation.

The book is not improved, in my opinion, by Christian's analysis of Russian society and of the institution of tax farming from a Marxist perspective. The damage is less than it might be because, to a large extent, Christian's Marxism is restricted to pronouncements ex cathedra at the beginnings of chapters, pronouncements that the judicious reader can ignore without losing the thread of the story. We are told, for example, that "the consumers' taste for vodka encountered the retailers' thirst for cash. Before arriving at these institutions, vodka was merely a source of wealth; once it left them, it was merely a source of gratification" and that "taxes, like commercial profits, are a form of revenue—a way in which wealth is transferred to social and political elites."

The real cost of this gratuitous Marxism is that an important question is overlooked. The czarist regime was undoubtedly autocratic and brutal in many respects, but not all of its actions in the fiscal realm were a direct manifestation of its brutality. Some aspects of its tax and expenditure policy might have been appropriate to a government that was not at all brutal or autocratic. The question that Christian might have asked and did not is, Which aspects of the story of the rise and fall of the tax farm are a reflection of policies that any government— good or bad—might have adopted in the economic and technical circumstances of nineteenth-century Russia, and which are specifically characteristic of the czarist regime?

DAN USHER

Queen's University
Kingston
Ontario
Canada

EDWARDS, JOHN CARVER. *Berlin Calling: American Broadcasters in Service to the Third Reich.* Pp. xi, 288. New York: Praeger, 1991. $21.95.

This is an unusual book. It deals very unevenly and somewhat confusedly with a fascinating subject: American men and women who served Germany during World War II by broadcasting Nazi propaganda to the United States. John Carver Edwards, a university archivist at the University of Georgia, has researched this subject intensely and well. He has made use of a wide variety of sources including trial records and Federal Bureau of Investigation files of his subjects, various manuscript collections, and numerous secondary works in German and English.

Unfortunately, his massive labors have not resulted in a well-rounded, integrated, finished work. He asks all the right questions, but the answers are confusing. We learn that some individuals fared better after the war than others, but we never learn why. We are told a great deal about the different broadcasters, but the context is so loose that it is difficult to understand just where they fit in. "Axis Sally"—one of the best-known of the broadcasters—is dealt with only in passing. The "ballyhoo artist" Edward Delaney is not given a chapter of his own but gets more space than Jane Anderson, who is the subject of a separate case study.

Edwards attempts to make clear why these men and women worked for the Nazis. He raises a series of interesting questions about their disaffection from an increasingly complex American society and about the dissolution of their ties to it after extended stays in Europe. But in the final analysis, it seems that what really moved them was an almost irrational fear of the Soviets and communism, anti-Semitism—although its intensity varied from individual to individual—an increasing hostility to the America being shaped by Franklin Roosevelt, and various individual quirks.

Edwards early on makes the important point that "among the great world powers Germany was the first to employ foreign nationals as propagandists to their respective countries" but does not follow up on it. He does present some very useful examples of the kinds of broadcasts that were made, and he does go into the bureaucratic infighting that hampered the broadcasters. Overall, there is much of interest in the book.

But the material does not hang together as it is presented. There is a lack of consistency. Two of the chapters appeared earlier as articles and are not fully integrated. The subject is an important one, and Edwards is to be commended for his energy, his diligence, and his research. But the finished product is one that probably will be mined by others who will use the material to much better ends.

DANIEL J. LEAB

Seton Hall University
South Orange
New Jersey

GILLINGHAM, JOHN. *Coal, Steel and the Rebirth of Europe, 1945-1955: The Germans and French from Ruhr Conflict to Economic Community.* Pp. xv, 397. New York: Cambridge University Press, 1991. $44.50.

John Gillingham has made an important addition to the recent literature on the reorganization of Europe after World War II. As he himself notes, the European Coal and Steel Community (ECSC), after some initial studies a generation ago, has received little critical analysis; no systematic study of the diplomatic origins of the ECSC, the aims of its founders, or the actual results of the negotiations has appeared. Gillingham has now filled this gap, his analysis extending to the Messina resolution of June 1955. Throughout, he has skillfully interwoven relevant published materials—including his own —with extensive use of public and private archival sources.

According to Gillingham, given the ECSC's historical antecedents during the interwar period, the important story of the ECSC in the post-World War II period is to be found not so much in new policy initiatives as in the constellation of factors and events that made the Paris agreement possible. Unquestionably, the role of the United States was indispensable. Apart from its general support of integration since the inception of the Marshall Plan, its tactical alliance with Monnet influenced the course of the Paris negotiations and helped bring them to a successful conclusion.

Monnet's initial plans were very much traditional French *Ruhrpolitik*, implying control and reform of the Ruhr in order to serve French interests and then gradually ever closer cooperation with Germany. Yet the final product of the Paris negotiations was quite different from this scenario; developments after the ECSC came into operation continued the trend away from the plans of European integrationists.

How can Gillingham claim therefore that the ECSC became all important in the subsequent construction of an integrated Europe? His answer dwells on the paradox that, despite the failure of Monnet's plans, the cause of European integration was nevertheless strengthened by such factors as the growing desire of Europeans for unity, German willingness to make concessions, and the learning process connected with participation in the functioning of ECSC institutions. Still, Gillingham is somewhat diffident about his answer, noting at one point that "the puzzle" calls for "intelligent speculation rather than rigorous structural analysis." His "speculation" should have been given more extended treatment, since it cannot be easily deduced from his detailed treatment of the ECSC's origins. But this observation should not detract from the book's solid merits. This is a superb study and deserves to join the classics by Alan Milward and Michael Hogan.

KARL H. CERNY

Georgetown University
Washington, D.C.

KENNETT, LEE. *The First Air War: 1914-1918.* Pp. xii, 275. New York: Free Press, 1991. $24.95.

This is a most valuable and interesting book. The author is clearly fascinated by his subject, but at the same time very much on his guard against a tendency to make too much of it. If we often nostalgically exaggerate how important the airplane was in World War I, Lee Kennett attempts to set the record straight.

The book is certainly well researched and includes a valuable survey of the literature as an appendix. One finds numerous citations of actual combat records, but also some of the very intriguing speculations at the time on what air power might be able to do, and even such speculations from before World War I (but fewer from after—more on this). The narrative is well written throughout and offers a series of macroscopic overviews and summaries, interspersed with just

enough anecdotal material and detail to make the story quite interesting, but avoiding letting the "flying stories" produce any distortion of the overall picture.

The overarching structure is very logical. Basically, it is organized by the kinds of uses to which airplanes were put, stressing first the supreme importance of the intelligence information-gathering function, and then somewhat debunking the impacts achieved otherwise from 1914 to 1918.

The one criticism that might be made of the book is that, by rejecting a romanticization of this first air war, it may also be understating the impression that bombing raids left on the governments and publics in the major powers between 1919 and 1939. Kennett somewhat quickly concludes, at the end of chapter 3, that the inhabitants of London, matching the pluck they were to display in the World War II blitz, did not show a great fear of the bombing they were suffering from 1914 to 1918. But there are other accounts that come to very different conclusions, and one can find many discussions after 1918 of how unbearable aerial bombardment was to be in the future.

Kennett may be right that World War I was nothing like what we have projected for World War III. But he may be dismissing too much the post-1918 analysts, of whom Douhet is only one example, who were making just such a projection.

GEORGE H. QUESTER

University of Maryland
College Park

MERRIMAN, JOHN M. *The Margins of City Life: Explorations on the French Urban Frontier, 1815-1851.* Pp. x, 318. New York: Oxford University Press, 1991. $45.00.

The city, as many have observed, is a stage, and the play that runs ordinarily is, appropriately enough, called civilization. The metaphor applies also if one enlarges the view to include the surroundings. The backstage or periphery, is often larger, busier, and more populous than the visible stage or city, but it lacks the latter's veneer of glamour, and a rougher drama plays out there than in the limelight.

France as a whole urbanized slowly in the first half of the nineteenth century, although large cities and places touched by emerging industrialization expanded faster. Paris more than doubled in population, Le Havre and Saint-Étienne grew lustily, and such industrial towns as Roubaix emerged from insignificance. While rapid urban growth led to infilling, crowding, and land-use transformation in city centers, it chiefly affected the periphery. Settlement pressed against any remaining barriers before leaping over them or hastening their destruction. Walls or no, the urban fringes accumulated the human and physical by-products of urbanization: vagrants, paupers, outcasts, new arrivals; dumps, noxious processes, shantytowns.

It is this margin of cities, fast-growing or not, that draws John Merriman's attention. Using mainly archival materials —police documents and military surveys that document the seedy side of life much as the press does today—he focuses on marginality as a social, spatial, and political process. His organizing idea is that the urban establishment's concern shifted over the period: feared as a source of disorder, the urban margin—faubourg or suburb—came to be seen as a hatchery for insurrection, the nesting place for a social alternative subversive of the property-respecting bourgeois order.

Given the inescapable parallels with urban issues today—the very adjective has become a code word for social pathology—certain aspects of the story in Restoration and July Monarchy France strike the reader. One is the gap between the aspirations to social control, as defined by what was thought proper and by the minimal legal-political restraints on the use of state power, and the means in fact available to enforce control. Spies and a compliant judiciary did not compensate for tight budgets and the lack of a professional police force. Merriman nonetheless has to draw heavily on establishment fears to flesh out the story, since the actual record of crime and conflict is remarkably spotty. Finally, while the urban margins appeared to threaten society, they, like the sprawl of Los Angeles, also prefigured the urban future. Not only would the agglomeration swallow its one-time outskirts, but, already on the fringe, precapitalistic restrictions on commerce in goods and labor were absent or ineffective, while proto-industry flourished.

Merriman devotes chapters also to well-established peripheral communities and to their conflicts, notably around religion: Red and White Catalans in Perpignan, Protestants and Catholics in Nîmes. Yet even here, his underlying concern is with politics, with the local fact of the contention among regimes and with the struggle of working-class radicalism to recapture the glory of 1792 in a crasser time. While the White Terror and July 1830 occasioned unrest here and there, 1848 and its harsh aftermath come in for the most emphasis. What we can call the Second Thoughts Republic, from June 1848 to the coup of 2 December 1851, saw urban property gradually suppress largely suburban labor, which had mistakenly taken the joint February uprising for the dawn of an age of social justice. Yet even this painful disillusion, Merriman argues, served to integrate new proletarians into the agglomerated world of industrial society.

PAUL M. HOHENBERG

Rensselaer Polytechnic Institute
Troy
New York

UNITED STATES

BELLAH, ROBERT N., RICHARD MADSEN, WILLIAM M. SULLIVAN, ANN SWIDLER, and STEVEN TIPTON. *The Good Society.* Pp. 347. New York: Knopf, 1991. $25.00.

A variety of recent studies have indicated that Americans seem to feel less allegiance to the society at large than in the past. We have in some respects become a nation of individualists with little concern for the common good. A continuation or intensification of this trend can have a devastating effect for the body politic and can lead to a brokered society with races and social and economic classes allied against each other. Results of statewide elections in New Jersey, Louisiana, and Mississippi in 1991 offer evidence that a form of balkanization can indeed be a possibility in our nation.

What is the role of institutions in American society, and how can they be utilized to halt the trend toward an America lacking a central core? This is the key question posed by the five writers of *The Good Society*, who are also the authors of the 1985 volume *Habits of the Heart*, which dealt with the theme of individualism and social commitment in modern society.

It is through institutions, the authors write, that we maintain the delicate balance between individual liberty and social order. Sadly, however, the major American institutions are failing in their task. They have often adopted narrow and parochial viewpoints and advocated single-issue politics at the expense of compromise and common themes. The institutions that matter most are those that deal with religion, international relations, government, education, and political economy.

The authors provide excellent analyses of the decision-making processes of these institutions, and they blast the view that individual autonomy must be the only social goal, arguing that social responsibility should also be a major factor in public life.

They advocate many specific reforms aimed at bringing about greater social responsibility in our national institutions. For instance, they recommend that we examine the European approaches to the issue of abortion; they suggest a greater sharing of authority and responsibility by workers and managers in the workplace; they promote the idea that political parties should be strengthened at the expense of individual candidates in order to promote more responsive candidates and elected officials; and they urge the development of a democratic administrative state able to support and extend a vital public sphere rather than supplant it.

The foregoing are a few of the many suggested reforms that could help make institutions more responsive to the promotion of a greater social harmony. The suggestions are in the most part practical and utilitarian. The question now, however, is to find the mechanisms—whether they be public or private—that could take these suggestions and those from other public policy analysts and begin to implement them with the goal of achieving some very necessary reform in American communal life.

FRED ROTONDARO

Congressional Affairs Press
Alexandria
Virginia

CARSON, MINA. *Settlement Folk: Social Thought and the American Settlement Movement, 1885-1930.* Pp. xiii, 280. Chicago: University of Chicago Press, 1990. No price.

Mina Carson's *Settlement Folk* is a comparative welfare history dealing with the confluence of Victorian English social radicalism and the U.S. urban progressive movement. In this elegantly written and researched academic book, Carson communicates her scholarly passion for the social welfare movement while effectively integrating newer bottom-up social history and gender issues with elite American social thought.

The reaction to crude mid-nineteenth-century English capitalism produced both Karl Marx and the Christian socialism of Thomas Carlyle and John Ruskin, who pioneered "practicable socialism," a mixture of paternalism, idealism, and aesthetic and educational inspiration—an attempt to soften class conflict and the utilitarian Darwinian ethos of Victorian Britain through voluntarism.

When social welfare and social science joined the growing professionalism of the new American university in the mid-1880s, cultural literacy and an obligation to build "character" became the foundation of the new liberal education. Social investigation offered a professional livelihood for the university-educated woman. New religion and new science merged in 1890s Britain when Charles Booth and Mrs. Humphry Ward published popular books that influenced Fabians like Beatrice Potter Webb. Christian socialism's "religion of humanity" was nurtured in American colleges by middle-class women, convinced that social science could solve the problems of an urban industrial ethos. American vernacular "plasticity" helped balance the inherent paternalism of educated outsiders helping the poor.

Lillian Wald's Henry Street settlement, in New York, established a visiting nursing service so that immigrants could avoid unnecessary hospitalization for routine illness; Jane Addams's Hull House, in Chicago, insisted that making the place pretty was more important than establishing "a sociological laboratory." One is more impressed by the courage of the settlement workers than appalled by their naïveté and by the magnitude of the problems they faced, especially with sensitive new immigrants. Addams and President Theodore Roosevelt made a political alliance based on their mutual conviction in "possibilism" as the best way to deal with the threat of social unrest.

With World War I, the generous settlement-folk impulse fragmented. One extreme was the militaristic paternalism of Robert Woods, who saw society's ills through the eyes of the social worker as epidemiologist. For Woods, prohibition was a necessary medicine.

Settlement Folk is an extremely useful study of how well-educated American idealists grappled with the modernism that challenged all of the pre-World War I world. The footnotes—regrettably, located at the back of the book—are as engaging as the well-written text.

RICHARD H. COLLIN

University of New Orleans
Louisiana

CORNELIUS, JANET DUITSMAN. *When I Can Read My Title Clear: Literacy, Slavery, and Religion in the Antebellum South*. Pp. xiii, 215. Columbia: University of South Carolina Press, 1991. $29.95.

Janet Cornelius's important contribution to the literature on African American slavery in the antebellum South explains why literacy was so important to the slave: it was not just for "practical uses—learning to read and write to help facilitate escape—but because literacy, especially the ability to write, signified an establishment of the African's human identity to the European world." After having been defined as inferior and subhuman, the slaves' demonstration of the intellectual capacity to be literate, like the Europeans, was a powerful boost to their self-esteem and pride.

Beyond this, slaves wished to learn to read and write so that they might read the Bible. While the important role played by religion within the African American slave community has already been established, Cornelius takes this discussion one step further by showing the connection of the quest for religious solace with literacy and the connection of both religion and literacy to leadership, secular and spiritual, in the African American community.

Cornelius establishes that a much larger number of slaves than previously estimated could read and write, although problems in determining an accurate rate of literacy remains. Slaves learned to read through their own efforts, picking up words here and there, and sometimes through the efforts of sympathetic whites. The ability to read clearly represented a perceived threat to the autonomy of the white slaveholding establishment, who enforced clear and rigid sanctions against slaves' acquiring such skills. Using Charleston as an example, Cornelius points out how working-class whites as well feared slave literacy, because of the ensuing competition for jobs.

Cornelius has written a well-researched, well-documented, and insightful work that will be must reading for all those interested in African American history, slavery, education, and political leadership. Alongside such works as Loren Schweninger's *Black Property Owners in the South, 1790-1915*, Cornelius's book should cause us to begin rethinking our assumptions about African American slaves and their accomplishments. As both authors reinforce for us, slaves were not merely workers but complex people who, like us, wanted to and did live their lives with dignity and self-respect.

KENNETH W. GOINGS

Florida Atlantic University
Boca Raton

HAYWOOD, C. ROBERT. *Victorian West: Class and Culture in Kansas Cattle Towns*. Pp. ix, 325. Lawrence: University of Kansas Press, 1991. $29.95.

WILLIAMS, MARILYN THORNTON. *Washing "The Great Unwashed": Public Baths in Urban America, 1840-1920*. Pp. xiv, 190. Columbus: Ohio State University Press, 1991. $40.00.

"Cleanliness is next to godliness" and, as John Wesley might have added, "dirt is next to disease and death." It was originally a fear of fever that encouraged philanthropic and then municipal enterprise to provide baths and washhouses in urban centers throughout the Western world in the nineteenth century. In developing the theme of respectability, C. Robert Haywood, in his book on "class and culture in Kansas cattle towns," has something in common with Marilyn Williams's book on public baths. Both are describing aspects of middle-class lives as Victorians strove to better themselves. Both books are also about women's efforts to keep the clothes and the bodies of their families clean.

Victorian West is a labor of love as the author examines the culture of three Kansas cattle towns, Caldwell, Dodge City, and Wichita. Of these, Wichita is the only one to have become a sizable town at the present time, with a population of nearly 300,000 persons. Caldwell is nowadays a village, while Dodge City is a small regional center with 20,000 inhabitants. The book will be warmly welcomed as it examines the social mores of these towns in the wild years after the 1880s.

However, Haywood's espousal of Bernard Bailyn's suggestion, to explain the "presence of great violence coupled with an equally persistent drive for gentility" in American society, such that it might relate to the "high proportion of colonists brought as transported criminals" seems wide of the mark. Surely these "criminals" were in reality the poor, ordinary men and women struggling to survive in the Old World, where draconian laws banished them to the New World for petty offenses. Would it be any more plausible to suggest that the two poles represented male and female elements in society?

Robert Haywood makes much of the divide in cattle-town society between respectable and fallen women. But it was women's low wages that determined their fate; prostitution was for many a necessary—but last—resort. Haywood argues that such women lived wild and hectic lives and died young. But Dr. William Acton, the least sensational and most sensible Victorian English commentator, wrote, "Prostitution is a transitory state through which an untold number of British women are forever on their passage." Were American women very different?

Marilyn Williams develops with skill and understanding the role of the philanthropist in putting pressure on municipal authorities to take on themselves the responsibility for public cleanliness. Her work is illuminating as she demonstrates that the provision of public bathing and washing facilities proved not to be an end but only a beginning as respectable families aimed for private bathrooms within their own homes rather than use public facilities, even good public facilities.

Although Williams examines with care the greater success of the Boston public baths, because they provided for leisure activities, she does not explore the bath, or washing house, as a social center. But in Glasgow, Scotland, the public washing and bathing facilities—never known as anything but "the steamie"— were the center of a strong and sustaining female fellowship that has been wonderfully portrayed in Tony Roper's play *The Steamie* (circa 1985). A lament for the closing of the last of the public baths and washhouses, this play, written for an all-female cast, reveals the strength of the female community in supporting each other. As the women scrub and pound on the washing board, soap, and plunge the dolly up and down, wrapped in swirling steam from the glorious hot water, they talk. They help and encourage the elderly widow, they chide the young girls for their silliness, and they consider, endlessly, the behavior of their menfolk. It is a telling image as they mourn the passing of the steamie, a symbol of warmth and indeed comfort in the harsh world they inhabit.

OLIVE CHECKLAND

University of Glasgow
Scotland

SCHUMAKER, PAUL. *Critical Pluralism, Democratic Performance, and Community Power.* Pp. xvii, 258. Lawrence: University Press of Kansas, 1991. $29.95.

A study of democratic governance in Lawrence, Kansas, this book is likely to be received by specialists as a major contribution to the theory and analysis of community power, and by others of us, perhaps, as a way of enhancing democracy—of a sort—in American cities. This towering achievement in empirical research offers in "comparative issues" an innovative method; and in "responsible representation," "complex equality," and "principle-policy congruence" it suggests analytical tests for evaluating the democratic performance of urban governments.

Critical Pluralism takes us beyond the elitist-pluralist debate and beyond the economistic and regime paradigms—all of which Schumaker examines closely— promising to specify democratic ideals, measure the extent to which they have been achieved, and suggest how they might be more faithfully realized. It is the last part of this promise that is likely to be most controversial. Modestly stated but clear enough, it is Schumaker's claim that his study is a significant step toward making good on the much-heralded but largely neglected postbehavioral project of fusing the empirical and the normative in the study of politics.

I agree that his book is just such a step, and an empirical study of such obvious depth and rigor that is also expressly normative is indeed a welcome achievement. Unreconstructed behavioralists will fulminate, and devout positivists cry heresy. The rest of us, however, while admiring the elegance of his science, may wish to quarrel with his philosophy, to ask, specifically, whether "critical pluralism" is right about democratic ideals.

Complex equality, for example, a concept borrowed from Michael Walzer, seems to me partly misapplied in Schumaker's analysis. Rather than part of a theory of justice that might challenge the reigning conceptions of justice in Lawrence—utilitarian and Rawlsian—both of which are tolerant of a great deal of political passivity and also of just the sort of dominance—money and commodities, here "economic growth"—that Walzer says we need to reduce, complex equality is used mostly to explain (away) the political inequality that Schumaker documents.

Again, principle-policy congruence threatens to mask if not legitimate a kind of majority tyranny, where the majority, formed by the alliance between middle and upper classes, are relatively well off and powerful and the minority are relatively poor and powerless. (The weak and poor win just often enough to make it possible to speak of complex equality.) Representatives, who tend to come from the well-to-do classes, of course "respond" to the "principles" of the majority more often than not. The resulting policies may not always be "progressive," as Schumaker concedes at one point; they may also represent a distorted or corrupted form of democracy when the principles from which they proceed are hardly debated and seem, moreover, tacitly to spurn democratic politics.

Lawrence appears to embody many of Progressivism's characteristic prejudices: economic growth—"progress"—over communal integrity, rule by experts rather than politicians, and a moralistic but unorganized citizenry. We also know that Progressivism rather quickly muted its clamorings for equality as it embraced economic efficiency. Welcome as Schumaker's taking a normative stand is, his political science as a whole seems itself to be rooted in that same Progressivism, certainly in its laudable—in my view—and avowed commitment to democracy but also in its limited and "realistic" view of democracy's possibilities. Schumaker cites as "promising" Stephen Elkin's insistence that a democratic urban regime must, most importantly, cultivate the citizen embedded in every private individual, but this evidently is not one of Schumaker's ideals of democracy. Throughout the study, two kinds of persons are mentioned over and over: those who act, are informed, and make things happen, called notables, representatives, or participants; and those who mostly behave and are passive, uninformed, and the objects, not makers, of policy, called—citizens! In short, critical pluralism is scarcely critical at all of prevailing American political culture, whose celebration of privatism and individualism counsels withdrawal from public life and renders "citizens" a synonym for "masses."

Finally, there is the disquieting suggestion that while a given community may pass the test set for it by critical pluralism, it will be political scientists and not citizens themselves who will have devised the questions and graded the examination. Hence the criticism of Elkin's acceptance of a "subjective" public interest in need of debate and democratic determination and the call instead for one "objectively" ascertained, presumably by the appropriate experts.

Whatever the merit of these observations, they should not obscure the overall point that this is an important book, political science that really matters. It seems certain to set a new agenda for research and thinking about democracy writ small in America.

ROBERT E. CALVERT

DePauw University
Greencastle
Indiana

WHITE, SHANE. *Somewhat More Independent: The End of Slavery in New York City, 1770-1810.* Pp. xxix, 278. Athens: University of Georgia Press, 1991. $35.00.

Shane White, lecturer of history at the University of Sydney, Australia, has written an extraordinary view of the United States' "peculiar institution." He analyzes the public documents and private data on the slaveholders and slaves in New York City during the last decades of slavery's legal existence there. His study also questions traditional assumptions about the benevolence of non-Southern American whites who granted emancipation to blacks.

While data on New York slavery in this period are far from copious, Professor White's use of extant sources reveals that, among Dutch and English New Yorkers, slavery was strongly embraced. Gradual emancipation followed a 1799 state law that stipulated that those already enslaved were to remain so and that the slave children born after 4 July 1799 were bound to the owner of their mother until their middle twenties. After enactment of the law, some New York slaves negotiated with their masters for freedom while others challenged the proprietary rights of slave owners.

Subsequently, slave ownership in New York City became a more complex, ambiguous socioeconomic institution. One example of this was John Jay, who served as president of the New York Manumission Society yet kept his slaves after the passage of the 1799 law. Upper- and middle-class New Yorkers such as Jay were not concerned about the incongruity of ending slavery and owning slaves; to them, slave owning was a symbol of economic achievement.

Professor White also argues that black culture—whether slave or free—significantly influenced the New York colonial society in adjusting to a nonslaveholding status. In this period, white New Yorkers became accustomed to the gradual rearrangement of master-slave relationships. Some New York slaves influenced their owners in the selection of new owners while others found their own buyers. Thus white and black New Yorkers made accommodation with the process of gradual emancipation.

Yet, black New Yorkers had no illusions about the alleged mildness of their slavery before and after the 1799 law. Violence toward slaves and violent resistance—such as the 1712 slave rebellion— were not uncommon. Slaves and free blacks were victimized by working-class white New Yorkers who resented the African presence.

Although this well-crafted book focuses on New York, it suggests that scholars still do not understand the complex social, economic, and political manifestations of chattel slavery in American cities in general. The book is troubling at some points; for example, it provides too little discussion of the black church and the role that Peter Williams of New York played in the establishment of African Methodist Episcopal Zion Church. Despite this, the volume is a useful analysis of New York City in the late eighteenth and early nineteenth century and of how that city maintained institutionalized slavery and, paradoxically, also sought to disestablish it.

JOHN A. HARDIN

Western Kentucky University
Bowling Green

SOCIOLOGY

ANDERSON, ELIJAH. *Streetwise: Race, Class, and Change in an Urban Community.* Pp. xii, 276. Chicago: University of Chicago Press, 1990. $19.95.

In this readable and interesting book, Elijah Anderson offers his insights into the continuing poverty and crime that afflict urban neighborhoods, especially those with a concentration of blacks. His focus is entirely upon the areas adjoining the University of Pennsylvania and Drexel University in Philadelphia, and his approach is exclusively ethnographic.

The book has two unusual assets. During the 1980s, when Anderson carried out his fieldwork, this heterogeneous locale included students from the universities; survivors of the antiwar and counterculture movements of the 1960s; middle-class whites and blacks involved in gentrification; a few newly arrived Asians; the remnants of a previous middle-class black group; and another few blocks with an impoverished black population, a group many would identify as the urban underclass. A unique contribution is Anderson's detailed description of how these groups shared their space, that is, how they behaved toward each other on the streets and in the meetings they held that sought to deal with pressing community issues. Quite clearly, there was a class dimension, but it was complicated by race, by the commitment some residents had to liberal ideologies more popular a generation ago, and by the hope of others for profits as land values went up.

For readers who are interested in public behavior in an intriguing neighborhood, such as how individuals determine whether it is safe to go for a walk or how the police perceive the area or whether a black skin protects a person from street crime, this is the book. It is the work of a perceptive and thorough ethnographer. The portrayal of the values of the struggling black working class is exceptionally good.

Anderson also makes a contribution by carefully examining the idea that structural changes in the economy and in the welfare system produced substantial changes in the values and behavior of those blacks who lacked the training and skills to secure good jobs. As blue-collar employment declined in Philadelphia, a drug culture emerged and some young black men regarded the opportunity to become rich selling drugs much more highly than taking the low-level jobs for which they were qualified. In Anderson's view, this reshaped their views of work and led them to disparage the older black men in the community who held solid blue-collar jobs. Young black women hoped they could marry a man who would work diligently, become a model father, and buy a home in the suburbs. They realized this was improbable, and welfare gave them an opportunity for independence. Thus the availability of payments from Aid to Families with Dependent Children, Anderson suggests, created a new set of values among poor women and helped to further isolate men and women by making them economically more independent.

I stress that Anderson does not prove that the values of lower-class blacks have been fundamentally reshaped by the absence of good blue-collar jobs, by the possibility for wealth by merchandising drugs, or by governmental welfare payments. Rather, he presents a plausible and thoughtful discussion of these issues.

Few social scientists are willing to take on the task of describing how social values change, especially when the new ones are seemingly much more deleterious to everyone than were the previous ones.

Three issues might have been treated differently. First, much of the book focuses upon the lower-class black residents and their interactions with the police or with the gentrifiers, both black and white. Anderson is careful not to generalize, but a reader might infer that he describes a pattern of change common in many black urban neighborhoods. He suggests that the area formerly housed a stable middle- or working-class black population, and readers will infer that what happened in this Philadelphia neighborhood probably occurred elsewhere. In particular, Anderson implies that there was a social cohesion in the black community that disappeared because of job loss, drugs, and welfare. Supposedly, older black men and women once socialized their children, monitored their neighbors' children, and taught young blacks how to be upstanding citizens who would take working-class jobs and raise stable families. Was this ever the case? Perhaps, but there is nothing in this volume to document it. Certainly, the descriptions of Washington's black ghettos a generation ago provided in Elliot Liebow's *Tally's Corner* (Boston: Little, Brown, 1967) and in Ulf Hannerz's *Soulside* (New York: Columbia University Press, 1969) do not match the image Anderson provides. Nor did W.E.B. DuBois, in *The Philadelphia Negro* (Philadelphia: University of Pennsylvania Press, 1899), describe much social cohesion when he lived and wrote about an adjoining Philadelphia area nine decades ago. Philadelphia's black community has been studied extensively, and Anderson might have drawn upon previous investigations and census data to provide several pages or a chapter about the actual status in 1950 or 1960 of the area he studied.

Second, I would appreciate more specification about what distinguishes the values and behaviors of the lower-class blacks in this book. For example, an interesting chapter describes sex codes and family life, reporting that young black men use many verbal games and strategies in their efforts to seduce young women, who have their own wily ways to obtain what they want from a relationship. Perhaps the same game is also played across the street by the middle-class and upper-class college students. Similarly, is there anything unique about the conflict over the functioning of the local public school?

Finally, there are problems in the last chapter, which discusses possible public policies. There is something for everybody in this discussion. Running throughout the book is the powerful idea that young black men with limited skills can no longer locate high-paying jobs, jobs that were readily available to their fathers. This agrees with the idea of William Julius Wilson and John Kasarda that male joblessness is the key cause of current black poverty. But Anderson also states that the work ethic has been lost and that young black men are often reluctant to accept the physically demanding, dirty jobs that may be available. In this regard, he endorses the views of Lawrence Mead. Interestingly, there is little in this book about the apparently improving job prospects for black women. Anderson's interpretation of the consequences of governmental transfer payments—especially benefits for unmarried women with children—seems consistent with those of Charles Murray and George Gilder.

This lucid book is stimulating and will be widely cited in the continuing thriving discussion of black poverty and urban decline. It clearly reports that the process of gentrification will hardly uplift neighboring poor areas. Similar to Alan Kotlowitz's *There Are No Children Here* (New York: Doubleday, 1991), the book is basically very pessimistic. After reading *Streetwise*, one appreciates that there are no easily implemented policies that will facilitate upward mobility by impoverished blacks, that might make urban areas safe, or that might encourage the residential integration of blacks and whites or the rich and the poor.

REYNOLDS FARLEY

University of Michigan
Ann Arbor

GOODWIN, MARJORIE HARNESS. *He—Said—She—Said: Talk as Social Organization among Black Children.* Pp. x, 371. Bloomington: Indiana University Press, 1990. $49.95. Paperbound, $19.95.

For eighteen months, anthropologist Marjorie Goodwin, armed with a tape recorder, followed a group of 49 black youngsters who lived on a street she calls Maple Street in Southwest Philadelphia. Early on, she became an invisible member of the group and diligently recorded their activities and conversations. The 26 boys ranged in age from 5 to 14; the 23 girls, from 4 to 13. The original focus of her investigation, part of a Ph.D. dissertation at the University of Pennsylvania, centered on how children from working-class families interacted and socialized, but, a decade later, after immersing herself in the literature on children by sociologists, anthropologists, psychologists, linguists, folklorists, ethnologists, and others—the appendices, notes, and bibliography of the book under review comprise nearly 20 percent of the volume—Goodwin turned her attention increasingly to how everyday talk could be analyzed to understand the social interaction —and by extension, the social organization—of the Maple Street youngsters.

By examining the conversations of youngsters in their social environment— rather than their speech patterns when they are with adults or in a caretaker setting—the study concentrates on, as Goodwin writes, "children as *actors actively engaged* in the construction of their social worlds rather than as *passive objects* who are recipients of culture." The social world the children created, as revealed in their talk, is discussed under such rubrics as "directives" (how one child attempted to get another to do something); "pretend play" (how boys used a hierarchical social organization to coordinate their activities and girls had minimal concern about status); "disputes and gossip" (how the children dealt with their differences of opinion); "he—said—she—said" gossip disputes, a form used almost exclusively by the girls and including accusations or a particular breach, such as one girl's talking behind another's back; and, perhaps most important, "stories," or how speakers created what was in essence "a vernacular theatrical performance" with the storyteller mimicking the exploits of participants, gesturing to set the scene, and providing necessary background information.

Although at times didactic, and occasionally pedantic, what emerges from the pages of this volume is an analysis of the remarkable diversity and complexity of activities and talk among a group of inner-city youngsters, who, despite age and gender differences, created a social environment that was at once exciting, complicated, engaging, and meaningful. Cooperation and competition existed across age and gender groupings. In the process of socialization, age, sex, and, by inference, race were not as important as what the children had in common—their shared humanity. By focusing on the social world of the children themselves, Goodwin breaks new ground.

LOREN SCHWENINGER

University of North Carolina
Greensboro

JENCKS, CHRISTOPHER and PAUL PETERSON, eds. *The Urban Underclass*. Pp. xiv, 490. Washington, DC: Brookings Institution, 1991. $34.95. Paperbound, $14.95.

This book is a collection of papers presented at a conference on the urban underclass at Northwestern University in 1989. The papers discuss the theories and hypotheses set forth by the sociologist William Julius Wilson. Although other research is also mentioned in the book, most of the papers revolve around Wilson's book *The Truly Disadvantaged*.

The book is divided into five sections. In part 1, Paul Peterson defines the concept of the urban underclass and discusses the paradox of poverty amid plenty. Christopher Jencks reports that, in the 1980s, dropout rates and reading and mathematical skills improved for the urban poor, teenage parenthood and poverty stopped improving, welfare dependency and violence stopped getting worse, and male joblessness and unwed parenthood became more severe. The paper is an excellent survey of the data and literature on the issues discussed throughout the book.

Part 2 deals with the economic conditions of the urban underclass. The titles of the articles are indicative of the issues discussed, for example, Richard Freeman's "Employment and Earnings of Disadvantaged Young Men in a Labor Shortage Economy" and Greg Duncan and Saul Hoffman's "Teenage Underclass Behavior and Subsequent Poverty."

Parts 3 and 4 cover the rationale of inner-city life and the causes and consequences of concentrated poverty. In this section, Elijah Anderson's and James Rosenbaum and Susan Popkins's papers are recommended for their originality.

Part 5 is concerned with the policy responses to poverty and whether the programs to combat it should be targeted exclusively on the poor or should be more universal in their application. Wilson dis-

cusses the latter issue in this part, and he restates his views in the last chapter.

Although the book contains valuable research, it lacks coherence. According to Jencks, what is considered underclass can be disaggregated into what he labels the impoverished underclass or undeserving poor, the jobless underclass, the educational underclass, the violent underclass, and the reproductive underclass or unwed mothers. He then finds that some problems are getting better and some are getting worse depending on whether the numbers in each category are increasing or decreasing. Wilson's approach to the phenomenon is holistic. According to him, what differentiates the urban underclass from what is traditionally called the lower class is their neighborhood or social milieu, specifically, living in urban census tracts with poverty rates exceeding 40 percent. He then rightly dismisses Jencks's paper as being irrelevant to the issue. For Wilson, individuals in their spatial context, their neighborhood, are the units that can be referred to as underclass. But as pointed out by Peterson, only 1 percent of the total U.S. population and 9 percent of the poor live in census tracts with poverty rates over 40 percent. Wilson's insistence on restricting the definition of the urban underclass has the effect of doing what he is afraid would happen to the concept, namely, making it a pejorative term for a small part of the poor.

A. REZA VAHABZADEH

University of Pennsylvania
Philadelphia

KADISH, MORTIMER R. *Toward an Ethic of Higher Education*. Pp. viii, 205. Stanford, CA: Stanford University Press, 1991. $29.50.

Mortimer Kadish's thesis posits that "there are choices of higher education that might produce a virtue that puts it to people to choose for themselves the better from the worse." He calls this "education for virtue." In 13 chapters, he tries to lay out his image of the possible shape of an ethic of higher education. Although he succeeds in this venture, many questions arise that need to be addressed.

To begin, questions regarding who has the power to define what is ethical, what is virtuous, what is better or worse are not adequately resolved. For example, in developing his framework, Kadish states that higher education's problem is to determine the objects most deserving appreciation. What he does not discuss is how we go about determining those objects. What power relations are involved in the process of making those decisions? He argues that through rational resolution, differences of opinion will be settled on their merits. But again, where do power, hegemony, and control fit into this equation?

The student's positional self-interest is also a central concept in his framework, but Kadish has not considered the collective interest of students or subgroups of students as alternative ways of defining positional interest. For instance, he states that nationalisms—ethnic or gender—break fraternities apart; however, he never discusses the history of exclusion related to these fraternities. Might these nationalisms be a rational response to historical exclusion?

Although Kadish argues against education for either the cultural connoisseurs or the technological marketplace, he does not adequately describe his education for virtue. What would these institutions look like—their faculties, students, and curricula? Kadish uses the ballet of higher education as a metaphor for describing his education for virtue, but his dance is very individualistic, a dance of positional self-interest. One could argue for a communal dance as an alternate description. For instance, in a polka one might be individually creative, but the real beauty is in its collective creativity: individuals working together for the collective good. Moreover, can one imagine an ethic of higher education without examining the populations served and those not served?

Kadish calls for an opening of the campus in advance of necessity, and the need for and importance of raising divisive issues, instead of waiting for them to strike. Despite this opening, he does not discuss how the critical issues of diversity, ethnic studies, affirmative action, gender, and sexuality on college campuses fit into his ethic of higher education.

Last, if we are working toward an ethic in higher education, then should we be producing students who have a sense of community interest or responsibility? Or should we be developing, as Kadish posits, students who are individualistic and self-interested albeit virtuous, democratic, nonauthoritarian, and nonspecialized—liberal? Kadish asks us what type of human beings we wish to work for. I would hope that we would work for students who have a sense of agency—those who can act on their own behalf—but who do so with a self- and community interest.

DANIEL G. SOLORZANO

University of California
Los Angeles

PESHKIN, ALAN. *The Color of Strangers, the Color of Friends: The Play of Ethnicity in School and Community.* Pp. xiii, 304. Chicago: University of Chicago Press, 1991. Paperbound, $15.95.

Alan Peshkin's study is a readable narrative. In eight chapters, it is "the story of a school and community that transcended a decade and more of ethnic strife to become a place of abiding mingling," with "ethnic conflict" lessened.

Peshkin combines techniques of anthropological ethnography, while using the tools of sociology, namely, theory, survey methods, questionnaires, participant observation, and interviews. He focuses on community residents and their school, with special emphasis on ethnic groups like blacks, Asians, and Hispanics. Peshkin gleans insightful glimpses into the intimacy of this community and school.

Chapter 2 shows the Riverview community to be a pluralistic mixture of ethnic groups. It is not a melting pot of harmony but one of conflict, woven into the belief in Americanization and assimilation. Chapter 3 demonstrates that what happened in Riverview was "what happened in the United States as a whole. Riverview is a microcosm." The rise and fall of ethnic conflict in Riverview from 1968 to 1980 paralleled that in the United States during the civil rights movement and the aftermath of ethnic strife. For Riverview, the change resulting from that period brought about a transformation and a new outlook—that ethnic differences could be tolerated and strife resolved.

The transformation of Riverview and its high school to consistently maintain this acceptance of ethnic differences can be summed up as follows:

1. Academic rather than ethnic considerations emerged, cutting across all ethnic barriers; the standard yardstick of grades, test results, overruled in most cases the intervention of ethnic identity.

2. At Riverview High School, assimilation into the mainstream is neither demanded nor supported by groups seeking to maintain ethnic identity by means of enforcement, but it still exists as a principle to follow.

3. The success of ethnic mingling, with minimal conflict, is due to the circumstances of the school setting. Individuals accept the legitimate authority of the school system to make decisions.

Overall, Alan Peshkin's study has one weakness. The sociological concepts of ethnicity introduced to examine this particular setting are inconsistently applied to the data, presenting a vacillation in the style of presentation. Also, the results of his analysis seem to be dictated by his subjective interpretation of the setting and data. As a participant observer, Peshkin allowed his bias to select informants amenable to his perception. He did, however, admit to his subjective analysis of data, writing, "I run the risk of presenting a study that has become blatantly autobiographical."

Alan Peshkin's book is designed to interest the general public and those concerned about the ongoing problems and turmoil in American communities and high schools. It is well researched and highly readable.

DANIEL MITCHELL

Silver City
New Mexico

SNOW, CATHERINE E., WENDY S. BARNES, JEAN CHANDLER, IRENE F. GOODMAN, and LOWRY HEMPHILL. *Unfulfilled Expectations: Home and School Influences on Literacy.* Pp. 251. Cambridge, MA: Harvard University Press, 1991. $29.95.

While it is obvious that children's skills in reading are developed both at home and in school, the process by which this happens is not at all obvious. How these two sources of reading development complement or compete with one another for children from low-income families—the topic of this excellent book—has been especially poorly understood. The authors, all faculty or students at the Harvard Graduate School of Education, studied intensively a relatively small number of low-income children and families—32—residing in a small Northeastern city. The children, in second, fourth, and sixth grades at the outset of the study, were followed longitudinally at three time points over two school years; an epilogue describes their academic and family conditions five years after the onset of the study.

This book, the second of two describing the results of this ambitious study, uses both quantitative and qualitative—or ethnographic—methods to relate gains in children's literacy status to factors in their homes and classrooms. (The complementary volume is J. W. Chall, V. A. Jacobs, and L. E. Baldwin, *The Reading Crisis: Why Poor Children Fall Behind* [Cambridge, MA: Harvard University Press, 1990].) The data base is very rich in terms of describing two models of home influence: "the family as educator" and "the resistant family," with case-study portraits of particular families and children provided for each model. Parent-school relationships are given full treatment, again enriched by case-by-case information. While less detailed, the descriptions of the children's classrooms help complete the picture of the two sources of literacy development for this sample of low-income children.

The most interesting findings involve comparisons of gains in reading comprehension for children whose homes were more or less supportive of literacy and whose classroom experiences in literacy development were rated as high, mixed, or low. Home and classroom experiences interacted strongly. All children in classrooms with strong ratings made expected or higher gains in reading comprehension, regardless of their home environment, as did most of those in low or mixed classrooms from highly supportive homes. However, none of the children in low-rated classrooms whose homes were also rated low on support for literacy made expected gains. Only 25 percent of children from low-literacy homes and a mixed classroom environment made expected gains. Two findings are noteworthy. The more important is that, for poor children, strong school experiences may compensate for literacy-poor homes, or vice versa. Second, not all low-income households are impoverished in terms of their support for their children's literacy development.

The very ambitiousness of this study, unfortunately, contributes to its major weakness. The authors were intent on presenting both quantitative and qualitative analyses of the data they had collected. Thirty-two children and families at three grade levels and three time points is a very large sample on which to collect such a wide array of observations, interviews, and elaborate literacy evaluations. On the other hand, 32 is a very small sample for conducting quantitative analysis, particularly considering variation in age, classrooms, schools, or family economic and social conditions. The major method, therefore, is necessarily bivariate—correlation—which provides no opportunity for statistically controlling for the multiple factors that might provide alternative explanations to those findings that the authors report.

Despite the weakness of the quantitative analyses presented in this book, the compelling nature of the findings about the ability of schools to compensate for literacy-poor homes in developing children's reading skills is heartening. The descriptions of the actual classroom experiences of many of these poor children, on the other hand, provides little hope that schools are actually providing the compensatory educational boost that this study shows is especially beneficial for children from low-income families. The long-term educational development of these children, demonstrated by their experiences in high school, is even more disheartening. This study demonstrates clearly that schools can make a difference in the literacy development of poor children, but the schools these children typically attend seldom fulfill this challenging task.

VALERIE E. LEE

University of Michigan
Ann Arbor

TYACK, DAVID and ELISABETH HANSOT. *Learning Together: A History of Coeducation in American Public Schools.* Pp. xii, 369. New Haven, CT: Yale University Press, 1990. No price.

Learning Together analyzes the history of American education from the viewpoint of women or gender policy and practice. Since it wrestles with an issue—coeducation—that most Americans take for granted, the authors imagine that it might have been otherwise. They show that coeducation sometimes became the target of vigorous debates, particularly when "women and men and cultural beliefs about gender were in transition." More specifically, this book explores the emergence of coeducation from the colonial period through recent years, emphasizing the complex relationships between what Tyack and Hansot call "silence, policy talk, and educational practice."

Learning Together shows that the system of coeducation took a variety of paths. Although most communities eventually pursued the pattern of mixing boys and girls in the same classroom, teaching them the same subjects, and subjecting them to the same rules and rewards, mixed schools followed different patterns at the local level. Some districts mixed sexes in the primary grades but separated them in secondary grades; others initiated coeducation in the high schools and only gradually extended it downward to the grammar schools.

This study demonstrates that the education of girls was not only a variegated but also a slow process. During the colo-

nial period, prohibitions against the education of females led to the smuggling in of girls after the boys had completed their lessons in New England towns. Under the impact of the American Revolution and the advent of evangelical Protestantism, however, women gained increasing access to education as consistent with the requirements of life in a republic, piety, and, above all, the fulfillment of conventional female roles as mother and wife. By the eve of the Civil War, the coeducation of boys and girls in rural America had become an established fact, largely devoid of acrimonious debate. While coeducation was much more contentious in the cities, it had nonetheless won out there, too, by 1890.

Although educating boys and girls together had become the norm in American society by the 1890s, Tyack and Hansot show how the Progressive Era posed the greatest challenge to the idea of coeducation. As growing numbers of women entered the teaching profession and as high schools expanded during the period, key educational leaders—particularly Dr. Edward H. Clarke of Harvard Medical School and G. Stanley Hall, president of Clark University—attacked coeducation as too masculine for girls and too feminine for boys and advocated schooling that separated the sexes. Yet, this resistance to coeducation and women teachers failed to halt the rising numbers of women in the profession or to turn the tide against coeducation. Although schools introduced a variety of new programs—especially vocational courses and athletic activities for boys and domestic science classes for girls—designed to segregate children by sex within the structure of coeducational environments, Tyack and Hansot convincingly argue that such efforts had little impact on the prevailing relatively undifferentiated learning experiences of male and female students.

Learning Together also documents the impact of the women's movement of the 1960s and 1970s on American coeducation. It shows how the feminist movement discovered "hidden injury" to women in the coeducational system. Building upon the lessons of the civil rights movement, women activists emphasized the impact of institutional sexism: gender-biased textbooks, classroom interactions that favored males over females, unequal access to athletic programs, and the dearth of women in positions of real power. Still, Tyack and Hansot conclude, because public schools historically provided greater equity for males and females than other institutions did in American society, they "proved to be a more responsive target for feminist reformers than many other institutions." In a brief but telling concluding chapter, Tyack and Hansot analyze the unraveling of this liberal agenda, as traditionalists mobilized against treating boys and girls alike and some feminists lost faith in the efficacy of coeducation itself.

This study provides a valuable synthesis of coeducation in America, but significant aspects of the story are inadequately developed. African American, Southern, and immigrant experiences receive uneven treatment. While the study gives some attention to the South and black education before the 1930s, there is little discussion of this from the 1930s onward. Indeed, the civil rights movement is treated mainly as a model for explaining the feminist attack on gender inequality in the schools. The complicated intersection of race and gender in the development of coeducation during the period is not explored. Much the same is true of immigrants and the question of ethnicity. Asian and Hispanic Americans barely receive a footnote, indicating insufficient attention to the West and Southwest.

Until a variety of neglected groups and regions are brought more fully into the story, our understanding of the history of coeducation is only partial. Thanks to Tyack and Hansot, however, *Learning Together* provides an indispensable scaffolding for building a broader synthesis.

JOE W. TROTTER

Carnegie Mellon University
Pittsburgh
Pennsylvania

ECONOMICS

BURTON, LLOYD. *American Indian Water Rights and the Limits of Law*. Pp. xiii, 174. Lawrence: University Press of Kansas, 1991. $22.50.

Lloyd Burton's sympathetic, carefully researched case law study of the erosion of Indian water rights reminds us that because one purpose of law is sanctifying the rights of particular groups, that which entitles some disenfranchises others. Courts cannot defend without destroying. Three issues are at the center of water conflicts between Native Americans and white settlers: (1) diametrically opposed values—limited-use rights to a resource on behalf of a collective good versus doctrines of perpetual private ownership; (2) states' rights—the federal government has acquiesced in the allocation of surface water rights to non-Indian interests, knowing that states compete with tribes over economic benefits of resources; and (3) a "morally indefensible conflict of interest" within the Department of the Interior between the Bureau of Reclamation, responsible for western water resource development, and the Bureau of Indian Affairs, charged with stewardship over Indian interests. Theories of constituency-based decision making in water policy—sometimes called "subsystem" policymaking—

perhaps explain this third issue better than ethical inconsistency does.

Examining a litany of cases, Burton contends that federal court rulings have in most cases defended the superiority of Indian rights, a position first affirmed in *Winters* v. *United States* (1908). Congress and the executive branch have subverted these rights by being more sympathetic to, and more subject to the influence of, states-rights advocates. Negotiation has not functioned equitably because, in the past, it was used to get tribes to relinquish water; this dilemma is compounded by the fact that unlike whites, indigenous Americans have never been concerned with how much money they could receive for their water but with how much water they could receive through negotiation.

Historically, erosion of Indian rights parallels growth in the white settler population. After the Civil War, westerners won the outright sale of federal lands to private parties for nominal fees, a pattern accelerated after World War II when explosive growth resulted in further disenfranchisement of Indians. With the end of the reclamation era, and decisions over allocation revolving around existing resources such as the Central Arizona Project, the water-rights game cannot be played the same way. While few can disagree with Burton's conclusion that prospects for improving the climate of equitable negotiations toward nonlitigated dispute settlements are better when both sides to a conflict share "similar economic perspectives" over efficiency, it will remain for future studies to determine if regional basin management systems or true water markets based on the environmental costs of misuse could produce fairer outcomes.

DAVID LEWIS FELDMAN

Oak Ridge National Laboratory
Tennessee

University of Tennessee
Knoxville

SLOANE, ARTHUR A. *Hoffa*. Pp. xi, 430. Cambridge: MIT Press, 1991. $24.95.

At a time when American labor finds itself on the fringes of American society, Arthur Sloane's absorbing chronicle of the life and times of James Riddle Hoffa reminds us of the central role labor leaders once played in the equation of American power. Chronologically last on a list that includes Samuel Gompers, John L. Lewis, Phillip Murray, Walter Reuther, and George Meany, Hoffa remains perhaps the best known of all. Unfortunately, this notoriety stems not from his considerable accomplishments in collective bargaining but from his completely amoral exercise of power in the corrupt, Byzantine precincts of the International Brotherhood of Teamsters.

Unlike former books on corruption in the Teamsters, Sloane's is a full-blown biography of an American original—a man who combined a single-minded, often violent pursuit of power with a private life of rectitude and familial devotion. One of the strengths of this biography is Sloane's picture of the private Hoffa, who lived simply, was generous to his friends, cared little for what money could buy, eschewed alcohol and tobacco, and was devoted to his wife and family.

Students of labor relations will appreciate the book because of the attention it pays to Hoffa as a labor leader. Hoffa, with all of his troubles with the law, was probably as popular with his rank and file as any union chief in American history. The reasons for this are not complex. Hoffa delivered for the members. Yet Sloane adeptly shows us that Hoffa's greatest collective bargaining triumph, the nationwide master freight agreement, was fashioned in a decentralized, low-profit, and regulated industry—the perfect setting for a system of union-dominated industrywide bargaining. Nevertheless, it was Hoffa who accomplished it, to the undying gratitude of the truck drivers and the almost universal admiration of the employers.

What Sloane does not solve is the riddle of Jimmy Hoffa. We are taken through Hoffa's rise to power, his feud with Robert Kennedy, his endless legal problems, imprisonment, and, finally, his mysterious disappearance. But the biographer draws few conclusions about the motivations of this complex man. Although Hoffa took advantage of his position in the union to enrich himself to some degree, he had no real interest in money. He used the mob when he needed them, and he accepted their penetration of the union at all levels as normal, but he does not seem to have been their creature. Although he learned organizing tactics and strategy at the feet of the Trotskyists Farrel Dobbs and the Dunne brothers in Minneapolis, he rejected all variants of socialism. When the time came, he ruthlessly destroyed his Minnesota mentors without a second thought.

Nor, in fact, does Hoffa appear to have had any political convictions. He was, in the final analysis, an extreme but logical product of the American system of bread-and-butter unionism. Hoffa relished power. Because of the circumstances of his life, the arena in which he came to exercise it was organized labor. He loved being president of the union, and he knew that as long as he kept the members happy, they would keep him in power. He saw no social reform role for trade unionism and did not want to change society. To Hoffa, a union was a business whose job was to sell the members' labor at the top dollar. In this regard, he resembled John L. Lewis, and it is not surprising that the great leader of the coal miners was one of his role models.

That Hoffa succeeded in his narrow vision of the role of a labor leader is unquestionable. This success allowed him to run the union as he saw fit. Although Sloane shows that there was already plenty of corruption in the union when Hoffa became president, under his leadership the word "Teamster" came to be synonymous with organized crime for most Americans. Whatever Hoffa's considerable success in collective bargaining, it hardly compensated for the damage his tenure at the head of the Teamsters did to the reputation of organized labor in this country.

RONALD L. FILIPPELLI

Pennsylvania State University
University Park

OTHER BOOKS

ABBOTT, DAVID W. and JAMES P. LE-
VINE. *Wrong Winner: The Coming De-
bacle in the Electoral College.* Pp. xiii,
168. New York: Praeger, 1991. Paperbound, $13.95.

ALLARD, C. KENNETH. *Command,
Control, and the Common Defense.*
Pp. xiii, 317. New Haven, CT: Yale
University Press, 1990. $25.00.

AVERCH, HARVEY. *Private Markets and
Public Intervention.* Pp. xiii, 221.
Pittsburgh, PA: University of Pittsburgh Press, 1990. $29.95. Paper-
bound, $14.95.

BANERJEE, NIRMALA, ed. *Indian
Women in a Changing Industrial Sce-
nario.* Pp. 319. Newbury Park, CA:
Sage, 1991. $35.00.

BARKAI, AVRAHAM. *Nazi Economics:
Ideology, Theory, and Policy.* Pp. xii,
291. New Haven, CT: Yale University
Press, 1990. $27.50.

BAUMAN, ZYGMUNT. *Modernity and
Ambivalence.* Pp. vii, 285. Ithaca, NY:
Cornell University Press, 1991. $43.50.

BAXTER, CRAIG et al. *Government and
Politics in South Asia.* Pp. xv, 416.
Boulder, CO: Westview Press, 1990.
$55.00. Paperbound, $24.95.

BECKER, THEODORE L. *Quantum Politics: Applying Quantum Theory to Political Phenomena.* Pp. xvi, 232. New
York: Praeger, 1991. $45.00.

BIRNBAUM, PIERRE and JEAN LECA,
eds. *Individualism: Theories and
Methods.* Pp. vi, 340. New York: Oxford University Press, 1990. $79.00.

BOGGS, DAVID L. *Adult Civic Education.* Pp. xii, 140. Springfield, IL:
Charles C Thomas, 1991. $29.75.

BOTT, ALEXANDER J. *Handbook of
United States Election Laws and Prac-
tices: Political Rights.* Pp. xxi, 535.
Westport, CT: Greenwood Press, 1990.
$75.00.

BOULDING, ELISE et al., eds. *Peace
Culture and Society: Transnational
Research and Dialogue.* Pp. xii, 308.
Boulder, CO: Westview Press, 1991.
Paperbound, $29.95.

BRAMS, STEVEN J. *Negotiation Games:
Applying Game Theory to Bargaining
and Arbitration.* Pp. xviii, 297. New
York: Routledge, 1991. $49.50. Paper-
bound, $15.95.

BROWN, LESTER R. et al., eds. *State of
the World.* Pp. xvii, 254. New York:
Norton, 1991. Paperbound, $10.95.

BROWN, NEVILLE. *New Strategy
through Space.* Pp. xi, 295. London:
Pinter, 1989. Distributed by Columbia
University Press, New York City. $35.00.

BRYNEN, REX. *Sanctuary and Survival:
The PLO in Lebanon.* Pp. xiv, 255.
Boulder, CO: Westview Press, 1990.
$28.50.

BUELL, EMMETT H., Jr. and LEE
SIGELMAN, eds. *Nominating the
President.* Pp. xix, 300. Knoxville: University of Tennessee Press, 1991. Paperbound, no price.

CALDWELL, LYNTON KEITH. *International Environmental Policy: Emergence and Dimensions.* 2d ed. Pp. xvii,
460. Durham, NC: Duke University
Press, 1991. $35.00. Paperbound, $18.95.

CAPUTO, RICHARD K. *Welfare and
Freedom American Style: The Role of
the Federal Government, 1900-1940.*
Pp. xvi, 174. Lanham, MD: University
Press of America, 1991. $41.25.

CASTRO, GINETTE. *American Femi-
nism: A Contemporary History.* Pp. xii,
302. New York: Columbia University
Press, 1990. $55.00. Paperbound,
$12.50.

CHENG HSIAO-SHIH. *Party-Military
Relations in the PRC and Taiwan:
Paradoxes of Control.* Pp. xiv, 178.
Boulder, CO: Westview Press, 1990.
Paperbound, $28.50.

CHRISTEN, YVES. *Sex Differences:
Modern Biology and the Unisex Fal-

lacy. Pp. 141. New Brunswick, NJ: Transaction, 1991. $29.95. Paperbound, $21.95.

CLARK, BARRY. *Political Economy: A Comparative Approach.* Pp. xii, 313. New York: Praeger, 1991. $24.95.

COHEN, BENJAMIN J. *Crossing Frontiers: Explorations in International Political Economy.* Pp. x, 336. Boulder, CO: Westview Press, 1991. $49.95.

DENNIS, EVERETTE E. et al., eds. *Beyond the Cold War: Soviet and American Media Images.* Pp. 180. Newbury Park, CA: Sage, 1991. $36.00. Paperbound, $17.95.

DEVLIN, ROBERT. *Debt and Crisis in Latin America: The Supply Side of the Story.* Pp. xvi, 320. Princeton, NJ: Princeton University Press, 1990. $35.00.

DINNERSTEIN, LEONARD and KENNETH T. JACKSON. *American Vistas.* 6th ed. Pp. x, 371. New York: Oxford University Press, 1991. Paperbound, $14.95.

DONALDSON, THOMAS. *The Ethics of International Business.* Pp. xvi, 196. New York: Oxford University Press, 1989. $24.95.

DREZE, JEAN and AMARTYA SEN. *Hunger and Public Action.* Pp. xviii, 373. New York: Oxford University Press, 1989. No price.

DUNCAN, DAYTON. *Grass Roots: One Year in the Life of the New Hampshire Presidential Primary.* Pp. 436. New York: Viking, 1991. $22.95.

EDWARDS, RICHARD and PAOLO GARONNA. *The Forgotten Link: Labor's Stake in International Economic Cooperation.* Pp. x, 132. Savage, MD: Rowman & Littlefield, 1991. $42.50. Paperbound, $17.95.

ERIKSEN, VIKING OLVER. *Sunken Nuclear Submarines.* Pp. 176. New York: Oxford University Press, 1991. $35.00.

EYERMAN, RON and ANDREW JAMISON. *Social Movements: A Cognitive Approach.* Pp. 184. University Park:

Pennsylvania State University Press, 1991. $35.00. Paperbound, $14.95.

FONES-WOLF, KEN. *Trade Union Gospel: Christianity and Labor in Industrial Philadelphia 1865-1915.* Pp. xx, 266. Philadelphia: Temple University Press, 1989. No price.

GABEL, JOSEPH. *Manheim and Hungarian Marxism.* Pp. xii, 122. New Brunswick, NJ: Transaction, 1991. $34.95. Paperbound, $25.95.

GIAVAZZI, FRANCESCO and ALBERTO GIOVANNINI. *Limiting Exchange Rate Flexibility: The European Monetary System.* Pp. xi, 230. Cambridge: MIT Press, 1989. $27.50.

GIBNEY, MARK, ed. *World Justice? U.S. Courts and International Human Rights.* Pp. xiv, 178. Boulder, CO: Westview Press, 1991. $39.95.

GILL, STEPHEN. *American Hegemony and the Trilateral Commission.* Pp. xiii, 304. New York: Cambridge University Press, 1990. No price.

GOTTFRIED, KURT and PAUL BRACKEN, eds. *Reforging European Security: From Confrontation to Cooperation.* Pp. xiii, 226. Boulder, CO: Westview Press, 1990. Paperbound, $26.95.

GRAZIANI, GIOVANNI. *Gorbachev's Economic Strategy in the Third World.* Pp. xx, 116. New York: Praeger, 1990. $34.95.

HAAS, PETER M. *Saving the Mediterranean: The Politics of International Environmental Cooperation.* Pp. xxiv, 303. New York: Columbia University Press, 1990. $42.00.

HALE, CHARLES A. *The Transformation of Liberalism in Late Nineteenth-Century Mexico.* Pp. xi, 291. Princeton, NJ: Princeton University Press, 1990. $37.50.

HANRIEDER, WOLFRAM F. *Germany, America, Europe: Forty Years of German Foreign Policy.* Pp. xviii, 509. New Haven, CT: Yale University Press, 1991. $35.00. Paperbound, $18.00.

HEADY, FERREL. *Public Administration: A Comparative Perspective.* 4th ed. Pp. x, 472. New York: Marcel Dekker, 1991. $49.75.

HESS, GARY R. *Vietnam and the United States: Origins and Legacy of War.* Pp. xvi, 205. Boston, MA: G. K. Hall, 1990. $26.95.

HIERONYMI, OTTO. *Economic Policies for the New Hungary: Proposals for a Coherent Approach.* Pp. xiii, 121. Boulder, CO: Westview Press, 1990. Paperbound, $18.85.

HIXSON, WALTER L. *George F. Kennan: Cold War Iconoclast.* Pp. xiii, 381. New York: Columbia University Press, 1991. Paperbound, $14.50.

HOLLIS, MARTIN and STEVE SMITH. *Explaining and Understanding International Relations.* Pp. vi, 226. New York: Oxford University Press, 1990. $55.00.

HULME, DERICK L., Jr. *The Political Olympics: Moscow, Afghanistan, and the 1980 U.S. Boycott.* Pp. xi, 179. New York: Praeger, 1990. $39.95.

HUNT, WILLIAM R. *Front-Page Detective: William J. Burns and the Detective Profession 1880-1930.* Pp. 222. Bowling Green, OH: Bowling Green University Popular Press, 1990. $39.95. Paperbound, $19.95.

HUTTMAN, ELIZABETH et al., eds. *Urban Housing Segregation of Minorities in Western Europe and the United States.* Pp. xiii, 431. Durham, NC: Duke University Press, 1991. $59.95.

JACOBS, FRANCIS and RICHARD CORBETT. *The European Parliament.* Pp. xxi, 298. Boulder, CO: Westview Press, 1991. $58.00.

JANOWITZ, MORRIS. *On Social Organization and Social Control.* Pp. vii, 324. Chicago: University of Chicago Press, 1991. $34.95. Paperbound, $17.50.

KEGLEY, CHARLES W., Jr. and KENNETH L. SCHWAB, eds. *After the Cold War: Questioning the Morality of Nuclear Deterrence.* Pp. xi, 276. Boulder, CO: Westview Press, 1991. $55.00. Paperbound, $16.95.

KELLER, WILLIAM W. *The Liberals and J. Edgar Hoover.* Pp. xiii, 215. Princeton, NJ: Princeton University Press, 1989. $25.00.

KELSO, LOUIS O. and PATRICIA HETTER KELSO. *Democracy and Economic Power: Extending the ESOP Revolution through Binary Economics.* Pp. 202. Lanham, MD: University Press of America, Kelso Institute for the Study of Economic Systems, 1991. $45.25. Paperbound, $27.25.

KITSCHELT, HERBERT and STAF HELLEMANS. *Beyond the European Left: Ideology and Political Action in the Belgian Ecology Parties.* Pp. viii, 262. Durham, NC: Duke University Press, 1990. $39.50.

KOBURGER, CHARLES W., Jr. *Narrow Seas, Small Navies, and Fat Merchantmen.* Pp. xxi, 157. New York: Praeger, 1990. $39.95.

KRUGMAN, PAUL R. *Rethinking International Trade.* Pp. viii, 282. Cambridge: MIT Press, 1990. $25.00.

LAIDI, ZAKI. *The Superpowers and Africa: The Constraints of a Rivalry, 1960-1990.* Pp. xxv, 232. Chicago: University of Chicago Press, 1990. $45.00. Paperbound, $14.95.

LASATER, MARTIN L. *A Step toward Democracy: The December 1989 Elections in Taiwan, Republic of China.* Pp. vii, 100. Lanham, MD: AEI Press, 1991. Paperbound, $7.95.

LAVIE, SMADAR. *The Poetics of Military Occupation.* Pp. ix, 397. Berkeley: University of California Press, 1991. No price.

LESSNOFF, MICHAEL, ed. *Social Contract Theory.* Pp. 233. New York: New York University Press, 1990. Paperbound, $19.00.

LIEVEN, DOMINIC. *Russia's Rulers under the Old Regime.* Pp. xxii, 407. New Haven, CT: Yale University Press, 1991. $40.00. Paperbound, $18.95.

LIPARTITO, KENNETH J. and JOSEPH A. PRATT. *Baker and Botts in* the Development of Modern Houston. Pp. xi, 253. Austin: University of Texas Press, 1991. $24.95.

LIPSHITZ, LESLIE and DONOGH McDONALD, eds. German Unification: Economic Issues. Pp. xv, 171. Washington, DC: International Monetary Fund, 1990. Paperbound, $10.00.

MacDONALD, STUART. Technology and the Tyranny of Export Controls: Whisper Who Dares. Pp. xi, 206. New York: St. Martin's Press, 1990. $55.00.

MARDER, ARTHUR J. et al. Old Friends, New Enemies. Pp. xxx, 621. New York: Oxford University Press, 1990. $69.00.

MASTERS, ROGER D. The Nature of Politics. Pp. xvii, 298. New Haven, CT: Yale University Press, 1991. $30.00. Paperbound, $12.95.

MESA-LAGO, CARMELO, ed. Cuban Studies. Vol. 20. Pp. xi, 245. Pittsburgh, PA: University of Pittsburgh Press, 1990. $32.95.

MINARIK, JOSEPH J. Making America's Budget Policy: From the 1980s to the 1990s. Pp. xv, 229. Armonk, NY: M. E. Sharpe, 1990. $39.95. Paperbound, $15.95.

MISHEL, LAWRENCE and DAVID M. FRANKEL. The State of Working America 1990-91. Pp. xiv, 315. Armonk, NY: M. E. Sharpe, 1991. $29.95.

MOLLENKOPF, JOHN H. and MANUEL CASTELLS, eds. Dual City: Restructuring New York. Pp. xiv, 477. New York: Russell Sage, 1991. $39.95.

MORALES-GOMEZ, DANIEL A. and CARLOS ALBERTO TORRES. The State, Corporatist Politics, and Educational Policy Making in Mexico. Pp. xxiv, 197. New York: Praeger, 1990. $39.95.

MULGAN, G. J. Communication and Control. Pp. 302. New York: Guilford Press, 1991. $35.00.

NASSAR, JAMAL R. The Palestine Liberation Organization: From Armed Struggle to the Declaration of Independence. Pp. xii, 242. New York: Praeger, 1991. $42.95.

NEEDLER, MARTIN C. The Concepts of Comparative Politics. Pp. xiii, 156. New York: Praeger, 1991. $39.95. Paperbound, $14.95.

NIELSEN, KAI. After the Demise of the Tradition: Rorty, Critical Theory, and the Fate of Philosophy. Pp. x, 278. Boulder, CO: Westview Press, 1991. $38.50.

PATTERSON, GRAEME. History and Communications. Pp. 251. Buffalo, NY: University of Toronto Press, 1990. $40.00. Paperbound, $16.95.

POHLMAN, H. L. Justice Oliver Wendell Holmes: Free Speech and the Living Constitution. Pp. ix, 265. New York: New York University Press, 1991. $45.00.

PROVENZO, EUGENE F., Jr. Religious Fundamentalism and American Education. Pp. xix, 134. Albany: State University of New York Press, 1990. Paperbound, $10.95.

RABKIN, RHODA P. Cuban Politics: The Revolutionary Experiment. Pp. xvi, 233. New York: Praeger, 1990. $39.95.

RASKIN, MARCUS G. Essays of a Citizen: From National Security State to Democracy. Pp. xiii, 321. Armonk, NY: M. E. Sharpe, 1991. $27.50.

ROGERS, PAUL P. The Bitter Years: MacArthur and Sutherland. Pp. xvi, 348. New York: Praeger, 1990. $49.95.

ROGERS, PAUL P. The Good Years: MacArthur and Sutherland. Pp. xix, 380. New York: Praeger, 1990. $49.95.

SANDOZ, ELLIS, ed. Eric Voegelin's Significance for the Modern Mind. Pp. xi, 218. Baton Rouge: Louisiana State University Press, 1991. $25.00.

SANDOZ, ELLIS, ed. Political Sermons of the American Founding Era, 1730-1805. Pp. xxxvii, 1598. Indianapolis, IN: Liberty Press, 1991. $38.00. Paperbound, $12.00.

SCHRECKER, JOHN E. The Chinese Revolution in Historical Perspective. Pp. xx, 240. New York: Praeger, 1991. $45.00. Paperbound, $17.95.

SHAH, GHANSHYAM. *Social Movements in India*. Pp. 222. Newbury Park, CA: Sage, 1991. $27.50.

SPRAGENS, THOMAS A., Jr. *Reason and Democracy*. Pp. xi, 281. Durham, NC: Duke University Press, 1990. $39.50. Paperbound, $17.95.

STEPHENSON, D. GRIER, Jr., ed. *An Essential Safeguard: Essays on the United States Supreme Court and Its Justices*. Pp. xii, 178. Westport, CT: Greenwood Press, 1991. $42.95.

STERLING, CLAIRE. *Octopus*. Pp. 384. New York: Simon & Schuster, 1991. Paperbound, $10.95.

STOKES, GALE, ed. *From Stalinism to Pluralism*. Pp. xi, 267. New York: Oxford University Press, 1991. $35.00. Paperbound, $12.95.

STROTHER, RAYMOND. *Cottonwood*. Pp. 285. New York: E. P. Dutton, 1991. $18.95.

VILLE, SIMON P. *Transport and the Development of the European Economy, 1750-1918*. Pp. xiii, 252. New York: St. Martin's Press, 1990. $59.95.

WATANABE, MASAO. *The Japanese and Western Science*. Pp. xiv, 141. Philadelphia: University of Pennsylvania Press, 1991. $28.95.

WATTS, MEREDITH W. et al. *Contemporary German Youth and Their Elders: A Generational Comparison*. Pp. xv, 193. Westport, CT: Greenwood Press, 1989. $39.95.

WENNER, LETTIE McSPADDEN. *U.S. Energy and Environmental Interest Groups: Institutional Profiles*. Pp. xxvii, 358. Westport, CT: Greenwood Press, 1990. $55.00.

WESTON, BURNS H., ed. *Alternative Security: Living without Nuclear Deterrence*. Pp. xv, 283. Boulder, CO: Westview Press, 1990. $45.00. Paperbound, $14.95.

YOON, DAE-KYU. *Law and Political Authority in South Korea*. Pp. xiii, 247. Boulder, CO: Westview Press, 1991. $40.00.

INDEX

'Abduh, Muhammad, 34-35
Addi, Lahouari, 11
ADDI, LAHOUARI, Islamicist Utopia and Democracy, 120-30
al-Afghani, Jamal al-Din, 33-35
AFRICAN CASE STUDY OF POLITICAL ISLAM: NIGERIA, AN, John Hunwick, 143-55
Akhavi, Shahrough, 11
AKHAVI, SHAHROUGH, The Clergy's Concepts of Rule in Egypt and Iran, 92-102
Alfarabi, 30-31
Algeria
  democracy, 127-29
  militant Islam, 55-58
  see also Islamic Salvation Front; National Liberation Front
Averroes, 32-33
Avicenna, 32
Ayubi, Nazih N., 11
AYUBI, NAZIH N., State Islam and Communal Plurality, 79-91

Bangladesh, political Islam in, 165
al-Banna, Hasan, 35
Bhutto, Zulfikar Ali, 116
BUTTERWORTH, CHARLES E., Political Islam: The Origins, 26-37
BUTTERWORTH, CHARLES E. and I. WILLIAM ZARTMAN, Preface, 8-12

Christians in Islamic states, 88-90, 91
CLERGY'S CONCEPTS OF RULE IN EGYPT AND IRAN, THE, Shahrough Akhavi, 92-102
CONSERVATIVE AND TRADITIONAL BROTHERHOODS, John Obert Voll, 66-78

Deeb, Mary-Jane, 10
DEEB, MARY-JANE, Militant Islam and the Politics of Redemption, 52-65
Democracy, 125, 137, 186-91
DEMOCRACY AND ISLAM: THE CULTURAL DIALECTIC, I. William Zartman, 181-91
Egypt
  clergy's concepts of rule, 93-99
  Muslim Brotherhood, 74
  Sufi brotherhoods, 74-75

Europe
  discrimination against Muslim immigrants, 175-76
  Muslim immigrants, 170-80
  pan-European immigration policy, 177-79

Fadhlallah, Muhammad Hussain, 63-64, 87
Faraj, Muhammad 'Abd al-Salam, 94-96
Fudi, Uthman b., 145-46

Gaffney, Patrick D., 10
GAFFNEY, PATRICK D., Popular Islam, 38-51
GOLDEN AGE: THE POLITICAL CONCEPTS OF ISLAM, THE, Ira M. Lapidus, 13-25
Gummi, Abubakar, 151

Hamas, 62
al-Haqq, Jadd al-Haqq 'Ali Jadd, 96-99
Hizballah, 63-64, 87
Hunwick, John, 12
HUNWICK, JOHN, An African Case Study of Political Islam: Nigeria, 143-55

India
  Muslims, 161
  political Islam, 165-66
Indonesia, political Islam in, 162, 166-67
Iran
  clergy's concepts of rule in, 99-102
  as an Islamic state, 20, 105-6, 110-13
Iraq
  Shiites, 82, 86-87
  Sunnites, 82
Islam
  militant Islam, 52-65
  personal religious belief, 17, 24-25, 77
  political opposition, 25, 39, 40, 183-86
  political paradigms and theory, 14-17, 26-37, 92-102
  popular Islam, 38-51, 105, 132, 133
ISLAM IN THE STATES OF THE FORMER USSR, Vitaly Naumkin, 131-42
Islamic Jihad, 62, 63
Islamic Salvation Front (FIS) (Algeria), 57-58, 127-28, 149-50, 189, 190
Islamic sects, 81-83, 86, 89, 90-91
Islamic states, 79-91, 103-19, 141, 149-50
Islamic Tendency Movement (MTI) (Tunisia), 58-60

ISLAMICIST UTOPIA AND DEMOCRACY, Lahouari Addi, 120-30

Jews in Islamic states, 88, 90, 91

Karawan, Ibrahim A., 11
KARAWAN, IBRAHIM A., Monarchs, Mullas, and Marshals: Islamic Regimes? 103-19
Kazakhstan, Islamic factors in politics, 140-41
Khomeini, Ruhollah, 35-36, 99-101, 106

Lapidus, Ira M., 10
LAPIDUS, IRA M., The Golden Age: The Political Concepts of Islam, 13-25
Lebanon
  militant Islam, 63-64
  Shiites, 86-87
  see also Hizballah; Islamic Jihad
Leveau, Rémy, 12
LEVEAU, RÉMY, Maghrebi Immigration to Europe: Double Insertion or Double Exclusion? 170-80
Libya, militant Islam in, 60-62

MAGHREBI IMMIGRATION TO EUROPE: DOUBLE INSERTION OR DOUBLE EXCLUSION? Rémy Leveau, 170-80
Maitatsine disturbances, 153-54
Malaysia, political Islam in, 167-68
Marsot, Alain-Gérard, 12
MARSOT, ALAIN-GÉRARD, Political Islam in Asia: A Case Study, 156-69
al-Mawdudi, Abu A'la, 35
Middle Eastern non-Islamic polity, 17-18, 23
MILITANT ISLAM AND THE POLITICS OF REDEMPTION, Mary-Jane Deeb, 52-65
Modernity and modernism, 123-24, 130
  and religion, 124-26, 168-69
MONARCHS, MULLAS, AND MARSHALS: ISLAMIC REGIMES? Ibrahim A. Karawan, 103-19
Morocco, as an Islamic state, 19-20
Muslim Brotherhood, 35, 74
Muslim Students Society (Nigeria), 151-52

National Liberation Front (FLN) (Algeria), 57, 190
Nationalism
  and Islam, 24, 70
  of Middle Eastern states, 21-22, 44-46, 47
  in Turkic regions, 138-40
Nationalist movements, 187

Naumkin, Vitaly, 11
NAUMKIN, VITALY, Islam in the States of the Former USSR, 131-42
Nigeria, 69, 143-55
  relationship of Islam to politics, 143-55
  Sufi brotherhoods or tariqas, 69, 150-52
Numayri, Ja'far, 75-77, 113-15

Occupied Territories, militant Islam in, 62-63

Pakistan, as an Islamic state, 20, 115-18, 161-62, 163-65
POLITICAL ISLAM: THE ORIGINS, Charles E. Butterworth, 26-37
POLITICAL ISLAM IN ASIA: A CASE STUDY, Alain-Gérard Marsot, 156-69
POPULAR ISLAM, Patrick D. Gaffney, 38-51

Saudi Arabia, as an Islamic state, 19, 105-6, 107-9
Schengen agreement, 178-79
Shiism, 83-86, 99-100
South Asia, political Islam in, 156-69
Southeast Asia, political Islam in, 156-69
Soviet Central Asia
  Islam, 131-42
  Sufi brotherhoods, 72-73, 132
STATE ISLAM AND COMMUNAL PLURALITY, Nazih N. Ayubi, 79-91
Sudan
  Islamic regime, 113-15
  Sufi brotherhoods, 75-77
Sufi brotherhoods or tariqas, 66-78, 132, 150-52
Sufism, 43, 45
Sunnism, 80-85, 89

Tunisia, militant Islam in, 58-60
Turkey, as a secular national state, 21
Turkic nationalism, 138-40

'Ulama', 42-43, 50-51, 85, 92-102, 108-9

Voll, John Obert, 10
VOLL, JOHN OBERT, Conservative and Traditional Brotherhoods, 66-78

Zartman, I. William, 12
ZARTMAN, I. WILLIAM, Democracy and Islam: The Cultural Dialectic, 181-91
ZARTMAN, I. WILLIAM, see BUTTERWORTH, CHARLES E., coauthor
Zia ul-Haq, 116-18